THE GATHERING OF REASON

Second Edition

JOHN SALLIS

STATE UNIVERSITY OF NEW YORK PRESS

Published by
STATE UNIVERSITY OF NEW YORK PRESS
ALBANY
2005

Printed in the United States of America

For information, address
State University of New York Press
194 Washington Avenue, Suite 305, Albany, NY 12210-2365

Production and book design, Laurie Searl
Marketing, Michael Campochiaro

Library of Congress Cataloging-in-Publication Data

Sallis, John, 1938–
The gathering of reason / John Sallis. — Sec. ed.
p. cm. — (SUNY series in contemporary continental philosophy)
Includes bibliographical references and index.
ISBN 0-7914-6453-9 (hardcover : alk. paper) — ISBN 0-7914-6454-7 (pbk. : alk. paper)
1. Kant, Immanuel, 1724–1804. Kritik der reinen Vernunft. 2. Knowledge, Theory of. 3. Reason. 4. Imagination. 5. Dialectic. 6. Transcendentalism. I. Title. II. Series.

B2779.S25 2005
121—dc22 2004022718

10 9 8 7 6 5 4 3 2 1

THE GATHERING OF REASON

SUNY SERIES IN

CONTEMPORARY CONTINENTAL PHILOSOPHY

DENNIS J. SCHMIDT, EDITOR

for Lauren and Kathryn

"C'est l'imagination qui étend pour nous la mesure des possibles soit en bien soit en mal, et qui par consequent excite et nourrit les desirs par l'espoir de les satisfaire."

J.-J. ROUSSEAU, *Émile*

CONTENTS

PREFACE TO THE FIRST EDITION

In this text I trace a way to the issue of imagination. It is intended to be a way around that closure of the issue, which, in play throughout the history of metaphysics, now obtrudes in the utter conflation of the difference that once separated imagination from fancy and in the allied displacement of them, indistinguishably, into an innocuous self-entertaining activity of conjuring up mental images. Radical measures are required in order to elude that closure: They must be capable of measuring out to imagination a space in which the traditional conceptual oppositions predetermining it can be thrown out of joint, infused with indeterminacy, anarchy.

The particular way traced runs through reason, through the problem of reason (in its Kantian form), which coincides with the problem of metaphysics. Or rather, it is a matter of treading carefully along the edge of a certain deforming of reason—a phenomenon which, at a different level and in that unconditioned form manifest today, might well be called "nihilism." At certain decisive turns on this way I shall also allude to certain other elements belonging to the relevant conceptual configuration, e.g., the oppositions between reason and experience and between reason and madness; and I shall take some steps toward transposing them in a direction that gives space to the issue of imagination, e.g., that of the oppositions between presence and absence and between self-possessed positing and self-dispossessed ecstasy.

In a sense this way remains peripheral, a merely "historical" complement, a critical preparation for a direct approach to the issue itself.

But is it merely a matter of restoring the issue, of reopening the question of imagination within a new, indeterminate space? Would not even the most rigorous direct approach to the issue be compelled by its very rigor to reproduce within itself a movement within the same torsion in which the present critical preparation is almost directly engaged—the torsion between reason and imagination, the movement between a (rational) theory of imagination and an application of imagination to itself, a releasing of imagination's own intrinsic reflexivity? Is it yet possible even to envisage the radical measure that such movement would require?

Portions of this text were presented in a paper, "Imagination and Truth," which I delivered at a colloquium in memory of Martin Heidegger that was held at Pennsylvania State University in April 1977; in a paper "Immateriality and the Play of Imagination," read at the meeting of the American Catholic Philosophical Association in April 1978; and in several graduate lecture courses given at Duquesne University. For their generous contributions at various stages and in various ways I am grateful to the Sankt Ulrich scholarly community, David Krell and Kenneth Maly, Charles Sherover, James Risser, Karen Barson, Marshell Bradley, and my wife. I owe special gratitude to the Alexander von Humboldt-Stiftung for support during the year in which the present text first began to take shape.

Mill Run, Pa.
August 1978

PREFACE TO THE SECOND EDITION

With only the slightest fancy one could envisage this book as a tissue of translations. Most comprehensively it translates Kant's *Critique of Pure Reason*, not only exposing it to the drift of another language but also reinscribing it in this language in such fashion as to remark the breaks, connections, and openings of the critical discourse. The reinscripted text is, in turn, carried over to other hermeneutical levels, the translation being governed at each level by a different directionality, by a different turning. Thus *The Gathering of Reason* not only doubles the critical discourse but also ventures to project it, to invert it, and to subvert it.

The network of translations is composed with the aim of laying out a way to imagination, to what at the time of composition I called the issue of imagination, thereby designating, at once, the emergence, lineage, and manifestation of imagination. This way necessarily leads through the critique of reason, yet not simply in order to arrive at Kant's theory of imagination, as though this theory could be set apart and developed independently of critique as a whole. Neither does this way through critique lead finally—as Kant had hoped—out of critique into a beyond where it would become possible to institute, in place of crisis, a system of pure reason, the true metaphysics. It is rather a way that swings indecisively between two sites, on the one side, a site where reason seems—to its detriment—to be abandoned by imagination and, on the other side, a site where the very potency of reason in its failure appears to derive from imagination's complicity in the production of dialectical illusion. It is as if, in the gathering of reason, imagination were to efface its operation while remaining nonetheless the very force most responsible for the dialectic in which pure reason is ensnared. Kant insists that this dialectic is natural and unavoidable, even though—paradoxically—it would seem most remote from nature, even though it would seem to trace precisely those lines along which metaphysics would always have sought to transcend nature and everything merely natural. Kant himself tacitly broaches the paradox by declaring dialectical illusion to be just as irrepressible (even after its detection by critique) as is the illusion that the moon is larger at its rising (even after its astronomical explanation).

In its title *The Gathering of Reason* announces another translation in which it is, as a whole, engaged, a translation belonging to another order. It is a double translation: of reason into λόγος and of λόγος into gathering—in both cases a translation both of sense and of word. In strict terms it would need to be called a double countertranslation, since it runs backward, reversing or undoing translations effected in the history of metaphysics and before that history. This countertranslation would confront reason with its largely forgotten origin; it would draw both the crisis of reason and the resultant task of critique back toward the Greek beginnings. Thus it would let that origin both inform the sense of reason and open it to deconstruction.

From the translation of reason a web of further translations extends. Among the most decisive is the translation of the two stems that Kant identifies as arising from the common root of the power of knowledge. These two stems, the rational and the empirical, are directly translatable—or rather, countertranslatable—into the terms by which the Platonic Socrates delimited the inauguration of philosophy. This delimitation is carried out in the *Phaedo* in the guise of a second sailing (δεύτερος πλοῦς): it consists in having recourse to λόγοι, as, in the absence of wind, sailors have recourse to the oars. It is a turn from things in their sensible presence that seeks their truth by engagement with λόγος. As such, it comes to be translated ever again in the course of the history of metaphysics, translated, most notably, into the metaphysically definitive turn from the empirical to the rational. The inaugural move thus becomes and remains one of having recourse to reason. Confronted with the fragmentation of experience and of experience-based knowledge, unable to see beyond the plethora of things, blinded by their presence, metaphysics has recourse to reason as its means of conveyance beyond. Or rather, metaphysics is precisely this having recourse to reason's power to convey one's vision on beyond the mere shards strewn across the site of human experience, on toward sense and coherence.

Recourse to reason may also be had—doubled—in the guise of critique. Reinscribing the inaugural move systematically, according to the inner law of reason itself, critique brings reason before a tribunal that would determine the very possibility and limits of purely rational knowledge. Thus critique translates the recourse to reason by staging the scene of a trial in which judgment would be pronounced regarding the lawfulness of reason's claims to power. Yet the tribunal can be nothing other than reason itself and, as Kant recognizes, critique nothing other than reason's self-knowing. As critique is itself, in turn, reiterated, retranslated—as it has been from Fichte's *Wissenschaftslehre* to *The Gathering of Reason* and beyond—the tribunal cannot but be exposed to the recoil of the very limits it determines, the recoil of these limits upon itself and upon the determinations it carries out. At the limit of the reiterating translation, what becomes manifest is the inevitable operation of spacing within reason, of spacings of reason. My later work on Kant is situated at this limit.

But in *The Gathering of Reason* the distinctness of the hermeneutical strata is rigorously maintained, and this separation serves to defer the recoil, to hold subversion at bay until, at the end, its force can be released without compromising—except retrospectively—the outcome at the other levels. Strict separation is sustained throughout even between, on the one hand, the most direct transcription of Kant's text, the commentary on the Transcendental Dialectic, and, on the other hand, the projection in which the translation of reason as gathering is carried through. The separation prescribes also that nothing further be ventured, that no other directionality be brought into play, until the projective translation has been carried through to the point of showing just how the gatherings of reason fail. What comes to be shown is that in each case, whether the idea posited by reason be that of the soul, of the world, or of God, the actual gathering of the manifold falls short of the unity of the idea. Only in relation to this result does inversion come into view and open the possibility of exposing still another, more concealed layer of critical thought. For the gathering of pure reason proves to be precisely the inverse of the gathering of pure understanding, which is assured its fulfillment by the operation of transcendental schematism, that is, by the synthetic power, the gathering force, of imagination. Yet if reason fails to gather into unity, it fails even more obtrusively to gather *into presence*. Only in the case of the cosmological idea, which uniquely is posited within the domain of appearances, does the pertinent gathering have linkage to a gathering into presence. And though, as in every case, the gathering—especially as a gathering into presence—goes unfulfilled, it is presumably because of this unique linkage that the sole reference to imagination in the entire Transcendental Dialectic occurs in the discussion of the cosmological idea. Retrospectively, the working out of the inversion serves to complete the translation of reason as gathering, since it brings into play the character of gathering as gathering into presence, into manifestness. At every level, whether the gathering be that of intuition, of understanding, or of reason and whether the gathering be fulfillable or not, it would be a gathering of a manifold in such a way as to make something manifest in its articulated coherence.

It is in the elaboration of inversion that the way to the issue of imagination comes to swing between two extreme sites. At one of these sites it would seem that what is lacking almost completely in the gathering of reason is imagination, that in any case it is this lack that decisively determines the character of such gathering as the inverse of the gathering of understanding. In its arrival at this site, the way would seem to have come to a dead end; it would have proven to be a way, not to the issue of imagination, not to the emergence, the manifestness, of imagination in its lineage, but only to the absence of such force and to the consequences of this absence. And yet, there is another site to which this way crosses over, a site where imagination proves to be in complicity with reason in the production of dialectical illusion. At this site it would turn out that thought alone never suffices for setting before our minds such ideas as those of the soul, of the world, and of God, that such ideas would always have been brought forth in and through imagination, rendered effective through the force of imagination, even through a lawless and ecstatic imagination alarmingly akin to madness. But once this encroachment of imagination upon reason is released, subversion is inevitable: critique will be driven in the direction of spacings, subjectivity will be submitted to thorough dismantling, and imagination will be redetermined through its most exorbitant traits.

Two occurrences following the publication of the first edition of this book deserve mention here. The first was a public discussion of the book in which, among others, Reiner Schürmann took part. Some record of the discussion is preserved in *Delimitations* (chapter 3). What I want to attest to here is the force of the questions that were posed. Most provocative was Schürmann's question as to whether the various forms of the subject's fragmentation (of subject and object, of intuition, of thought, and of intuition and thought) originate from a basic hiatus, from a radical breach that would constitute the very finitude of human knowledge. By developing this question, Schürmann brought the discussion, by quite another route, to the edge of the same abyss at which I had sought to compose the book.

The other occurrence was a matter of surprise. It came about when, shortly after the book appeared, a German translation was undertaken. What came as a surprise had to do with the word *gathering*, with the resonances it proved capable of evoking and with the semantic resources it was able to bring into play. For in the preparation of the German translation, the title proved virtually untranslatable; thus an extended note had to be added at the beginning of the book explaining how the word *gathering* was to be understood in the English title, how it had no German equivalent, and how it had been, only inadequately, translated into German. This note also provided indirect justification for the disparity between the English title and the title adopted for the translation (*Die Krisis der Vernunft*). It would be difficult to imagine a more provocative attestation to the wonder of translation: having taken up the word in order to translate effectively certain turns of phrase in a German text on Greek thought, having taken it over into a discourse on Kant aimed at translating critique, as it were, back into Greek, having sought to bring into play the full resources of the English word—its force, its δύναμις—I then had finally to acknowledge that it could not be translated back into the German from which it had come.

Hofheim am Taunus
January 2004

INTRODUCTION

1.

Reason—the very word now bespeaks crisis, failure of every available sense to fulfill what cannot but be intended. The crisis is radical, for in every other instance reason would serve as that to which recourse would be had in order to isolate and resolve crisis, in order to open up and appropriate a fulfilling sense. Even to thematize the conceptuality of crisis is already to lay claim in deed to a certain resolution of the crisis of reason—that is, such crisis withdraws, renders provisional, the very possibility of its being thematized as such. The crisis is so radical that even this schema itself, that of crisis, has been emptied in such fashion as to accommodate almost anything that becomes somehow problematic; the schema of crisis has itself entered upon a crisis.

Recourse to reason in the face of crisis (to use this schema provisionally) is a strategy deeply embedded in the Western tradition. More precisely, it defines the turning by which this tradition was founded and subsequently constituted. The founding turn is traced in the Platonic dialogues—most openly, in that swan song sung by Socrates in the *Phaedo* in hope of charming away fear in the face of death, the absolute crisis. Among the Socratic incantations there is one in which Socrates, looking back into himself, back into his past, away from death, retraces the way to philosophy: he tells of how he began with a wondrous desire for the wisdom to be had by investigating natural things, of how, disillusioned, he turned in vain to the teachings of Anaxagoras, of how finally he came to set out on a "second sailing in search of causes." This second sailing, the founding turn of the tradition, commenced through a turning away from the immediately present, in which Socrates foresaw a threat of blindness: fearing that he might suffer such misfortune as befalls those who look at the sun during an eclipse, fearing that his soul might be blinded should he look directly at things with his eyes, he decided, as he tells his interlocutors, that he "must have recourse to λόγοι and examine in them the truth of beings."[1]

In the tradition thus founded, the Socratic recourse to λόγοι was translated into a recourse to *ratio*, reason. The translation served to establish the recourse in a definitive course: Withdrawal from the immediately present for the sake of a reappropriation of those beings in their truth became a matter of recourse from the sensible (τὸ αἰσθητόν) to the intelligible (τὸ νοητόν). Through recourse to reason the shallowness of inarticulate immersion in the immediate and particular was replaced by the depth and comprehensiveness of theoretical knowledge. Man was translated into rational animal.

Today that translation has become radically questionable. It is not primarily a matter of man's now proving resistant to the translation, not a matter of a contemporary testimony to an inevitable resurgence of irrationality. On the contrary, contemporary man, technological man, attests to an insistent rationality of unprecedented consistency, reconfirms the translation through the pervasive rationalization of all sectors of human life. What has become questionable in the highest degree is not the rationalization of man but rather the very rationality that defines that translation; it is reason itself that has come into question, that has become suspect. The juridical metaphor is appropriate—or rather, its very inappropriateness serves to announce the abyss opened up by the crisis of reason: Reason, previously constituting the tribunal before which all disputes, all differences, were to be resolved, is itself in dispute, appears to harbor difference within itself; it is itself to be summoned before a tribunal and required to give proof of its identity against the charge that it is sheer prejudice, a mask for other interests. But the very demand for proof—to say nothing of the demand for resolution of difference—is inconceivable apart from reason, and the possibility of a sufficiently detached judgment and resolution is threatened from the very moment the summons is issued to reason. Could reason ever be so detached from itself as to be capable of constituting its own tribunal? Can such distance ever be opened up within reason?[2]

Without suppressing the difference, one may nonetheless discern in the Platonic-Socratic turn an image of the crisis of reason. Even before the translation into reason, the profound ambivalence that haunts all recourse to λόγοι was experienced as the problem of *sophistry*: Socrates, allied with the sophists in having recourse to λόγοι, found in those sophists his most formidable opponents, most formidable precisely because of the alliance. He was compelled to reiterate continually the almost self-effacing difference, to reestablish Socratic recourse, hence discourse, in its integrity, to differentiate philosophy from sophistry. The trial and condemnation of Socrates attest to the political limit of that differentiation—that is, to the depth of the crisis.

The crisis has also its images within the tradition, and it is to one of these, the Kantian image, that I propose to attend. More precisely, I shall initiate a reflection on that *critique* of reason with which Kant responds to the *crisis* of reason, to the "conflict of reason with itself."[3] In this critique the problem of sophistry is quietly renewed:[4] It is a matter of determining to what degree the inferences of reason "are sophistications not of men but of pure reason itself" (A 339/B 397). It is a matter of exposing the sophistry that belongs to pure reason itself, of measuring the division of reason against itself. Such measuring is traced in the Transcendental Dialectic of the *Critique of Pure Reason*, which will accordingly serve as the focal text for the reflection.

2.

Metaphysics—this too bespeaks crisis, no less than does *reason*. It bespeaks the same crisis: Almost from the beginning, recourse to reason has understood itself to be, correlatively, an establishing of the distinction between intelligible and sensible. Through this establishing, metaphysics was inaugurated.

The distinction is not, however, simply constituted by such establishing; it is constitutively linked neither to reflection nor to history. Rather, it is a distinction already in force in the very event of speech, which both reflection and history presuppose; it is a distinction opened up once and for all in that moment when speech first transgressed the limits of sense, a moment in principle irretrievable, an absolute past. Such is the radicalness with which we are bound to the distinction. We are not given the choice of relinquishing it—not even in silence, which, always coming too late, is nourished precisely by the possibility of speech.

One might, in face of crisis, attempt to isolate from history a reflection on this prehistorical distinction—that is, to bring to bear upon the premetaphysical origin of metaphysics a reflection freed from history, from metaphysics, from the history of metaphysics—that is, to secure outside metaphysics a tribunal for metaphysics. Or rather, one might be tempted, did not the attempt so quickly betray itself. For such reflection is inextricably bound to expression and thereby to history: From the moment that one *expresses* the distinction, one has already broached a relation to the history in which are entangled the language and conceptuality which such expression cannot help but invoke. To express the distinction precisely *as* a distinction between intelligible and sensible is already to place the reflection within the history of metaphysics. It is to resume that history—necessarily, since we have no other choice except that silence of nonreflection which would deliver us over to a more inexorable necessity. We *must* resume that history. But can we?

Any simple resumption of the metaphysical tradition is today out of the question—even granting a quite genuine sense of resumption, granting, for instance, that resumption always requires an element of renewal, adaptation, reanimation. Why out of the question? Because one cannot today simply resume the expressed distinction that inaugurates that tradition, the distinction between intelligible and sensible, the distinction which, as expressed, compels our reflection to grant its rootedness in the metaphysical tradition. Or rather, one could simply resume the distinction, and thus the metaphysical tradition it inaugurates, only at the cost of putting out of question what is today most questionable, only at the cost of blinding oneself to the crisis of metaphysics.

Permit me here merely to allude to an historical phenomenon without attempting anything like a demonstration of it; I ask this because to determine in this case whether and in what sense a demonstration is even possible, to determine what sense demonstration could have here, would not only lead into an interminable analysis but would rather quickly get entangled in the very phenomenon that is here in question. What phenomenon? Nietzsche called it the advent of nihilism. I would prefer to allude to it with the word "occlusion"—to speak of the occlusion of the distinction between intelligible and sensible, and correspondingly, of the occlusion, hence crisis, of metaphysics. Central to this phenomenon is the recurrent emptying of every refuge in which a pure intelligibility would be secure—that is, the recurrent appropriation of every alleged intelligible to the sphere of the sensible. Recall some moments of this attack: the reduction of the intelligible, in its theological aspect, to the human, all-too-human at the hands of Feuerbach, Nietzsche, Freud; the reduction of the noumenal, first in German Idealism and then radically in Nietzsche and in phenomenology; the reduction of the ideality of meaning, its empirical reduction in psychologism, its transcendental reduction in Husserl, and its reduction to a system of differences in structural linguistics.

In referring to the occlusion of the distinction I want to retain all three senses of the word. There is, first, the sense of *absorption* as when in chemistry one says that a certain gas is occluded, for example, by charcoal; the distinction between intelligible and sensible is in this sense occluded in the absorption, the appropriation, of the intelligible by the sensible. There is, secondly and consequently, a *closing* of the distinction. Thirdly, this closing *obstructs*, blocks our passage; specifically, it obstructs that movement in which, resuming our metaphysical heritage, we would carry it onward. We, by contrast, are both too much within and too much without metaphysics—that is, suspicious of its every means, yet lacking any others. The occlusion of the metaphysical distinction recurs in each dimension in which the distinction gets reopened, and the examples cited allude to some of these dimensions. Occlusion recurs so insistently that one might well want simply to yield to it, were that choice open short of relinquishing reflection once and for all. But as soon as we reflect, as soon as we invoke the only conceptual and linguistic means really at our disposal, we have already reopened the metaphysical distinction and, if we require that the reflection be radical, have set for ourselves the task of reconstituting the distinction.

Here perhaps we can begin to discern a parting of ways: in one direction ever recurrent occlusion, indefinitely reiterated oscillation between means and end of reflection, from within metaphysics to without, exhaustion both manifest yet prohibited. But let us not retreat too quickly, too dogmatically. It seems to me that, instead, we ought to exercise a certain reticence about this direction—at least as long as we have not passed beyond its mere schema and made the effort to follow it up in a concrete and systematic way. Especially, I should want to postpone, perhaps indefinitely, the conclusion that this direction is *simply* one of hopelessness and anarchy; for nihilism is precisely *not anything simple* but a phenomenon of such complexity as to escape perhaps all previous measures. I would perhaps even want to grant that for some time yet it might be imperative to follow this direction—to linger on its way until one sees everywhere only the countenance of "this uncanniest of all guests."[5] Granted a certain sense of economy and strategy, one can in a limited context defer occlusion in such fashion as to turn metaphysics against itself. Who can yet say whether, beyond such deconstruction, an abrupt, eruptive leap outside the metaphysical tradition might be possible? Has such "active forgetfulness" as Nietzsche invoked yet been put to the test? Can we yet even envisage how Zarathustra might prove himself?

Nevertheless, the leap beyond the tradition, from man to overman, even if an alternative, is not the only one. There is another way—a way which *turns back* into the tradition, without, however, becoming either a mere resumption of that tradition or, at the other extreme, a deferent turning of the tradition against itself. To adumbrate this other way let me use the title *archaic reflection*.

Such reflection is a regress to an ἀρχή, a return to a beginning, to an originary phase of the tradition, to a phase in which something decisive originated. It is distinctive of such phases that within them matters are never so secure as they become subsequently; and that very insecurity is what secures them against the alternatives of being either (emptily) repeated or else (anarchically) abandoned. Within an originary phase there is an unsettling openness, and, in a reflective return to the texts in which such a phase is traced, in a desedimenting reading of those texts, we can bring again into play the manifoldness suppressed by subsequent tradition; we can stage again that play of different levels, different directions, different dimensions, which, irreducible to a closed structure, constitutes precisely the openness in which something decisive can originate. Yet we stage the play only in order that it might reflect something to us—that is, archaic reflection turns back into such an originary phase in order to let something at issue today be reflected in that beginning, in order to trace out in that beginning an image of the issue enriched by the openness of the beginning. Ultimately it is a matter of recovering and elaborating the undeveloped possibilities freed through the tracing. Reflection would thus bring the means gained from the beginning to bear upon the issue from which and for the sake of which the reflection commenced.

3.

My intention is to initiate an archaic reflection with respect to the crisis of reason and, correlatively, of metaphysics, a reflection of these issues in that originary phase of the tradition that is traced in Kant's major texts. The reflection will be focused primarily on the Transcendental Dialectic of the *Critique of Pure Reason*, for it is in this text that Kant most openly exhibits the crisis besetting reason and metaphysics.

But is it appropriate to regard the state in which the problems of reason and of metaphysics are taken up by Kant as one of crisis? Is there here even an image of crisis in that radical sense that I have outlined above in reference to our own time? There can be no doubt but that Kant intended his destruction of traditional metaphysics to be in service ultimately to a constructive project through which metaphysics would eventually be reconstituted beyond the threat of crisis.[6] In this sense Kant set out not to destroy metaphysics but to complete it, as Aristotle had completed logic. He would establish metaphysics as science by examining that metaphysics which, in a fundamental sense, belongs to human nature, that propounding of questions to itself into which pure reason is impelled. Established metaphysics, he says, would be "nothing but the *inventory* of all our possessions through *pure* reason, systematically ordered" (A xx). Its completion is guaranteed by reason's relation to itself: "Here nothing can escape us, because what reason produces entirely out of itself cannot conceal itself but rather is brought to light by reason itself as soon as one has discovered the common principle" (A xx). Reason's pure products, reason cast as product for itself, cannot remain concealed from itself.[7] Not even that concealment that has rendered metaphysics a battleground of endless controversies (A viii) is intrinsically necessary; it is merely the consequence of the fact that "the common principle" had not previously been discovered—sheerest accident astray at the very source of all necessity. Nothing essential separates reason from total self-presence—only that "trial, practice, and instruction" that it happens to require "in order gradually to progress from one level of insight to another."[8] With regard to reason's self-disclosure, enlightenment is assured: "if only freedom is granted,"—"freedom" signifying here release from constraints external to reason, constraints which "lie not in lack of reason but in lack of resolution and courage," so that correspondingly the preceding conditional is driven outside the following conditioned:—"enlightenment is almost sure to follow."[9] It is almost as though the history of metaphysics ought not to have been, as though it were, at most, the passage of reason through childhood. Having now reached the maturity marked by the inception of critique, reason would establish its own self-possession beyond the reach of any radical crisis.[10] Through the labor of transcendental criticism a new edifice secured from the ground up would be erected alongside the ruins of the old metaphysics. Crisis would thus be resolved, its resolution conforming entirely to the classical schema of recourse to reason—that is, the crisis would in the end prove not to have been radical.

Everything hinges upon the issue of reason's essential self-presence. Only the assurance of essentially total self-presence can entitle reason to serve as its own tribunal. Only such assurance can vindicate repeating with respect to the problem of reason itself the classical schema of recourse to reason. Only such assurance can excuse this "metaphysics of metaphysics"[11] from reflecting what is problematic in metaphysics back upon itself; for if, on the contrary, reason could be essentially concealed from itself, such concealment could then invade critical reflection itself and haunt it at every level, robbing it of that security with which crisis would be finally suppressed.

In this connection one can only be astounded at how consistently Kant's texts invoke, defend, and circumscribe such self-concealment: most notably in the theories of inner sense and of freedom. The discontinuity is obtrusive: That assurance of self-presence that is required for the Kantian recourse is decisively withdrawn in the execution of that recourse—that is, the very condition of critique is withdrawn by critique. The issue of self-presence thus constitutes the hinge connecting two conflicting strata of Kant's discourse. There is a turning on this hinge: a turning back into crisis. This turning, this subversion of metaphysical security, is what, at the deepest level, gives the Kantian beginning its distinctive openness.

4.

Archaic reflection, focusing upon certain texts, is interpretive, hermeneutical. It is detached from its texts in such a way as to open up the possibility of original access to what is traced in the text, to traces at various, possibly discordant levels of the text, perhaps even to certain traces that remained imperceptible to the author of the text. In the *Critique of Pure Reason* Kant openly grants such hermeneutical space:

> I need only remark that it is by no means unusual, upon comparing the thoughts which an author has expressed in regard to his subject, whether in ordinary conversation or in writing, to find that we understand him better than he has understood himself; as he has not sufficiently determined his concept, he has sometimes spoken, or even thought, in opposition to his own intention (A 314/B 370).

It is not without significance that this remark is inserted into a portion of text devoted to consideration of Plato's use of the word "idea."

Two general hermeneutical principles can be gleaned from Kant's text, in which they are generated, whether overtly or not, by transposition of complementary methodological principles (governing the relation: writer-text) to the dimension of interpretation (thus made to govern the relation: interpreter-text). The first such principle is a canon of classical hermeneutics; it pertains to the relation between part and whole. The complementary methodological principle is formulated in one of Kant's letters to Garve: "Another peculiarity of this sort of science is that one must have a conception [*Darstellung*] of the whole in order to rectify each of the parts, so that one has to leave the thing for a time in a certain condition of rawness, in order to achieve this eventual rectification."[12] This methodological principle, prescribing that the progression from parts to whole be followed by a regression from whole to parts, i.e., prescribing a circling in which each would be determined through the other—this principle is transposed in the Preface to the *Critique of Practical Reason* into its hermeneutical form:

> When it is a question of determining the origin, contents, and limits of a particular faculty of the human soul, the nature of human knowledge makes it impossible to do otherwise than begin with an exact and (as far as is allowed by the knowledge we have already gained) complete delineation of its parts. But still another thing must be attended to which is

> of a more philosophical and architectonic character. It is to grasp correctly the idea of the whole, and then to see all those parts in their reciprocal interrelations, in the light of their derivation from the concept of the whole, as united in a pure rational faculty [*Vernunftvermögen*]. This examination and the attainment of such a view are obtainable only through a most intimate acquaintance with the system. Those who are loath to engage in the first of these inquiries and who do not consider acquiring this acquaintance worth the trouble will not reach the second stage, the synoptic view [*Übersicht*], which is a synthetic return to that which was previously given only analytically (V, 10).[13]

The second principle connects that of whole and parts to the question of definition. It is found in the same text, in the form of a precaution:

> Such a precaution against making judgments by venturing definitions before a complete analysis of concepts has been made (usually only far along in a system) is to be recommended throughout philosophy, but it is often neglected. It will be noticed throughout the critiques (of theoretical as well as of practical reason) that there are many opportunities for supplying inadequacies and correcting errors in the old dogmatic procedure of philosophy which were detected only when concepts, used according to reason, are given a reference to the whole (V, 9n).

The precaution is against venturing definitions and thereby final particular determinations prior to the return from the whole to those parts; one cannot begin with definitive determinations but must rather grant a stratification of the text corresponding to different degrees of determinacy. Such stratification is especially suited for systematic appropriation of traditional concepts, allowing them to be taken over with a certain suspension of determinacy so as then to be progressively redetermined at several successive levels of determinacy. Such rigorous appropriation is of course typical of Kant.

It goes almost without saying that the archaic reflection to be focused on the Transcendental Dialectic is to be attentive to that hermeneutical space in which it is to be cast. Likewise, it is to be accordant with those hermeneutical principles gleaned from Kant's texts. However, these principles, pertaining to such concepts as part, whole, and determination, are merely formal and by no means suffice to generate the complex and various structures that can be exhibited by hermeneutical spaces. For the most part, the relevant structures are materially determined—that is, they are generated from the manifest structure of the text itself, from the matter put at issue in that text, and from the interplay of reflection, matter, and text. To this degree rigorous predetermination of the hermeneutical space is precluded. Yet one could hardly even initiate reflection without some anticipation of the structures that are to govern that reflection. An anticipatory sketch is indispensible.

Let me distinguish four differently structured spaces, each corresponding to a particular interpretive strategy.

The first is that of *duplex interpretation* or *commentary*. It is as though a loose, half-blank page were to be folded (*plicare*) in two (*duo*), an image of the original text then being inscribed on the previously blank half. Such interpretation, doubling the Kantian text, remains within the horizon explicit in that text itself, the horizon constituted by the author's expressed conception of the problems and aims animating the text; it remains thus within a traditional conceptuality and is shaped to and by that conceptuality. Yet, even within the simple twofold, distance is already installed, the space of reflection opened up between the text and its double, between original and image.

The second strategy, that of *projective interpretation*, is determined by a subordinate reflection to which I have already alluded: the reflection of the Kantian concept of reason back into its Greek origin, the translation of reason back into λόγος. This reflection presupposes a certain recovery of that origin; it presupposes that, reversing the direction of tradition, one has translated λόγος back into Greek. Here I can only outline this recovery.[14] It is a recovery which carries the verb form λέγειν back behind that sense ("to speak") which eventually gained dominance and from which the sense of λόγος came largely to be determined. It carries λέγειν back to the sense: to lay—specified as: to let things lie together before us, to let them be manifest, to collect them, gather them, into presence. Λόγος means originally: gathering into presence—and it is only because speech was experienced as such gathering that λόγος could acquire a specifically linguistic sense. As a gathering, λόγος is neither a mere circumscribing that would leave unmarked the elements thus gathered; nor, on the other hand, does it impose uniformity on these elements. Rather, it lets opposed elements come together, and thus from this original sense are generated the concepts of synthesis and of articulation. Λόγος, as the gathering of opposed elements, composes them *all* into *one*, yet without suppressing their mutual opposition. Λόγος occurs as: Ἓν Πάντα.

It is, then, a matter of reflecting the Kantian problem of reason back into the original issue of λόγος as gathering, of uncovering those traces of the original sense which continue to operate, subliminally, within the concept of reason. It is a matter of positing reason as gathering, the gathering of reason, and of thereby orienting the Kantian text in such a way as to assemble from its elements an interpretive horizon that is not overtly operative in that text. Projective interpretation, taking over the results of duplex interpretation, consists then in the projecting of these results upon that horizon in such a way that they get understood from it, mirrored back, reflected, from it.

The third strategy, that of *inversive interpretation*, broadens the textual base while still retaining the focus on the Transcendental Dialectic. Its space is one of inverse imaging, of inversion; and within this space it is a matter of exhibiting various texts as inversions (in various differentiated regards) of the focal text. It is a matter of letting this text, the Transcendental Dialectic, be inversely imaged, reflected, in a series of other Kantian texts in such a way that, through the play of imaging, through the reflection, a concealed stratum of the focal text can be unearthed.

The final strategy, that of *subversive interpretation*, re-installs the Kantian texts within the history of metaphysics in such a way as to constitute the space of a complex series of turnings: a turning within the metaphysical gathering of reason; the counter-turning of critique; and a turning which, subverting metaphysics, turns the reflection finally away from the Kantian texts.

CHAPTER I

INTERPRETIVE HORIZONS

1. THE PROBLEM OF METAPHYSICS

> . . . we begin from the point at which the common root of our power of knowledge divides and throws out two stems, one of which is *reason*. By reason I here understand the whole higher faculty of knowledge and am therefore contrasting the rational with the empirical (A 835/B 863).

This point marks also the beginning of metaphysics: The division gets retraced through that movement in which, turning away from the immediately present, one comes to have recourse to reason; thereby the division gets established in a certain overtness and the immediately present differentiated, retrospectively, as the (merely) empirical. Because it marks the beginning of metaphysics, Kant can, near the end of the *Critique of Pure Reason*, begin from this point "to project the architectonic of all knowledge arising from *pure reason*"—that is, to project the architectonic of that metaphysics for which that entire Critique is the requisite preparation, that metaphysics in which the cultivation of human reason would be consummated (A 850/B 878). And it is from this same point, strategically engraved at the end of the Introduction (". . . there are two stems of human knowledge, namely, sensibility and understanding, which perhaps spring from a common, but to us unknown root"—A 15/B 29), that the entire critical propaedeutic begins. From this point, which thus punctuates the Kantian text, one can invoke, perhaps most directly, with fewest strokes, the horizon explicitly governing that text. This same horizon is to govern the duplex interpretation to be made of a major segment of that text.

From this point of division arises the traditional distinction between historical knowledge and rational knowledge.[1] Kant formulates this distinction in terms of the origin of knowledge: "Historical knowledge is *cognitio ex datis*; rational knowledge is *cognitio ex principiis*" (A 836/ B 864). Even at this level of mere appropriative reformation, a peculiar shift is already in play (one which will eventually prove decisive for placing Kant's text within the history of metaphysics): Delimiting historical knowledge as that kind which is given from "elsewhere" (*anderwärts*), he thus shifts the locus of the immediately present; what was originally a turn away from the immediately present has become a turn to something present in a more profound and no less immediate sense; it has become a turn *from* the presence of objects (an imperfect presence because of the very difference separating objects from the subject) *to* reason's presence to itself, a turn from presence to self-presence.

But what is more decisive in the present connection is the problematic generated by the concept of purely rational knowledge and confirmed by a cursory glance at the history of metaphysics. The problem is one which Kant never ceased to reiterate: If metaphysics consists of purely rational knowledge, knowledge *ex principiis*, knowledge purely through concepts (in distinction from historical, i.e., empirical knowledge, but also from mathematical knowledge which, though not empirical, involves construction in intuition), then how is it possible for metaphysics to be legitimated as a knowledge of things, as synthetic knowledge? How can there be knowledge of something that is "elsewhere" (outside the mere thought, the concept) without that knowledge having come from "elsewhere"? How is purely rational synthetic knowledge possible? Only if this problem is resolved in a rigorous, binding way can metaphysics, that "battlefield of . . . endless controversies" (A viii), be placed upon the secure path of science. Hence, the *problem* of metaphysics: How is metaphysics as science possible?

If this problem is regarded with sufficient generality, if it is formulated in terms not only of theoretical knowledge (determining of objects) but also of practical knowledge (self-determination), then it may be deemed the horizon of critique as such, of the entire enterprise to which the three critiques are devoted. By resolving this problem, critique is to prepare the ground for metaphysics (as science), for a system of pure reason:

> For if such a system is one day to be completed under the general name of metaphysics (which it is possible to achieve quite completely and

> which is of highest importance for the use of reason in every connection), the ground for the edifice must be explored by critique as deep down as the foundation of the faculty of principles independent of experience, in order that it may sink in no part, for this would inevitably bring about the downfall of the whole.[2]

On the other hand, the same problem, regarded in terms of theoretical knowledge only, forms the horizon of the *Critique of Pure Reason.*

What, then, does the resolution of the problem require, taking it now in its more restricted form? The answer is given by the title which Kant assigns to that portion of the *Critique of Pure Reason* that encompasses almost the entire text, excluding only the Prefaces, the Introduction, and the concluding Doctrine of Method: what is required is a Transcendental Doctrine of Elements. A doctrine of elements: an analysis of human knowledge into its elements, an exhibiting of its fundamental articulation. A *transcendental* doctrine of elements: an analysis distinguishing those elements which, constitutive of objects, belonging to the very conditions of the possibility of objects, are therefore sources of purely rational knowledge of those objects; an analysis distinguishing them especially from those elements which only *seem* to supply such knowledge, through such semblance drawing us instead into self-dissimulating error and onto that battleground of endless controversy thereby prepared. This dividing of the analysis into a delimiting of constitutive elements *and* a distinguishing of them from semblant elements broaches that division of the entire Transcendental Doctrine of Elements (hence of nearly the entire *Critique of Pure Reason*) which contrasts the Transcendental Dialectic, the negative component, with the entire remainder. Although this is not the only articulation at this level—another cuts across it, the division stemming from the division of the common root, the division into Transcendental Aesthetic and Transcendental Logic—it nonetheless establishes the most immediate, explicit horizon of the Transcendental Dialectic and so is of focal significance for the corresponding duplex interpretation.

2. GATHERING

In the case of projective interpretation the horizon has a quite different character. Not explicit in the text itself, not already cast in its unity by the author's expressed conception of the problems and aims animating the text, it must rather be *assembled.* Yet it is anything but a matter of constructing independently of the text at issue a horizon then to be imposed on that text as an alien framework; against such external violence of interpretation the advantage will always be had, quite rightly, by the counterdemand for a freeing, a restoration, of the text. Nevertheless, such restoration need not go to the extreme of hermeneutical positivism. Indeed the very schema that would then be implicit holds the issue of interpretation within an alien, not to say ontologically naive, framework, as though it were at most a question of various degrees stretching with utter continuity between two extremes: on the one hand, the text taken as it itself is (as though its objectivity were self-evident), on the other hand, the text taken in terms of some alien framework. It goes almost without saying that this schema effectively suppresses all genuine hermeneutical questioning.

To assemble a horizon for projective interpretation is a matter, not of preparing an alienation of that text, but rather of freeing a level of discourse submerged in that text and of establishing its unity by reference to a certain subordinate reflection—in the present instance, the reflection of the Kantian concept of reason back into its Greek origin, the translation of reason into λόγος, the posing of reason as gathering. But the horizon is to be assembled *from the text itself*, rigorously composed from elements of the proximate context of the text at issue.

Let me begin with the opening sentences of the Transcendental Aesthetic (A 19/B 33). Though outwardly cast as a mere series of definitions, this opening is of major systematic and interpretive import. Beginning from the point at which the common root divides, Kant sketches in these opening sentences the *beginning* of the *Critique of Pure Reason*, i.e., that configuration of the matter at issue from which the entire development of this text will proceed. It is from this beginning that the assembling of the horizon needs to proceed.

The matter to be put at issue is knowledge of objects. Thus Kant begins: "In whatever manner and by whatever means a mode of knowledge may relate to objects, *intuition* is that through which it is in immediate relation to them. . . ." This says: In all knowledge of objects, in all synthetic knowledge (regardless of its specific character), intuition has a certain primacy. Intuition is that by which knowledge stands in *immediate* relation to its object. Whatever may be involved in the full structure of the relation of knowledge to its object, whatever else this relation may involve, intuition is what gives it its element of immediacy. Intuition contributes the immediate content of knowledge. This peculiar primacy is held by intuition in *all* knowledge of objects; it extends over all distinctions between different kinds of knowing. In every case intuition is what provides knowing with its objective immediacy.

Whatever other elements may belong to knowledge must, accordingly, be considered in reference to the primacy held by intuition. Thus, in the first sentence Kant adds that intuition is that "to which all thought as a means is directed." At least at the level of the beginning, intuition and thought must not be regarded as coordinate stems; rather, at this level intuition has primacy over thought, which is no more than a means in service to intuition. But the limits of this opening determination need to be carefully established: Kant's posing of thought as a means in service to intuition does not consign it to a minor role within the structure of knowledge. On the contrary, thought is what is most problematic in that structure and what is most in need of the discipline of critique; correspondingly, the major part of the Transcendental Doctrine of Elements is a Transcendental Logic, i.e., an investigation of the role of (pure) thought in knowledge of objects. Nevertheless, if in the course of the *Critique of Pure Reason*—that is, in the *development* of the matter at issue, in contrast to its initial configuration—there emerges a respect in which thought enjoys a primacy within the structure of knowing, such primacy will be built, as it were, on the character of thought as a means in service to intuition and thus will complement rather than negate the distinctive primacy had by intuition.

Kant continues: "But intuition takes place only insofar as the object is given to us." In what ways can the object be given? How can such giving occur? What forms can it assume? Two forms may be specified, corresponding to the possibility that the giving may proceed from the side of the subject or from the side of the object. In the first case the subject would give itself the object; in the other case the object would give itself to the subject.

This distinction between two ways of giving, which is itself generated formally from the subject-object distinction, opens, in turn, onto the distinction between an essentially self-enclosed, unlimited knowing and the exposed, limited knowing to which man finds himself constrained. The former, though associated (in an emphatically empty way) with the concept of the divine, is thematized almost exclusively in structural terms. It is definitive of such unlimited or divine knowing that within it the intuition of the object is essentially free of any limitation by the object intuited, in no way dependent on (limited by) the object's giving itself. In limited, human knowing the intuiting is, by contrast, dependent on a giving which proceeds from the object.

This distinction between divine knowing and human knowing is decisive for the horizon to be assembled. Specifically, I shall go about assembling this horizon by elaborating structurally the opposed terms of this distinction and transforming it finally into a concept of the movement of human knowing. This elaboration of the distinction is a matter merely of unfolding the relevant concepts, of unfolding the possibilities contained in the concept of knowing and its modalization into limited and unlimited modes; in Kant's terms, this development falls on the side of thought rather than knowing.[3] Most emphatically, it is not to be understood theologically, as though it were a matter of knowledge about God; rather, it is a matter of developing the distinction in such a way as to situate human knowing and to pose the problem of human knowing.[4]

Each of the two modes of knowing needs to be elaborated in such a way that certain components of its full structure are made explicit. In the case of divine knowing, these components are forms of unity: It is a matter of exhibiting the *fourfold unity* that is prescribed by the concept of such knowing.

Divine knowing corresponds to that form of giving in which the subject gives itself the object. To give itself the object is to bring the object forth, to create it in the very act of knowing it. The intuition operative in such knowing Kant calls *original* intuition (B 72): It is original in the sense that it *originates* the very object intuited, that is, contains within itself the origin of that object and thus first lets the object come forth into existence. In the case of original intuition the object does not exist beyond (independently of) the intuition; it neither arises outside the sphere of that intuition nor, originating within the intuition, is it released from that intuition so as to stand in itself. Thus, original intuition is not separated from its object; and, to the extent that divine knowing coincides with such intuition, it is a knowing which forms an immediate unity with its object, a knowing immediately *present* to its object. This unity of subject and object constitutes the *first* of the four forms of unity prescribed by the concept of divine knowing.

The unity is comprehensive, for divine knowing is nothing but such original intuition, nothing else beyond it. Divine knowing coincides with original intuition: Kant declares that in thinking the primordial being, it is to be granted that "all his knowledge must be intuition, and not *thought*, which always demonstrates [*beweist*] limitations" (B 71). What are these limitations that would be demonstrated, shown, made manifest by thought? They are not only—and not fundamentally—limitations belonging properly to thought but limitations within intuition. Thought would demonstrate, show up, not so much its own limitations as rather the limitations in intuition. How? The demonstration lies in the connection between the very need for thought and the limitation of the corresponding intuition: the very need for thought, the very involvement of thought in a knowing, would attest to limitations in the intuition on which that knowing is built. Thought is a means in service to intuition, and the need for that means would testify to limitations in the intuition. Conversely, if intuition is unlimited, perfect, complete, there will be no need for thought; and so a knowing built upon an unlimited intuition will be purely intuition, will involve no thought.

Original intuition is precisely such an unlimited, complete intuition. It brings forth its object in immediate unity with itself and thus has the object totally within its purview, is utterly self-enclosed. From such intuition the object cannot be withdrawn, cannot hold itself in reserve. It is prohibited from giving itself in a merely *partial* way such that there would remain in it, as given, as turned toward intuition, a certain indeterminacy—an indeterminacy which would then need to be repaired through the determining power of thought. Rather, original intuition is such that from its very inception the object is posed in its *full presence*—that is, original intuition involves no need for the object to be *gathered into presence*. Posed in its full presence, the object is intuited in its *full* determinacy; it is spared that indetermination which, testifying to a withheld reserve, announcing (making manifest, making present) a certain *absence*, would shatter the mirror of full presence. Divine knowing is fullness of vision, its object a unity of presence immune to all indeterminacy, all fragmentation; and if God does not think, it is because his intuition is so complete that he has no need to think. This *unity of intuition* constitutes the *second* of the forms of unity prescribed by the concept of divine knowing.

The issue involved in this form of unity is also expressed through Kant's identification of original intuition as "intellectual intuition" (B 72). This expression is taken over from the *Inaugural Dissertation.* According to the earlier work, divine intuition is independent (i.e., not dependent on an object existing independently of it) and archetypal (i.e., brings forth its object); it is "on that account perfectly intellectual."[5] For an intuition to be intellectual means, within the context of the *Dissertation,* that it is intuition of intelligible things in contrast to sensible things, of things as they are rather than as they appear to an intuition that is sensible.[6] The connection is clear: Because divine intuition is original, its object is totally within its purview, that is, incapable of being in any regard withdrawn, absent, concealed, from that intuition; within such an intuition the object must show itself as it is, and consequently the intuition is intellectual.

The expression "intellectual intuition" points also to another issue, for there is something highly problematic about the conjunction posed in this expression. Within the structure of human knowing the intellectual is set over against the intuitive: Whereas intuition, as sensibility, is that receptivity of the subject by which objects appear to it, the intellectual is what is not capable of appearing but must rather be thought.[7] Thus, the expression "intellectual intuition" conjoins thought and intuition. Yet, how can these be so fused into unity that intuition not only uses thought as a means but is actually stamped by the character of thought, i.e., becomes intellectual? And how especially is such conjunction possible in divine knowing? How can divine intuition be intellectual if God does not think?[8]

The same problematic conjunction is also introduced in another form, namely, in the concept of an understanding which is also intuitive, an intuitive understanding. In the Transcendental Deduction (B 145) Kant refers explicitly to "an understanding which is itself intuitive" and then adds in parentheses: "as, for example, a divine understanding which would not represent to itself given objects but through whose representation the objects would themselves be given or produced." This explanation in reference to the example of divine understanding makes it clear that in this conjunction of intuition and understanding the issue is essentially the same as in the consideration of original intuition. But the issue has been transposed into the form appropriate to the Transcendental Analytic: whereas in the Transcendental Aesthetic

Kant considers divine knowing as an intuition so self-sufficient as to require no further contribution by thought, in the Analytic he regards it as an understanding—hence, as thought (cf. A 69/B 94)—so self-sufficient as to give itself its object, as an understanding thus in need of no separate faculty of intuition such as would otherwise be required to supply understanding with its object. In both cases it is a matter, not of one faculty to the exclusion of the other, but rather of their unity.[9] It is a matter of thinking that unity from two different perspectives: In the Transcendental Aesthetic the unity of intuition and thought is considered from the perspective of intuition; in the Transcendental Analytic this same unity is considered from the perspective of thought or understanding.

Kant offers a still more refined formulation for that conjunction expressed in the concept of intuitive understanding. He writes: "An understanding in which through self-consciousness all the manifold would *eo ipso* be given, would be intuitive"—and then he adds the contrasting concept: "our understanding can only *think* and for intuition must look to the senses" (B 135; cf. B 138–9). This formulation poses the major term of the conjunction in a more radical form: Transcendental apperception, self-consciousness, is the fundamental act of understanding, and a self-sufficient understanding would be such as to give itself its object through this fundamental act. For such an understanding all positing relative to something other than itself would be dissolved into its own self-positing. Especially in this formulation the peculiar completeness, wholeness, unity, of divine thought is evident; it is a unity which consists in self-sufficiency, in not being dependent upon, mediated by, an essentially detached intuition. This *unity of thought* constitutes the *third* of the forms of unity prescribed by the concept of divine knowing.

In Kant's formulation of the two principal concepts of divine knowing there is an apparent conflict: according to the concept formulated in the Transcendental Aesthetic divine knowing would be primarily intuition, whereas according to the concept given in the Transcendental Analytic it would be primarily thought or understanding. However, this conflict between the concept of original intuition and that of intuitive understanding is resolved to the extent that both concepts prove to involve the same issue merely considered from two different perspectives, namely, that of the unity of intuition and thought. But is the issue really the same in both cases? Can this sameness be maintained in view of the character of original intuition? Is not original intuition precisely such that it essentially excludes any admixture of thought whatsoever? Does Kant not stress precisely this exclusion of thought from original intuition? If God does not think, how can there be in divine knowing a unity of thought and intuition? How can it be maintained, then, that the concepts of original intuition and of intuitive understanding present the same issue?

It is necessary to consider more carefully what Kant would exclude in excluding thought from original intuition. The sole issue in the exclusion—what is to be preserved by it—is the unity, the completeness, of divine intuition; and so, what Kant would exclude is all thought that would be correlative to some limitation in the intuition. What kind of thought would this be? It would be a thought correlative to an *indeterminacy* on the side of intuition, a thought which as means in service to intuition would "repair" such indeterminacy. What Kant excludes is all thought that would assume the form of a *determining*, of an establishing of determinacy in a more or less indeterminate "given." Does this mean that *all* thought is excluded? It does not—as can be seen by examining more closely the concept of original intuition.

In original intuition the object is not only intuited but also brought forth, created, posited in its existence as an object. Furthermore, the positing is in thoroughgoing unity with the intuiting: the object is not posited and then intuited but rather is posited in its very being intuited and is intuited in its very being posited. However, intuition is as such receptive. Thus, if within original intuition there is to be a positing of the object, a positing in unity with the intuitive reception, there must be incorporated into that intuition a spontaneity which, despite the opposition between spontaneity and receptivity, is unified with that intuition. Such spontaneity, such power of positing (in contrast to mere receiving) is the power of thought.[10] Hence, in this respect thought must be integral to original intuition. However—and this is what Kant's exclusion enforces—such thought is not a determining thought, not a thought which establishes determinations in something, not a thought which posits relative to a "given," not a discursive thought.[11] It is rather a thought which posits *originally*,[12] which posits the object as such instead of merely positing determinacy in a pregiven object.

I conclude: In divine knowing—whether regarded as original intuition or as intuitive understanding—intuition and thought are not merely correlative, not merely two "stems," but rather are fused into an essential unity. Divine knowing is anterior to the point at which the common root divides,[13] anterior of course to metaphysics and critique—or rather, in another sense, divine knowing is precisely that point, that original unity posited by critique. This *unity of intuition and thought* constitutes the *fourth* of the forms of unity prescribed by the concept of divine knowing.

Thus unfolds from the concept of divine knowing—specified as original intuition and as intuitive understanding—a fourfold unity: unity of subject and object, of intuition, of thought, and of intuition and thought. These four forms of unity within the structure of divine knowing are the moments which the assembling of the (projectively) interpretive horizon is to take over from this term of the general distinction between divine knowing and human knowing. Taking them over, it is then a matter of extending the elaboration to the corresponding moments within the structure of human knowing—that is, of unfolding the fourfold disunity, the fourfold fragmentation, which within human knowing corresponds to the fourfold unity of divine knowing.

Let me rejoin the opening of the Transcendental Aesthetic: "But intuition takes place only insofar as the object is given to us." This says: Human knowing corresponds to that form of giving which proceeds from the object; in human knowing the object gives itself to the subject. The intuition involved in such knowing Kant calls "derivative intuition." Here the knowing subject is dependent on something not created by that subject, on its announcing itself, on its affecting the subject. Thus Kant continues: "This again is only possible, to man at least,[14] insofar as the mind is affected in a certain way." Such dependence on affection already indicates the relevant disunity between subject and object. This disunity is more specifically determined through Kant's concept of sensation and of the role played by sensations in human knowing: "The effect of an object upon the faculty of representation, so far as we are affected by it, is sensation." As mere effects, mere modifications of the subject's receptivity, sensations cannot be regarded as corresponding to anything in the object itself. What the object gives, the effects which it produces in the mind, does not coincide with the object as it is in itself; indeed the breach in the presence of subject to object is so radical that even the assertion of it is rendered problematic. This radical separation between the object (the thing-in-itself) and what is given on the side of the subject (sensation) constitutes the *first* of the forms of disunity, a *disunity of subject and object.*

To an intuition thus dependent on affection and thus separated from its object the inner nature of that object is not given. To such intuition is not given the substance of the thing, i.e., the inner essence which would make the thing what it, in its singularity, is. To human intuition is not given the thing in its singular intelligibility.[15] Rather, in place of the thing in its singular unity, there is given to human intuition only sensations, which not only are remote from the thing-in-itself but also, since they "occur in the mind separately and singly" (A 120), constitute a radically dispersed manifold. Sensations constitute only the "matter" of appearances; they are devoid of form, utterly fragmentary, utterly lacking wholeness and unity (cf. B 129–30; A 99). This *disunity of intuition* is the *second* of the forms of disunity. It is a disunity which shatters the full presence of divine intuition, leaving the object withdrawn, absent, and in its stead only scattered fragments. Here the need is obtrusive: the need for the object to be *gathered into presence.*

Because of its fragmentary character, its radical dispersal, its indeterminacy, human intuition requires thought as a means. Such intuition needs thought in order to be supplied with that determinacy which it itself lacks, in order thus to be raised to the level of a knowing; it needs thought in order for the object to be gathered into presence. In turn, the distinctive character of human thought derives from the peculiar directedness which it has to human intuition, to serving the need of human intuition. Specifically, human thought has the character of a determining; it is an establishing of determinacy in something pregiven to it, namely the indeterminate manifold of derivative intuition. Human thought is a positing *relative to* a "given"—not, as in the case of divine thought, a positing of the object itself.[16] At every level it is subject to a sensible condition. It is a positing which is thus dependent, partial, which requires that a content be supplied to it from elsewhere, and which remains fragmentary without that content.[17] This *disunity of thought* is the *third* of the forms of disunity.

Since human intuition is derivative, the object for such intuition is not simply posited through an act of positing thought fused into unity with the intuition itself. On the contrary, there is a separation between receptivity and spontaneity, between the intuited and the determination posited by thought for the intuited. In other words, there are two stems of human knowledge. Its division into these two stems, i.e., the *disunity of intuition and thought*, constitutes the *fourth* of the forms of disunity.

My intention in thus elaborating the terms of the general distinction, in exhibiting the fourfold unity of divine knowing over against the fourfold disunity within human knowing, has been to sketch in its basic structure the hiatus separating human from divine knowing. However, this separation is not a matter of a mere static gap between two immovable levels—or, rather, it is such only as the abstract framework of a movement. The transformation of the elaborated distinction between divine knowing and human knowing into a concept of the movement of human knowing constitutes the decisive final step in the assembling of the (projectively) interpretive horizon.

This transformation is a matter of granting human knowing its intrinsic movement: Human knowing is not simply situated once and for all on the lower side of the gap but is rather the movement across the gap, the movement of closing the gap. In other words, the fourfold disunity, the fragmentation within human knowing, constitutes only the *beginnings* of human knowing. Such knowing is not, however, merely subject to, and totally determined by, these beginnings but rather is a movement *from* the beginnings. It is a movement of ascent toward the level of divine knowing, a movement of self-perfecting. More precisely, it is a movement of gathering the fragmentary beginnings into unity, a movement of gathering through which the fourfold disunity of the beginnings would be repaired, a movement by which the object, gathered into its unity of presence, would be gathered into presence to the subject. It is a movement through which the initially dispersed, disunited, fragmentary, would be gathered up into a unity akin to that of divine knowing. Human knowing as a movement of gathering, is a movement toward re-creating out of the fragmentary beginnings of human knowing a unity akin to that of divine knowing.

The horizon for the projective interpretation is thus assembled: It is constituted by this complex concept of gathering—gathering of fragmentary beginnings into unity akin to that of divine knowing, gathering of object (and ultimately of self) into presence. Yet this gathering, in its highest aspirations, coincides with metaphysics itself. For critique it is accordingly a matter of carefully attending to the limit of the gathering ascent of human knowing, of rigorously establishing that point at which, in dramatic terms, the bond of human knowing to its fragmentary beginnings reasserts itself, threatening aspiration with tragedy and diverting philosophy into sophistry. The *Critique of Pure Reason* would determine this limit and, insofar as possible, provide means by which human knowing might be restrained within it.

3. MODES OF GATHERING

The horizon thus assembled is to serve for the projective interpretation of a text, the Transcendental Dialectic, which is itself part of a larger text, the Transcendental Doctrine of Elements of the *Critique of Pure Reason*. It is thus a text which has in the strongest and most literal sense its context. In order to prepare for the interpretation, this context needs, then, to be assimilated to the horizon—that is, the Transcendental Aesthetic and the Transcendental Analytic need to be referred to the issue of gathering. They need to be rendered (though only in a global, preparatory way) as presenting various *modes of gathering*.

The basic issue in the Transcendental Aesthetic is, as the title indicates, sensibility or intuition considered in reference to its *a priori* elements. The issue is *a priori* sensibility, i.e., pure intuition (A 21/B 35–6). How does pure intuition constitute a mode of gathering?

Within the context of the beginnings as constituted by the fourfold fragmentation, sensation may be designated as the *utter* beginning of human knowing both in the sense that the dependence of human knowing on sensation is at the root of all its forms of fragmentation and in the sense that sensation provides the beginning element of which human knowing is in a certain respect only a development. At the level of this beginning element there is utter disconnection, utter dispersal, utter lack of form, sheer content (cf. A 99; A 120; B 129–30). But this level, sensation, is only the beginning; it is not yet a knowing, not yet even intuition in the genuine sense. Rather, intuition and the knowing built upon it require a movement away from this beginning—that is, intuition takes place as a surpassing of this beginning level, as an informing of the sheer content, as bringing it under form. This informing, this provision of form, takes place, at the most elemental level, through *pure intuition*. Pure intuition serves to *gather* the dispersed manifold of sensations. As a constitutive moment within empirical intuition, it serves to gather the sheer "given" into the pure forms of space and time, forms which are so "essentially unitary" that, in contrast to the objects of empirical intuition, they admit manifoldness only by limitation (cf. esp. A 25/B 39; A 32/B 47–8). Pure intuition is a mode of gathering; it is the first mode of gathering, since within the structure of the gathering as a whole it is presupposed by all further modes.

In what way does this gathering serve to repair the disunity that constitutes the beginnings of human knowing? Just how does it serve to gather in unity what is fragmented? Which specific forms of fragmentation does it serve to repair? Clearly the disunity repaired is not one involving thought, neither that of thought itself nor that of thought and intuition, for the gathering in pure intuition occurs at a level at which thought is not yet installed, at the level where the matter for thought is first constituted.[18] Also, there is at this level no repairing of the disunity of subject and object but, at most, only remote preparations for such. The disunity that does get repaired through pure intuition is that of intuition itself (the second of the four forms). That utter fragmentation, so radical that even the title "intuition" is not yet appropriate, is surpassed through the gathering in pure intuition; what was utterly fragmented is gathered into unity, granted wholeness. In the case of *original* intuition such a gathering would of course not be necessary, for the very fragmentation thus repaired is lacking; it is in this connection that one should understand Kant's insistence that divine knowing does not involve any pure intuition: "We are careful to remove the conditions of time and space from his intuition" (B 71).

In the concept of pure intuition there is a peculiarity which needs to be noted. Because of its character *as intuition*, pure intuition is such that something is given to it. Yet, because of its character *as pure*, what is given to such intuition must be such as to originate, not from the side of the object, but rather from the subject itself. Thus, in pure intuition the subject gives something (a form) to itself—that is, what is given (intuited in pure intuition) is *posited* within that very intuition, in unity with it. In other words, the structure of pure intuition is the same as that of original intuition; in both cases there is unity of intuiting and positing.[19] The difference is that pure intuition brings forth only the formal constituents of the appearing object (space and time as the forms of appearances) whereas original intuition brings forth the object as a whole, is its sole origin. Thus, with pure intuition there is inscribed at the core of human intuition an image of original (divine) intuition. Within pure intuition itself, considered in abstraction from its role in empirical intuition and thus in knowing as a whole, all forms of fragmentation would be abolished and not just repaired; the gathering would be absolute (if I may for strategic purposes retain this contradiction). But, this image of original intuition is always inserted into the total structure of empirical intuition—indeed in such a way that its gathering power is carried over in limited form to the whole of empirical intuition (and the contradiction thereby decomposed).

At the level of the Transcendental Analytic or, more generally, at the level of thought there are several different modes of gathering. The distinction between them is rooted in a threefold distinction that emerges from Kant's initial delimitation of the concept of transcendental logic (cf. A 50/B 74–A 57/B 82): the distinction between *logical thought*, which, as in syllogistic reasoning, abstracts from all content so as to deal only with the form of knowledge; *empirical thought*, which deals with empirical content, as in ordinary empirical judgments; and *pure thought*, which involves a content that is pure, i.e., nonempirical. The modes of gathering corresponding to these types of thought need to be considered.

Kant avers that "we constantly have need of inference" (A 303/B 359). What is accomplished by means of inference? What need is satisfied thereby? One does not, strictly speaking, extend his knowledge of things, for inference (of the deductive kind at issue here) is purely formal. According to Kant, inference serves rather to establish connections between items of knowledge already in one's possession, that is, to give *formal unity* to knowledge, as, for example, when a proposition is brought under certain further conditions by means of a syllogism. Kant says that "in inference reason endeavors to reduce the varied and manifold knowledge obtained through the understanding to the smallest number of principles (universal conditions) and thereby to achieve in it the highest possible unity" (A 305/B 361). Thus, in logical thought items of knowledge already constituted, i.e., judgments, are gathered into formal unity. Logical thought is a mode of gathering.

This need for inference, the need for the gathering in logical thought, is rooted in the fragmentary beginnings to which human knowing is tied. In human thought there is a fundamental disunity, a lack of wholeness, of self-sufficiency, in the sense that such thought does not include its correlative intuition in unity with itself. Rather, it depends on an independent, essentially detached faculty of intuition which provides its content. Such thought takes the form of a *determining* of this content. Yet, a content can be determined in various regards; for example, one and the same thing can be determined as red, long, heavy, etc.; and so, *many* determinations arise. Instead of the single unified act of positing the object, as in divine knowing, there is a multiplicity of partial positings in which the object is determined *as* something, i.e., as having some definite character. Consequently, human thought is *dispersed* into a manifold of determinations. Because it is dispersed, there is need of that gathering which is accomplished in logical thought.

The gathering character of empirical thought is evident even at the level of mere conceptualization. In contrast to intuitions, concepts are never simply given but rather arise through the spontaneity of thought; whatever may be the source of their matter (content), that form by which they are specifically constituted as concepts is always made rather than given. Kant describes such form when he defines a concept as "a representation of that which is common to many objects."[20] Correspondingly, the basic act of conceptualization by which the form originates is an act of bringing many under a one; in his *Logic* Kant calls this basic act "reflection" and indicates how in its full structure it engages two other acts, the subordinate acts of comparison and abstraction.[21] In the *Critique of Pure Reason* Kant refers to the basic act not only as reflection (e.g., A 85/B 117) but also as function: "Whereas all intuitions, as sensible, rest on affections, concepts rest on functions. By 'function' I mean the unity of the act of bringing various representations under one common representation" (A 86/B 93). This basic act is a gathering of many under a one.

The *significance* of the gathering character of empirical thought is more evident in Kant's account of the way in which concepts are actually used in knowing things, namely, in empirical judgments of the kind that lie at the root of the need for logical thought, empirical judgments in which something is determined *as* having some definite character. The relevant significance is expressed when Kant writes: "Accordingly, all judgments are functions of unity among our representations; instead of an immediate representation, a *higher* representation, which comprises the immediate representation and various others, is used in knowing the object, and thereby much possible knowledge is collected into one" (A 69/B 93–4). Why is such recourse to a higher representation required? Why is a generic representation, a concept, used in knowing the object? Because the immediate representation does not suffice for knowing the object. In other words, since intuition (the immediate representation) does not present that inner essence of the object that would render it genuinely intelligible, recourse must be had to concepts (higher representations) in which the object is made intelligible through unification with others under a one. The lack of a singular unifying essence is compensated for by gathering the object together with others under a generic unity; lack of full presence is compensated for by a gathering which, having recourse to concepts, indirectly makes present.

It is clear that the fragmentation which the gathering repairs in the case of empirical judgments is that of intuition. But there is something peculiar about this gathering: Empirical thought does not simply gather the relevant manifold into that unity which it lacks but instead gathers it into a higher unity. Why does the gathering take this form? Why does empirical thought not simply gather the manifold into the unity of the thing's singular essence? Thought could gather the manifold in this direct way, into the singular essence, *only if* thought first of all *posited* that unity, since it is decisively not given to human knowing. But this is impossible: Thought cannot simply posit the singular essence of the object, for the object is so withdrawn from the subject that there is lacking entirely any ground that could render such positing objectively valid. Nevertheless, empirical thought must posit a unity for its gathering of the manifold, since none is given. But the unity which it posits is not that of a singular essence but rather a determination freed from intuition by conceptualization, a concept.[22]

Just as logical thought (inference) takes over what has already been accomplished by empirical thought in order that it might be brought to a higher level of unity, so empirical thought presupposes the accomplishment of pure thought. Indeed, the Transcendental Logic takes pure thought as its principal theme (as the title indicates), and all developments concerning empirical thought or logical thought are ultimately for the sake of dealing with the problem of pure thought. Yet, the Transcendental Logic is divided into an Analytic and a Dialectic, and this division corresponds to a modalization of pure thought, its division into the modes of understanding and reason. Most of Kant's initial presentations of this distinction are formulated in terms of the (formal) logical employment of the two faculties; but such employment provides no more than a clue for developing the distinction between pure understanding and pure reason. Such fundamental distinctions are never ready-made such that at the outset one could simply formulate them once and for all; they have rather to be worked out through the inquiry itself from whatever initial opening is available, however inadequate that initial grasp might eventually prove to have been. In the case of the distinction between understanding and reason, the deepening of the distinction through the inquiry itself can be made especially evident by projecting the issue upon the (projectively) interpretive horizon; it is then possible to grasp the distinction in terms of a fundamental difference between two modes of gathering. But such a grasp cannot be had at the outset.

The mode of gathering that is principally at issue in the Transcendental Analytic is that linked to pure understanding. Kant elaborates this mode of gathering at successively more fundamental levels, corresponding roughly to the three middle chapters of the Analytic (Transcendental Deduction, Schematism, Principles). In this preparatory sketch I shall limit consideration to the first of these levels.

The principal elements of the relevant gathering are first laid out at that point, prior to the Transcendental Deduction, where Kant introduces the categories by following the clue provided by the logical table of judgments (A 76/B 102 – A 83/B 109). Since pure understanding involves no empirical content, it cannot be related to objects in terms of any such content; its relation to objects cannot, as with empirical understanding, consist in determining objects with respect to some definite empirical content. Its relation to objects must be a pure, nonempirical relation. In general, understanding can relate to objects only mediately, only through intuition (cf. A 19/B 33); and so, in particular, the pure relation of pure understanding to objects must be mediated by intuition. Thus, at the level at which the Transcendental Deduction begins, Kant presents the relation of pure understanding to objects as simply mediated by *pure* intuition; since the Transcendental Aesthetic has at this point already worked out the relation of objects to pure intuition (pure intuition constituting the form of appearances), the central issue becomes that of the relation between pure understanding and pure intuition.[23]

How can understanding be related to pure intuition? It can relate to such intuition only by somehow applying its spontaneity to the material (content) provided by pure intuition—that is, by providing concepts under which this material can be unified. Thus Kant says that the manifold of pure intuition provides the "material for the concepts of pure understanding" (A 77/B 102). This manifold must, he continues, "be gone through in a certain way, taken up, and connected." He adds: "This act I name synthesis"—"the act of putting different representations together and of grasping what is manifold in them in one [act of] knowledge." Pure understanding provides the concepts for the synthesis of pure intuition, the concepts under which its manifold is gathered into unity. These concepts Kant calls pure concepts of the understanding or categories.

Thus, in that mode of gathering that is linked to pure understanding, the manifold to be gathered is that of pure intuition and the form of unity into which this manifold is to be gathered is that which is thought in the pure concepts of understanding. However, pure understanding does not itself gather the manifold into unity. What actually accomplishes the gathering is, not understanding, but imagination: "Synthesis in general . . . is the mere result of the power of imagination, a blind but indispensable function of the soul, without which we would have no knowledge whatsoever but of which we are scarcely ever conscious" (A 78/B 103). Thus, the gathering involves three elements: pure intuition, pure understanding, and imagination. It is clear that imagination, bringing the manifold of pure intuition under the concepts of pure understanding, is the mediating element.

Within the Transcendental Deduction the elaboration of the structure of this gathering proceeds in relation to the general task of the Deduction. This task itself comes, in the course of the Deduction, to be grasped at progressively more fundamental levels. According to the initial formulation the Deduction has as its task to settle a certain question of right (*quid juris*), namely, that with which certain concepts are applied to objects. Regarding which kind of concepts does there arise such a question of right? It arises with regard to those concepts which are not derived from the things of experience, i.e., those concepts which are nonempirical but which (it is claimed) apply to these things in other than a purely formal way. In other words, the task of the Deduction is to show how *pure* concepts can have objective validity. In

Kant's words, the Deduction is "the explanation of the manner in which concepts can thus relate *a priori* to objects" (A 85/B 117).

Kant delimits the relevant conditions of possibility: There are only two ways in which a concept and an object can have a necessary relation to one another: Either the object must make the concept possible or the concept must make the object possible. In the first case the relation is empirical, the concept an empirical, not a pure, concept. The case of pure concepts must fall under the other alternative: a pure concept, if it is to have necessary relation to an object, must be such as to make the object possible. Thus, the question becomes more specific: How do pure concepts make possible the object of experience? Kant excludes one alternative, implicitly bringing into play the distinction between human knowing and divine knowing: Pure concepts do not make the object possible in the sense of producing it, bringing it into existence. Rather, they make the object possible *as an object*, that is, they make possible its very character *as* an object, that is, they constitute its objectivity:

> The question now arises whether *a priori* concepts do not also serve as antecedent conditions under which alone anything can be, if not intuited, yet thought as object in general. In that case all empirical knowledge of objects would necessarily conform to such concepts, because only as thus presupposing them is anything possible as *object of experience*. Now all experience does indeed contain, in addition to the intuition of the senses through which something is given, a *concept* of an object as being thereby given, that is to say, as appearing (A 93/B 125–6).

Pure concepts make it possible for appearances to be experienced not merely as appearances but as appearances *of* something, *of* an object. It is in this connection that Kant describes the categories as "concepts of an object in general" (B 128; cf. B 146).

Two different descriptions of the categories have emerged. On the one hand, Kant describes them as concepts of synthesis, i.e., as concepts which define a unifying unity, a unity for a gathering. On the other hand, he calls them concepts of an object in general, i.e., concepts through which appearances are constituted as appearing objects. It needs finally to be seen how these two descriptions converge in the issue of the transcendental object.

This issue originates in the further determination of the way in which pure concepts make possible the object of experience. Kant proposes to clarify what is meant by object or, specifically, by "an object of representations":

> We have stated above that appearances are themselves nothing but sensible representations, which, as such and in themselves, must not be taken as objects capable of existing outside our power of representation. What, then, is to be understood when we speak of an object corresponding to, and consequently also distinct from, our knowledge? (A 104).

This says: Appearances alone, the material supplied by intuition, do not constitute objects; they lack objectivity, lack that character of standing over against knowledge. The problem is then: How can there be objects? How is an object constituted? Or, in a more detached formulation: What is that "objectifying function" by which appearances are referred to an object, that is, constituted as appearances *of* an object?

One might suppose this objectifying function to be merely a matter of referral, i.e., merely a connecting of appearances with the object. In the strict sense, however, such a connecting would be impossible, for the object is not given, is "nothing to us" (A 105). It is not as though appearances and object were equally present to intuition such that one could simply be referred to the other; it is not as though the subject would need only to supply the connection between the two terms.

What, then, must be the character of the objectifying function and of the object to which appearances are attached through this function? Kant continues: "It is easily seen that this object must be thought only as something in general = x, since outside our knowledge we have nothing which we could set over against this knowledge as corresponding to it" (A 104). Here there are two essential indications. (1) Since the object is not given, it can enter into the structure of experience only as *something thought*, as something posited by thought. But (2) as what is it posited? As having what specific determination? The point is that it is not posited as having any specific determinations, not posited as a specifically determined object; for there are no specific objective determinations given, such that it could then be posited as corresponding to them. Rather, it is thought only as something in general = x; it is posited as object in general, posited only as having those determinations which anything must have in order to be an object (in the most general sense).

The object thus posited may be identified as the *transcendental object*:[24]

> But these appearances are not things in themselves; they are only representations, which in turn have their object—an object which cannot itself be intuited by us and which may, therefore, be named the non-empirical, that is, transcendental object = x. The pure concept of this transcendental object (which actually throughout all our knowledge is always one and the same = x) is what can alone confer upon all our empirical concepts in general relation to an object, that is, objective reality (A 109).

In short, since the object is not given, it can only be posited as object in general, as transcendental object, to which, then, appearances would somehow be referred. Thus regarded, the objectifying function would involve two components: the positing of the transcendental object and the referral of appearances to this object.

The transcendental object is, then, simply the totality of those determinations that belong to any object whatsoever, that define the very sense "object." The crucial point is that these determinations are *forms of unity*; this is why Kant can write of "that unity which constitutes the concept of an object" (A 105). More specifically, these determinations are precisely those forms of unity represented by the categories; thus Kant writes that the categories "are fundamental concepts by which we think objects in general for appearances" (A 111). Pure thought (more precisely, pure understanding) is the thinking *of* the transcendental object, the thinking in which it is posited. Or, to cast the issue in terms of form/content, pure understanding represents the objective form for the matter of appearances; it posits the form under which that matter must be brought, by which it must be informed, in order to be objectified and thus constituted as appearance of an object.

These terms especially serve to clarify the other component of the objectifying function, the referral of appearances to the transcendental object. For, in a sense, it is not a referral at all but rather an informing, a unifying, of appearances:

> Now we find that our thought of the relation of all knowledge to its object carries with it an element of necessity; the object is viewed as that which prevents our modes of knowledge from being haphazard or arbitrary and which determines them *a priori* in some definite fashion. For

> insofar as they are to relate to an object, they must necessarily agree with one another, that is, must possess that unity which constitutes the concept of an object (A 104–5).

For appearances to be related to an object requires that they possess that unity, those forms of unity, that is thought in the transcendental object (or, correlatively, in the categories). In other words, appearances can be objectified only by being made to embody that unity, only through the synthesis of the manifold: "It is only when we have thus produced synthetic unity in the manifold of intuition that we are in a position to say that we know the object" (A 105). Even more directly: "an object is that in the concept of which the manifold of a given intuition is united" (B 137). The objectification of appearances, the constitution of appearances as appearing object, the bringing forth of the object into presence, takes place as the gathering of the manifold of appearances into the forms of unity defined by the concepts of pure understanding. But this gathering of the manifold of appearances is, according to the Transcendental Deduction, made possible—even, in effect, accomplished—by that gathering of *pure* intuition into these forms of unity. The entire issue of objectivity is brought back to the issue of the fundamental gathering.

This fundamental gathering, in its extension through pure intuition to the empirical manifold of which pure intuition is the form, serves to repair all those forms of disunity that constitute the beginnings of human knowing. First of all, through this gathering the intuited is gathered into the form of an object, constituted as an object. Thus, in place of that object in itself from which the finite subject is radically separated, this gathering constitutes an object correlative to finite subjectivity. Gathering the object to the subject, it repairs the disunity of subject and object. Yet, it repairs it only within limits; the gathering does not establish such absolute, self-enclosed unity as that which defines divine knowing but only a unity in which articulation is essentially preserved as trace of the gathering. Second, by this provision of an object *for* what is intuited the gathering also repairs the disunity of intuition, i.e., it brings the intuited appearances under the form (unity) of objectivity, brings the object forth into presence. Third, it grants a wholeness to thought. Within the structure of the gathering, thought is in a certain regard freed of dependence on empirical content, that is, thought accomplishes a genuine positing of the object, namely, of the transcendental object. To this extent, pure thought is an image of divine thought (just as pure intuition proved to be an image of original intuition). However, it is *only* an image of divine thought, for it is a positing which is subject to a sensible (though not an empirical) condition, the condition expressed in the schematism or, more generally, in its dependence on the power of imagination actually to accomplish the synthesis which it prescribes. Finally, this subjection of thought to a condition indicates that the gathering serves to repair the disunity of intuition and thought. Thought is not only dependent on imagination but, by virtue of that very dependence, is gathered together with intuition. Imagination, gathering the object into presence to the subject, binding intuition and thought together in a unity akin to that of intellectual intuition, nevertheless sets apart from the divine that unity of human knowing thus constituted, sets it apart by inscribing in it articulation (or, more precisely, the modes of articulation as such, the transcendental schemata).

CHAPTER II

THE TRANSCENDENTAL DIALECTIC

Let me proceed now to the duplex interpretation of the focal text, the Transcendental Dialectic. To the space of such interpretation belongs the horizon explicit in the text itself; I have thematized this horizon as the problem of metaphysics. Furthermore, the space of such interpretation prescribes that the conceptuality and even the style of the interpretation be shaped to the traditional conceptuality with which this horizon, enclosing the entire text, is infused. Indeed, the commentary which such interpretation will generate is eventually to be taken up into the projective interpretation, that is, projected upon the horizon that has been assembled, the horizon constituted by the issue of gathering. But the commentary has first to be prepared, and methodological clarity requires that this preparation be kept distinct from the projective interpretation.

1. TRANSCENDENTAL ILLUSION (A 293/B 349–A 299/B 355)

The Transcendental Dialectic belongs to the Transcendental Doctrine of Elements. Specifically, it constitutes that part of the transcendental analysis devoted to distinguishing those elements which *seem* to supply purely rational knowledge without actually doing so, those semblant elements which thus generate transcendental illusion.

It is not, however, from this partition of the Transcendental Doctrine of Elements that Kant begins, but rather from that other major division that cuts across it, the division into Transcendental Aesthetic and Transcendental Logic. The Transcendental Dialectic constitutes the Second Division of the Transcendental Logic. At the beginning of the

Transcendental Logic, where Kant develops the concept of such a logic in contrast to general logic, he characterizes transcendental logic as excluding from its purview, not all content (as does general logic), but merely all empirical content. Transcendental logic thus deals with "the rules of the pure thought of an object" (A 55/B 80). Its first part, the Transcendental Analytic, deals with this matter in a primarily positive way: It exhibits the elements of the pure thought of an object and establishes their character as such by reference to the possibility of experience. The second part, the Transcendental Dialectic, is primarily negative: Kant characterizes it as a critique of dialectical illusion. Also, he indicates that it takes the form of a critique of reason with respect to that kind of employment by which such illusion is generated (cf. A 63/B 88). The Introduction to the Transcendental Dialectic develops these preliminary indications.

In the first of the two parts of this Introduction Kant undertakes to delimit the sense of "dialectical illusion" or, as he now calls it, "transcendental illusion." He indicates first the sense which "illusion" ("*Schein*") as such is to be taken to have, a procedure required by the fact that the word "*Schein*" includes in its range of meaning the sense of "shine," "look," "appearance," "semblance," as well as that of "illusion"; the sense which Kant indicates for it corresponds closely to that of "illusion," and so it is necessary for Kant to exclude the other senses. Yet, in doing so, he also determines positively the sense which the word is to have.

Kant distinguishes illusion (*Schein*) from probability (*Wahrscheinlichkeit*): Probability is a matter of insufficiently grounded truth, whereas illusion falls on the side of error. In contrast to probability, illusion is a matter of deception, of something which serves to lead us into error or hold us in it. Indeed, illusion has as its generic character: seeming to be true. But the seeming which specifically constitutes it is one which diverges from the truth rather than coinciding in content with it.

Kant distinguishes illusion also from appearance (*Erscheinung*): Appearance is simply what is intuited in intuition, and in mere intuition there can be no truth or error, hence, no illusion.[1] Rather, it is only in judgment, not in mere sense, that these are to be found: "Truth and error, therefore, and consequently also illusion as leading to error, are only to be found in judgment [*Urteil*], i.e., only in the relation of the object to our understanding" (A 293/B 350). This does not mean, however, that the locus of truth, error, and illusion is fully constituted by understanding or thought. Understanding, taken alone, is no more capable of objective truth or error than are the senses: "Thus neither the understanding by itself (uninfluenced by another cause) nor the senses by themselves would fall into error" (A 294/B 350). The relevant locus lies rather in judging, in bringing what the senses offer (appearances) under what understanding provides (concepts). It lies "in the relation of the object to our understanding"—in the relation between sensibility, by which the object is given, and understanding, by which the object is thought.[2] The origination of illusion is thus to be considered in reference to this locus, in terms of the relation between intuition and thought; illusion arises when the proper relation between intuition and thought is disrupted in a certain way. Kant suggests that this disruption somehow proceeds from the side of sensibility: "Now since we have no source of knowledge besides these two, it follows that error is brought about solely by the unobserved influence of sensibility on the understanding, through which it happens that *the subjective grounds* of the judging flow together with the objective grounds and make the latter deviate from their determination [*Bestimmung*] . . ." (A 294/B 350–1). Kant elaborates only to the extent of drawing an analogy between his task and the analysis of a complex motion into the constituent forces that produce it; transcendental reflection has as its task to resolve that misdirection of judging from which error and illusion arise into those components pertaining respectively to sensibility and understanding. Presumably it is only through such transcendental analysis that the otherwise "unobserved influence of sensibility on the understanding" could be genuinely exhibited.[3] Only thus could it be shown how sensibility is "the ground of error" (B 351 n.).

Kant focuses next on specifically transcendental illusion, contrasting it with two other kinds. It is to be distinguished, in the first place, from empirical illusion, i.e., from that kind of illusion which we usually tend to regard as mere deception of the senses (e.g., optical illusions). In such illusion, however, the error does not arise from the senses—"the senses do not err" (A 293/B 350)—but rather from empirical judgment; as Kant later says, we "treat as being immediately perceived what has really only been inferred" (A 303/B 359). By contrast, transcendental illusion is linked to *pure* understanding rather than to empirical understanding and the employment of its concepts in empirical judgment. Transcendental illusion arises, not in empirical judging, but in a "deceptive extension of *pure understanding*" (A 295/B 352). In order to indicate the general character of this extension, Kant introduces two distinctions. He distinguishes, first, between immanent principles (*Grundsätze*), those the application of which is confined entirely within the limits of possible experience (as in the case of the principles of pure understanding exhibited in the Transcendental Analytic), and, on the other hand, transcendent principles, those which profess to pass beyond the limits of possible experience. The second distinction clarifies a term of the first: Kant distinguishes transcendent principles from the transcendental employment of the categories, i.e., from the mere application of the categories to things in general and in themselves. The point of the distinction is that the transcendental employment of the categories is merely an error of judgment regarding those limits marked out by the Transcendental Analytic; as in the case of empirical illusion, there is merely error in the subsumption of things under concepts. By contrast, transcendent principles are not simply a matter of error in judgment but rather are such as actually to incite one to trespass the relevant limits: "A principle, on the other hand, which takes away these limits or even commands us actually to transgress them is called *transcendent*" (A 296/B 353). It is with such transcendent principles that transcendental illusion arises. Thus, it is with such principles—and not with mere transcendental employment of the categories—that the Transcendental Dialectic is concerned.

Kant draws the further contrast between transcendental illusion and logical illusion. The latter, which he identifies as the illusion of formal fallacies, results from mere lack of attention to the formal rules of thought and is such that as soon as we attend to these rules the illusion disappears. Logical illusion is simply a matter of oversight, not something which positively forces itself upon us. Kant draws the contrast: "Transcendental illusion, on the other hand, does not cease even after it has been detected and its invalidity clearly revealed by transcendental criticism" (A 297/B 353). Here there is a *natural* and inevitable *illusion*, "a natural and unavoidable dialectic of pure reason," which is "inseparable from human reason" (A 298/B 354). Mere attention, mere exposure of such illusion, does not remove it; one can no more make such illusion disappear "than the astronomer can prevent the moon from looking larger at its rising" (A 297/B 354). Such illusion is not something "which some sophist has artificially invented" (A 298/B

354)—that is, it pertains to a sophistry of a different order, a sophistry which belongs so essentially together with philosophy as to be its constant threat. It is the task of the Transcendental Dialectic to expose the threat and to put into effect whatever precautions are available against the deception with which we are thus threatened; but there is no pretense of abolishing the threat.

How does transcendental illusion arise? Kant specifies the brief account already given regarding the origin of illusion as such. There are certain subjective rules for connecting our concepts in a way that serves the understanding; however, these rules look as though they were objective, they seem to be determinations of things. And so, "We therefore take the subjective necessity of a connection of our concepts, which is to the advantage of the understanding, for an objective necessity in the determination of things in themselves" (A 297/B 353). Kant does not indicate how it happens that the subjective rules come to look objective, how this seeming to be objective but not being so originates—or, rather, he indicates it in the only way appropriate at this preliminary stage, by naming reason as the locus of the issue.

The second part of the Introduction to the Transcendental Dialectic is thus entitled "Pure Reason as the Seat of Transcendental Illusion." It should be noted that only at this point, nearly halfway through the *Critique of Pure Reason*, does Kant finally address himself directly to what is named in the title of the work as the matter at issue—pure reason. One should, accordingly, proceed carefully and be especially attentive to the statement with which Kant begins: "All our knowledge starts from the senses, proceeds from thence to understanding, and ends with reason, beyond which there is no higher faculty to be found in us for elaborating the matter of intuition and bringing it under the highest unity of thought" (A 298/B 355–6). This statement is decisive for the duplex interpretation: It situates reason with respect to intuition and understanding, thus situating also the Transcendental Dialectic with respect to the Aesthetic and the Analytic. The statement is even more decisive as regards the preparation for the projective interpretation, for it is one of those statements (the first in the Dialectic) which point decisively beyond their immediate context to the horizon that has been assembled for the projective interpretation, the horizon consisting of the conception of human knowing as a movement from disunity toward unity, as a movement of gathering the fragmentary beginnings into unity. It should be noted how in this decisive statement Kant refers specifically to various elements of this horizonal conception: to knowing as movement, to the senses as constituting the beginning from which that movement proceeds, to the gathering character of the movement (i.e., its bringing the matter under unity). And it should be noted also how he gives a first, general articulation of this movement into two phases, one involving understanding, the other involving reason. Within the total movement of human knowing reason is thus linked to the final of the two principal phases.

2. REASON (A 298/B 355–A 309/B 366)

The Transcendental Dialectic is to work out the problem of transcendental illusion. The locus of this problem has been identified as pure reason. Kant's immediate task is to give a preliminary characterization of pure reason.

It was noted above that only at this point, nearly halfway through the *Critique of Pure Reason*, does Kant finally address himself directly to what is named in the title of the work as the matter at issue. Considered in this connection, the first half of the work appears as merely preparatory for the Transcendental Dialectic; in traditional terms the revolution in ontology (*metaphysica generalis*) that is brought about through the Aesthetic and the Analytic is for the sake of a critical confrontation with rational psychology, rational cosmology, and rational theology (the disciplines of *metaphysica specialis*). On the other hand, such a centering of the critical undertaking in the Dialectic is limited by an ambiguity in Kant's use of the word "reason." According to the broader of the two senses, the Aesthetic and the Analytic belong to the critique of pure reason no less than does the Dialectic, for this broader sense corresponds to the mere "contrasting [of] the rational with the empirical"—that contrast to which Kant comes by beginning "from the point at which the common root of our power of knowledge divides and throws out two stems" (A 835/B 863). This sense is to be distinguished from the narrower sense according to which reason is only *one* of the higher faculties of knowledge, to be contrasted especially with understanding.[4] In the Transcendental Dialectic "reason" is used in the narrower sense.[5] One ought surely to be provoked by the apparent outrage: The word which names the fundamental matter put at issue in the *Critique of Pure Reason* is left openly ambiguous! That the movement of reason (in the narrower sense) is the final phase through which the movement of reason (in the broader sense) would be brought to decisive fulfillment, that it is—or, rather, would be—the crowning mode of gathering, might well provoke one to suspect that the ambiguity is anything but a mere equivocation—that it is, rather, grounded in the issue of reason itself.

The second of the two parts of the Introduction to the Transcendental Dialectic is entitled "Pure Reason as the Seat of Transcendental Illusion." This part is divided into three sections.

It has been noted already how at the very beginning of his consideration of reason Kant identifies it as belonging to the final phase of that movement of knowing in which the matter of intuition is brought under the unity of thought. How is it, then, to be positively characterized? Kant confesses that the task of explaining this highest power of knowledge (*oberste Erkenntniskraft*) puts him in a certain perplexity (*Verlegenheit*). What is it about this task that prompts Kant to call attention to the perplexity in which it places him? What is especially perplexing about this task of explaining reason? No doubt there is manifold ground for perplexity in face of the issue of reason, as the Dialectic will amply confirm. But also there is a perplexity of a special order to which Kant's remark may be appropriately referred. It is a perplexity of a kind that attends the beginning of any fundamental inquiry: An initial characterization of reason is something perplexing, difficult, even hazardous, because the inquiry which Kant is to initiate thereby has as its aim to put reason *at issue* in a fundamental way. If the issue is to be decided genuinely, from the matter itself, the initial characterization must be such as to leave open the space for the decision; it must be sufficient for initiating the inquiry yet such as does not merely define reason in advance in a way that would close off the matter and, in effect, settle the issue before the questioning has even really begun. The *Critique of Pure Reason* is no *positive* science: It does not merely take as its theme something already posited in its basic determination but rather makes an issue of the basic determination of reason. Thus, it is not a matter merely of formulating a sufficiently precise statement of an already decided definition of reason.

Nevertheless, an initial characterization of reason is required, and it is to this task that Kant turns. He proceeds by characterizing, first, reason in general, subsequently considering its more specific forms. His characterization of reason in general involves three steps.

First, he indicates how, as reason in general, it has two specific forms. Thus, he distinguishes between the logical use of reason and its real use, i.e., between reason as a logical faculty and reason as a transcendental faculty. This division into two specific forms is analogous to the case of understanding; indeed, it is a distinction which goes back to the very beginning of the Transcendental Logic where Kant distinguishes between general logic and transcendental logic (cf. esp. A 55/ B 79–80). In the logical, i.e., merely formal, use of reason, abstraction is made from all content of knowledge; in this capacity reason is simply the faculty of making mediate inferences, syllogisms. In its real use there is likewise no empirical content involved; however, there is a content of another order, a pure content. What is the relation of transcendental (i.e., pure) reason to this content? Kant says that "it contains within itself the origin of certain concepts and principles, which it does not borrow either from the senses or from the understanding" (A 299/B 355). Thus, transcendental reason originates its pure content, just as pure understanding originates that pure content expressed in the categories. In fact, Kant proposes to proceed as he did in the analysis of understanding, namely, to use the logical faculty as the clue for uncovering the transcendental faculty: "Following the analogy of concepts of understanding, we may expect that the logical concept will provide the key to the transcendental and that the table of the functions of the former will at once give us the genealogical tree of the concepts of reason" (A 299/B 356). Nevertheless, Kant indicates that the logical faculty provides *only* a clue; having defined logical reason as the faculty of making mediate inferences, he observes that the other faculty (transcendental reason) "is not to be understood from this definition" (A 299/B 355). Consideration of the logical use of reason provides only an opening onto the problem of pure reason. Already one can anticipate another determining factor which utterly distinguishes pure reason: its relation to pure understanding, that relation which Kant has already indicated as being crucially involved in the origination of transcendental illusion (cf. A 297/B 353).

Granted the analogous division into logical and pure forms, how, then, is reason to be distinguished from understanding? The statement of this distinction forms the second step in Kant's characterization of reason in general. Referring to the characterization of understanding as the faculty of rules, he says: "reason we shall here distinguish from understanding by entitling it the faculty of principles [*Vermögen der Prinzipien*]" (A 299/B 356). What is a principle? Kant says: "Knowledge from principles is, therefore, that knowledge alone in which I apprehend the particular in the universal through concepts" (A 300/B 357). Two senses must be distinguished. According to the looser sense, "every syllogism is a mode of deducing knowledge from a principle" (A 300/B 357) and any proposition capable of serving as a major premise in a syllogism may be termed a principle. This sense corresponds to the logical use of reason in contrast to its real use. According to the other, stricter sense, a proposition can be termed a principle only if it is such *in itself* and according to its proper origin, not merely within a syllogism—that is, only if it itself expresses a knowing purely through concepts, a knowing dependent on thought alone. It is important to observe that the principles (*Grundsätze*) of pure understanding, as formulated in the Analytic, are to be distinguished from principles (*Prinzipien*) in this strict sense: Because the principles (*Grundsätze*) of pure understanding do not constitute a knowing purely through concepts, because they involve the requirement that concepts be brought under sensible conditions (schematized), because they must be supported "by conditions of a possible experience in general" (A 301/B 357), they are not principles (*Prinzipien*). How, then, is reason distinct from understanding? In their real use, toward which Kant orients the distinction, both are faculties of rational knowing in that broad sense to be contrasted with empirical knowing. Both are faculties of knowing through concepts, but in fundamentally different ways: Pure reason is a knowing *purely* through concepts, pure understanding a knowing through concepts *as* essentially linked up with intuition, i.e., *as* brought under the sensible condition expressed in the schematism.

The final step in Kant's characterization of reason in general is an elaboration of the distinction between reason and understanding:

> Understanding may be regarded as a faculty which secures the unity of appearances by means of rules, and reason as being the faculty which secures the unity of the rules of understanding under principles. Accordingly, reason never applies itself directly to experience or to any object but to understanding, in order to give to the manifold knowledge of the latter an *a priori* unity by means of concepts, a unity which may be called the unity of reason and which is quite different in kind from any unity that can be accomplished by the understanding (A 302/B 359).

This elaboration is decisive, for here again Kant's statement points beyond its immediate context to that horizon that has been assembled for projective interpretation. In this statement Kant, in effect, elaborates the character of the final phase of the gathering movement, that phase at which reason comes into play. The analogy with understanding, already posed in the initial articulation of the gathering (cf. A 298/B 355–6), remains intact: In both cases the function performed is structurally the same, namely, that of bringing a manifold under a unity, i.e., gathering. But the terms of the gathering, the specific unity and manifold, are different. In the case of understanding the unity is one of rules (i.e., of categories), the manifold that of appearances; in the case of reason the unity is one of principles, the manifold that which remains after the understanding has done its work, the "manifold knowledge" of understanding. Just as understanding takes over the manifold yielded by intuition and gathers it into certain forms of unity, so, likewise, reason takes over the manifold yielded by understanding and gathers it into still higher forms of unity.

Kant alludes again, in conclusion, to the fundamental difficulty of such characterization: "This is the universal concept of the faculty of reason insofar as it has been possible to make it clear in the total absence of examples" (A 302/B 359). The characterization is only preliminary. Already, in fact, it has tended to focus on a specific form, pure reason, rather than remaining at the level of full generality.

Kant compensates somewhat in the second section, "The Logical Employment of Reason." He distinguishes between immediate and mediate inference, correlating this distinction with that between understanding and reason (in their logical employment); he briefly discusses mediate inference or syllogism (*Vernunftschluss*), loosely correlating its three constituent propositions with understanding, judgment, and reason, respectively, and distinguishing the three types, categorical, hypothetical, and disjunctive.[6] He notes that the syllogism is to be regarded regressively ("If, as generally happens, the judgment that forms the conclusion is set as a problem . . ."—A 304/B 361) and that, correspondingly, reason in its logical employment engages in reducing the manifold of knowledge to the smallest number of general principles, thus bringing it under the highest possible unity.[7]

The final section focuses explicitly on the pure employment of reason. Kant poses the problem of *pure* reason: Does reason itself originate concepts by which it relates to objects?—i.e., Is it "objective" in the manner of pure understanding? Or, is reason merely a faculty for imposing logical form on knowledge? Kant proceeds to anticipate his answer, and his anticipation serves to indicate a third alternative between those of being objective (in the manner of pure understanding) and being merely, formally logical. According to this third alternative, reason would be applied to understanding just as the latter is applied to the manifold of intuition so as to bring it under a certain unity; reason would thus serve "to bring the understanding into thoroughgoing accordance with itself" (A 305/B 362). On the other hand, reason would not thereby prescribe any law for objects but rather would provide only "a subjective law for the orderly management of the possessions of our understanding" (A 306/B 362). One should recall Kant's previous indication that the origination of transcendental illusion consists precisely in the illicit transformation of such a "subjective law" into an objective principle that would determine things (cf. A 297/B 353).

Kant gives direction to the problem of pure reason by focusing, finally, on two features of logical reason and using them as clues for determining the character of pure reason. He notes that logical reason does not directly determine objects, as does empirical understanding; rather it takes the determinations yielded by understanding and unifies them through inference, connects them in syllogisms. Likewise, pure reason is not directly related to objects: "Accordingly, even if pure reason does not concern itself with objects, it has no immediate relation to these and the intuition of them but only to the understanding and its judgments" (A 306/B 363–4). Thus, the unity of reason is not that of understanding, that of a possible experience; and its principles will, consequently, be transcendent in relation to objects of possible experience.

The second relevant feature of logical reason lies in its bringing a certain judgment (the conclusion) under higher conditions (the premises), its bringing a conditioned under its conditions; this procedure can, in turn, be indefinitely reiterated by the construction of prosyllogisms. Analogously, pure reason seeks to trace the conditioned back through its entire series of conditions. On the other hand, the analogy is limited: "But this logical maxim can only become a principle of *pure reason* through our assuming that if the conditioned is given, the whole series of conditions, subordinated to one another—a series which is therefore itself unconditioned—is likewise given, that is, is contained in the object and its connection" (A 307/B 364–5). At this stage one can only wonder about much of what Kant alludes to in this cryptic anticipation: In what sense can a series of conditions be unconditioned? What does it mean to say that a series of conditions is given or contained in the object? What sense does containment have here? Although the passage leaves many questions unanswered, it serves as an important warning against expecting to gain full access to the problem of pure reason merely by extending the analogy with logical reason. The issues have rather to be developed from "deeply concealed sources."

3. IDEAS
(A 310/B 366–A 320/B 377)

The Transcendental Dialectic has commenced with a regress from the problem of transcendental illusion to that of pure reason. In the Introduction this regress is merely preparatory—that is, Kant merely points to pure reason as the seat of transcendental illusion in order that, subsequently interrogating what has thus been brought into focus, he might exhibit such illusion as it actually unfolds from its source.

The Introduction also supplies an initial characterization of reason. To summarize: This characterization yields three essential determinations, which, though they remain general in the way required of preparatory determinations, provide, nevertheless, the initial cast of the Dialectic, the structural formation of issues from which the subsequent interrogation will move. The first determination is closely related to Kant's way of distinguishing between logical reason and pure reason: pure reason is such as to *originate a pure content.* The second determination corresponds to the contrast between reason as a faculty of principles and understanding as a faculty of rules: The content which reason originates is *purely conceptual.* The third determination arises in Kant's elaboration of the analogy between reason and understanding; just as understanding, through the categories, provides forms of unity for the manifold of intuition, so reason, through its pure content, provides forms of unity for the manifold knowledge of understanding. Hence, this determination may be formulated: The pure content which reason originates consists of *forms of unity for the gathering* of the manifold of understanding.

Thus, the essential determinations of pure reason are determinations of it with respect to that pure content to which it is essentially related. Reciprocally, that content is itself determined as originated by pure reason, as purely conceptual, and as constituting forms of unity for the gathering of the manifold of understanding. Items of such pure content Kant designates as concepts of pure reason. Hence derives the title of the first of the two Books into which the Transcendental Dialectic as a whole is divided: The Concepts of Pure Reason. One of its concerns is with the other name to be given to these concepts of pure reason—"transcendental ideas."

In Book I Kant undertakes a more precise characterization and derivation of the concepts of pure reason, a "subjective derivation" of these concepts "from the nature of our reason" (A 336/B 393). The first two paragraphs, leading up to the beginning of Section 1, he devotes to elaborating two more specific determinations that are carried over from the Introduction, determinations which in effect develop the problem of reason and its content from the perspective of the distinctive gathering in which they are involved. The first of these determinations places the pure content, the concepts of pure reason, beyond objects of experience: pure reason has no immediate relation to objects. Thus unbound, pure reason is fit for engagement in a regression from the level of objects, which are thoroughly conditioned, back through the relevant conditions to something finally unconditioned. It is a matter now of elaborating reason's aloofness from objects of experience and its involvement in the regression from conditioned to condition. In the elaboration the correlativity of the two determinations comes especially into play.

Both determinations come together in Kant's characterization of the concepts of pure reason as "not merely reflected but inferred concepts" (*nicht bloss reflektierte, sondern geschlossenen Begriffe*). The characterization is meant to express a contrast: concepts of pure understanding *are* merely reflected concepts. What does Kant mean in designating certain kinds of concepts as reflected? What is a reflected concept? The proper sense can be grasped only in relation to Kant's analysis of conceptualization. According to that analysis a concept originates in an act by which a manifold content is brought under a one in which the many agree; this basic act Kant calls "reflection."[8] So, in conceptualization the manifold content is reflected into the concept that originates in that very act, and in this sense the concept is a reflected concept. It is clear how an empirical concept is always a reflected concept: It originates in an act of reflecting a manifold empirical content into a unity of form. But Kant insists that even the concepts of pure understanding are reflected concepts. Why? Because, in Kant's words, "they contain nothing more than the unity of reflection upon appearances, insofar as these appearances must necessarily belong to a possible empirical consciousness" (A 310/B 367)—that is, they are the unities into which appearances must be reflected *a priori* in order to satisfy the conditions for the possibility of experience and its objects. The categories are reflected concepts because in the *a priori* synthesis which is their effective origination they are precisely the unities into which a manifold, though *pure*, content is reflected.

By contrast, concepts of pure reason are not merely reflected concepts; they do not originate in a mere reflection of a given content into unity. Rather, they extend beyond anything that could be given (either *a priori* or *a posteriori*); and, on the other side, the manifold content, instead of being merely reflected into them, has rather to be assembled. This breach between such concepts and the manifold content which they would gather—this breach with respect to which one can detect already a twofold aspect correlative to the two terms—Kant expresses by calling these concepts "inferred." Without at this stage considering further distinctions, Kant says simply that a concept of reason is "something to which reason leads in its inferences from experience" (A 311/B 367). One consequence is already evident: A genuinely fundamental interrogation of the concepts of pure reason must focus on the *inferences* of reason through which these concepts originate. Thus, the problematic of the Transcendental Dialectic is decisively shifted toward the investigation of the dialectical inferences of reason. At the very outset Book I has proved to be merely preliminary to Book II.

The contrast in terms of reflection makes it clear that the aloofness of the concepts of reason, the indirectness of their relation to objects of experience, is of a radically different kind from that which concepts of understanding have (by virtue of the mediation of intuition). The concepts of reason are "concerned with something to which all experience is subordinate but which is never itself an object of experience" (A 311/B 367). Within experience no object adequate to such concepts could in principle be found: Because they are concepts of reason, "they have, in fact, no relation to any object that could be given as coinciding with them" (A 336/B 393). Nothing given in experience could ever correspond to what is represented in them.

At this point Kant gives the concepts of pure reason their other name—"transcendental ideas." The naming launches a consideration of ideas in general (Section 1), ostensibly centering on the word "idea," on the way in which it was used by Plato, and on its appropriateness as a designation for the concepts of reason. Through these general considerations, however, Kant accomplishes something more significant and much less self-evident than merely explaining the historical appropriateness of his using the word "idea": he situates the problem of reason as it occurs in the Transcendental Dialectic within a broader systematic context. Specifically, he subordinates the task of the Dialectic to a further end. The task of the Dialectic is, he says, "to level the ground," which has been "honeycombed by subterranean workings which reason, in its confident but fruitless search for hidden treasures, has carried out in all directions and which threaten the security of the superstructures" (A 319/B 376–7). In terms of Kant's metaphor, it is a matter of leveling the ground by making the work of reason cave in on itself. One can hardly help wondering at the irony: A discussion explicitly oriented to Plato's *Republic* is concluded by consigning dialectical reason to a kind of mole-tunnel (*Maulwurfsgang*), that is, to something like an underground cave in which genuine vision is lacking. In any case, the ground is to be leveled, made firm *for* something else that is to be built upon it (*baufest*). What is to be built? That which, according to Kant, gives philosophy its peculiar dignity. Referring first to the task of the Dialectic, he writes: "we must meantime occupy ourselves with a less resplendent, but still meritorious task, namely to level the ground and to render it sufficiently secure for moral edifices of these majestic dimensions" (A 319/B 376–7). What is to be erected on the leveled ground are principles of morality—that is, the criticism of dialectical reason has as its end a freeing of reason *for* its practical employment. One could appropriately recall Kant's declaration in the Preface to the second edition: "I have therefore found it necessary to deny *knowledge* in order to make room for *faith* [*Glaube*]; the dogmatism of metaphysics, that is, the preconception that it is possible to make progress in metaphysics without a critique of pure reason, is the true source of all that unbelief [*Unglaube*], always very dogmatic, which clashes with morality" (B xxx).

4. DERIVATION OF THE IDEAS (A 321/B 377–A 338/B 396)

After the introductory discussion of ideas in general, Kant turns his attention in the remainder of Book I to the derivation of the ideas. This derivation may be regarded as consisting of three main steps; in addition, there is inserted between the second and third steps an important further consideration of the relation between reason and understanding.

Prior to the first step Kant indicates the general principle or procedure which the derivation is to employ:

> The form of judgments (converted into a concept of the synthesis of intuitions) yielded categories which direct all employment of understanding in experience. Similarly, we may expect that the form of syllogisms [*Vernunftschlüsse*], when applied to the synthetic unity of intuitions under the direction of the categories, will contain the origin of special *a priori* concepts which we may call pure concepts of reason, or *transcendental ideas*... (A 321/B 378).

Here Kant is setting forth an analogy, he is positing a structural identity of the correspondence between logical reason and pure reason *with* the correspondence between logical understanding and pure understanding: Just as the categories derive from the forms of judgment, so the transcendental ideas derive from the forms of syllogism. On the other hand, he is also indicating here the limits of such correspondence: Just as the derivation of the categories involves reference to the manifold of intuition that is to be synthesized, so the derivation of the ideas involves reference of the forms of syllogism to the relevant manifold, that of understanding. Thus, the derivation of the ideas will involve two kinds of factors. On the one hand, it will involve *logical* factors; specifically, Kant will proceed both from the general nature of the syllogism and from the division of the syllogism into kinds. On the other hand, the derivation will involve what one might call *categorial* factors, i.e., those that pertain to the manifold of understanding which is to be brought under the idea; specifically, Kant will proceed by applying the logical forms to the manifold in general and by following the guide of the categories as expressing an essential differentiation within that manifold.

(1) Kant takes logical reason as his point of departure. In its logical employment, reason is the faculty of mediate, syllogistic inference; what

logical reason originates are syllogisms. The first step of the derivation consists simply in working out the relevant correspondence: Just as logical reason originates syllogisms, so pure reason originates transcendental ideas. In other words, it is a matter of determining what in general is accomplished by logical reason in its constructing of syllogisms and of then applying this result to the case of pure reason and its ideas.

What does logical reason accomplish in constructing syllogisms? What is its function in this regard? Kant answers: "The function of reason in its inferences consists in the universality of knowledge according to concepts, and the syllogism is itself a judgment which is determined *a priori* in the whole extent of its conditions" (A 321–2/B 378). Here there are two functions indicated. First, a syllogism serves to bring a judgment (the conclusion) under its *conditions* (the premises from which it follows). In describing the syllogism as "itself a judgment which is determined *a priori* in the whole extent of its conditions," Kant is referring to this function, this exhibiting of a judgment (the conclusion) *as* determined by its conditions (premises); he is not simply collapsing the difference between syllogism and judgment but, on the contrary, is positively setting forth that difference. There is also a second function identified in Kant's statement: the universality of knowledge. This function can be clarified by reference to Kant's example:

> All men are mortal.
> Caius is a man.
> Caius is mortal.

The point is that in the construction of the syllogism the predicate of the conclusion (the major term: "mortal") gets thought in a universal condition, referred back to a universal condition in which it is involved (the major premise: "All men are mortal"); in Kant's terminology, it is a matter of seeking a concept (the middle term: "man") "that contains the condition under which the predicate ['mortal'] . . . is given" (A 322/B 378), in order to refer the conclusion back to a universal condition.[9] The construction of a syllogism is a movement in the direction of greater universality, and in such condition logical reason thus performs two allied functions: something is referred to its conditions *and* to something more universal. In short, reason's constructing of the syllogism accomplishes a referral of something to its universal conditions; it brings something under universal conditions.

Kant applies this result to the manifold in general on which *pure* reason bears: "In the synthesis of intuitions there corresponds to this the *allness* (*universitas*) or *totality* of the conditions" (A 322/B 379). Kant is saying: Just as logical reason, in constructing syllogisms, brings something under *universal conditions*, so pure reason would bring something (namely, the manifold yielded by understanding) under the *totality of conditions*. In other words, the transition from logical reason to pure reason requires merely the transformation of the concept of universality into a corresponding concept appropriate to the manifold on which pure reason bears. Logical reason, originating syllogisms, brings things under universal conditions, whereas pure reason, originating transcendental ideas, brings items of the relevant manifold under the totality of conditions: "The transcendental concept of reason is, therefore, none other than the concept of the *totality* of the *conditions* for any given conditioned" (A 322/B 379).

This concept of the totality of conditions is itself initially delimited by reference to logical reason. With respect to any syllogism it is possible to construct, on the one side, prosyllogisms in which a premise of the given syllogism appears as conclusion, i.e., in which a condition is referred back to more remote conditions; and, on the other side, episyllogisms in which the conclusion of the given syllogism appears as a premise, i.e., in which something conditioned is referred ahead to something else of which it is a condition. Thus, it is possible to speak of a chain of interconnected syllogisms and of two directions of movement correlative to such a chain, either upward from syllogism to prosyllogism or downward from syllogism to episyllogism. In other words, from a given conditioned there are ascending series of syllogisms leading up to ever more remote conditions and descending series leading from the given conditioned down to that of which it is a condition.[10] The crucial point as regards *pure* reason is: The transcendental ideas are concepts of the totality of conditions only in the sense of the *ascending* series:

> If, therefore, knowledge be viewed as conditioned, reason is constrained to regard the series of conditions in the ascending line as completed and as given in their totality. But if the same knowledge is viewed as a condition of yet other knowledge, and this knowledge as constituting a series of consequences in a descending line, reason can be quite indifferent as to how far this advance extends *a parte posteriori* and whether a totality of the series is possible at all (A 332/B 388–9).

Kant refers, finally, to the connection between the totality of conditions and the unconditioned—both of these providing "equivalent titles for all concepts of reason" (A 324/B 380). At this stage such connection can only be regarded in a formal way: Since the totality of conditions contains *all* conditions, there cannot be any further condition that would condition (i.e., be a condition of) this totality, which must, therefore, be unconditioned. This connection prescribes, then, that a transcendental idea may also be regarded as a concept of the unconditioned.

(2) In the second step of the derivation Kant proceeds to determine the different kinds of transcendental ideas. In this determination both kinds of factors are directly involved: The differentiation between the ideas is derived both from the differentiation between kinds of syllogisms and from a certain categorial differentiation (a differentiation pertaining to the manifold). The categorial factor is taken up first: "The number of pure concepts of reason will be equal to the number of kinds of relation which the understanding represents to itself by means of the categories" (A 323/B 379). Kant is saying: There will be a transcendental idea corresponding to each of the basic ways of conditioning, to each of the basic kinds of relation possible between condition and conditioned within the relevant manifold. Thus, there will be a transcendental idea corresponding to each of the categories of relation: subsistence, causality, and community. Kant then adds the other factor: There is "precisely the same number of kinds of syllogism, each of which advances through prosyllogisms to the unconditioned" (A 323/B 379). The three transcendental ideas will correspond to the three kinds of syllogisms, categorical, hypothetical, and disjunctive. Combining the two factors, Kant expresses the character of the transcendental ideas thus: "We have therefore to seek for an unconditioned, first, of the *categorical* synthesis in a *subject*; secondly, of the *hypothetical* synthesis of the members of a *series*; thirdly, of the *disjunctive* synthesis of the parts in a *system*" (A 323/B 379).

Between the second and third steps of the derivation Kant inserts an important further consideration of the relation between reason and understanding, applying to the development of this issue the delimitation of the transcendental ideas. Already in the Introduction to the Dialectic he has indicated that reason has to do with a higher level of unity than that of understanding. Now he specifies this difference: In the ideas the unity of understanding is extended up to the unconditioned, up to what is absolutely (i.e., in all relations) unconditioned, up to the level of absolute unity. Reason extends the relative, conditioned unity achieved at the level of understanding up to the level of absolute unity. It is especially significant that this extension has two rather distinct sides. On the one side, "Reason concerns itself exclusively with absolute totality in the employment of the concepts of the understanding and endeavors to carry the synthetic unity which is thought in the category up to the completely unconditioned" (A 326/B 383). This says: Reason takes over the synthetic unity thought in the categories and extends such unity up to the level of the unconditioned. Reason extends the category into an unconditioned unity and thereby transforms it into a transcendental idea. Here Kant is giving a first indication of how the ideas originate, of the "inference" through which they arise. However, the extension to the level of the unconditioned also has another side. Kant says that reason occupies itself with understanding "in order to prescribe to the understanding its direction toward a certain unity of which it has itself no concept and in such a manner as to unite all the acts of the understanding, in respect of every object, into an *absolute* whole" (A 326–7/B 383). This says: Reason not only extends the formal unities of understanding (in such a way as to transform them into ideas) but also seeks *to gather* under these ideas the content yielded by understanding, its knowledge, determinations, and judgments. Most briefly expressed, the two-sidedness takes this form: Reason both posits the unconditioned unities (ideas) and seeks to gather the manifold of understanding into those unities.

Kant sketches two different ways in which the ideas of reason can be employed, one of them negative (dialectical), the other positive. On the negative side, there is the objective employment of the ideas, that is, the employment of them as though they were concepts of objects. Critical thought exposes them, on the contrary, as transcendent: "they are transcendent and overstep the limits of all experience; no object adequate to the transcendental idea can ever be found within experience" (A 327/B 384). On the positive side, Kant observes that ideas serve also as directive unities, that is, they serve to direct the understanding in such a way as to bring the latter "into complete consistency with itself" (A 323/B 380; cf. A 305/B 362). This means that without a directedness toward further unification there would be within understanding an inconsistency between, on the one hand, its character as unifying (gathering) and, on the other hand, the disunity, fragmentation, which remains in the knowledge supplied by understanding alone. Thus, reason has a positive function with respect to understanding: It provides understanding with directive unities which the latter can not give itself but which it needs for the sake of its very self-accord. This function of reason Kant calls its "regulative" function. It is by virtue of this, together with the practical function of reason, that the transcendental ideas are, in the end, not simply "superfluous and void" (A 329/B 385).

Kant insists, finally, that the ideas "are not arbitrarily invented; they are imposed by the very nature of reason itself" (A 327/B 384). They are not merely fictitious concepts which happen to have been concocted but which could just as easily not have been invented. Nor are they concepts with which one could simply dispense once critical thought has exposed their relation to dialectical illusion. On the contrary, they arise of necessity from reason itself, and with like necessity are imposed in reason's service to understanding. Here Kant takes a first step toward an answer to one of the questions that stands at the beginning of the *Critique of Pure Reason*: "How is metaphysics, as natural disposition, possible?" (B 22).

(3) Whereas the second step of Kant's derivation of the ideas characterized each of them as a concept of an unconditioned to be sought in a certain regard (corresponding to the categories of relation and the kinds of syllogisms), the final step determines the specific form which that unconditioned takes in each of the three cases. This determination brings into play another factor, which, however, is not without a certain intrinsic connection to the other two types. Kant classifies the relations to be found in our representations:

1. relation to the subject
2. relation to objects
   (a) as appearances
   (b) as objects of thought in general

He reformulates the classification into a simple threefold schema:

1. relation to the subject
2. relation to the manifold of the object in the appearance
3. relation to all things in general

Since it has been shown already that an idea is a concept of a totality of conditions, of unconditioned totality, of unconditioned unity, absolute unity, Kant needs for the purpose of deriving the ideas merely to extend to the level of absolute unity each of the three kinds of relations to be found in our representations:

1. absolute unity of the subject: soul
2. absolute unity of the series of conditions of appearance: world
3. absolute unity of the condition of all objects of thought in general: the being of all beings, God

Thus, the transcendental ideas represent the themes of rational psychology, rational cosmology, and rational theology, i.e., the themes of *metaphysica specialis*. Yet, as long as the actual unfoldings of the ideas (the "inferences" of pure reason) have not been exhibited, the determination of the ideas remains only preliminary; and so, at this stage the ideas may, especially in the highest case, still seem "utterly paradoxical" (A 336/B 393).

Near the end of Book I Kant writes: "Finally, we also discern that a certain connection and unity is evident among the transcendental ideas themselves, and that by means of them pure reason combines all its modes of knowledge into a system" (A 337/B 394). He goes on to refer to an advance from knowledge of the soul, to that of the world, and finally to that of God. These remarks point toward that abeyant horizon that has been assembled for projective interpretation and prompt a shift, in conclusion, to the level of such interpretation, a first, venturesome transposition into that hermeneutical space. Within it, human knowing is posed as a movement of gathering the fragmentary beginnings into a unity akin to that of divine knowing. Reason comes into play in the final phase of this movement and so would bring the movement to its completion; specifically, reason posits the transcendental ideas as absolute unities into which the manifold of understanding would be gathered. In the passage just cited Kant is observing, however, that, despite the drive toward unity, what reason posits is not *a* unity but rather *three* unities (soul, world, God), so that, even granted this positing, even granted the correlative gathering, a fragmentation into three would still remain. The sense of human knowing thus prescribes the need for reason to gather the ideas themselves, to carry the threefold over into unity—not, however, into some still higher idea (unity) but rather into the highest of the three. In order that it not involve some further idea, this gathering must be intrinsically prescribed by this highest idea of the three, that is, the gathering of the manifold into the idea of God must, at once, amount to a gathering of the other two ideas into it; in this sense there must be a final progression through them up to the highest unity (God). Hence, the movement of human knowing upward from its fragmentary beginnings to that unitary end in which there would be re-created such unity as belongs intrinsically to divine knowing—this movement would be, in its end, a knowing of God. The re-creating of the unity of divine knowing would come to completion precisely in knowledge of the divine. The question is whether human knowing can attain this level, whether it can even approximate to divine self-knowing, in view of its fragmentary beginnings, its radical finitude.

CHAPTER III

THE GATHERING OF REASON IN THE PARALOGISMS

Kant's actual critique of dialectical reason is entirely contained in the second of the two Books into which the Transcendental Dialectic is divided. Everything else is preparatory for the critiques of rational psychology, of rational cosmology, and of rational theology which he carries through in the course of this Book. The actual problematic, the locus where the issues of the Transcendental Dialectic are to be worked out, is named by the title of this Book: The Dialectical Inferences of Pure Reason. Appropriately, Kant introduces the Book by reiterating, in still another formulation, those two determinations of reason by virtue of which the problem of reason has its locus in the domain of dialectical inference, namely, reason's aloofness from all objects of experience and its correlative involvement in inference.

Already Kant has stressed that transcendental ideas do not correspond to any objects of experience, that, to state it conversely, nothing given in experience can correspond to what is represented in such ideas. This aloofness of reason Kant now formulates in a different way. He says that the object of a transcendental idea "is something of which we have no concept" (A 338/B 396). This formulation must be taken in its specific intent, for there is obviously a sense in which one *does* have a concept of the object of a transcendental idea: One has the transcendental idea itself, and it is a concept of that object. The specific intent of Kant's formulation is: Of such an object one does not have the kind of concept that could be exhibited in experience, that "allows of being exhibited and intuited in a possible experience" (A 339/B 396).

In other words, we have no concept of understanding (*Verstandesbegriff*) corresponding to such an object but only a concept of reason (*Vernunftbegriff*). An additional formulation makes this intent still clearer: "although we cannot have any knowledge of the object which corresponds to an idea, we yet have a problematic concept of it" (A 339/B 397).

Kant reiterates, secondly, the role played by inference in the origination of ideas: "The transcendental (subjective) reality of the pure concepts of reason depends on our having been led to such ideas by a necessary syllogism" (A 339/B 397). As executed by pure reason, such syllogisms will, Kant notes, have no empirical premises; nevertheless, they will begin with something known (*etwas, das wir kennen*)—presumably, therefore, with something known *a priori* rather than empirically—and will proceed to something else of which one has no concept, i.e., of which one comes to have a problematic concept only through the inference. In such inference an inevitable illusion is operative, an illusion through which one ascribes objective reality to that which is reached by the inference. Again Kant stresses that these conclusions are not merely invented but spring from the very nature of reason. They belong to the sophistry of pure reason.

Kant names the three kinds of dialectical inference corresponding to the three kinds of transcendental ideas derived in Book I. The idea of the soul is reached by transcendental *paralogism*, that of the world by the *antinomy* of pure reason, that of God by the *ideal* of pure reason. The task is to exhibit in their actual unfolding these forms of inferences, here hardly more than named, and to expose them as dialectical.

1. PARALOGISM IN GENERAL
(A 341/B 399–A 348/B 406; A 381–405; B 406–432)

(a) The Issues of Paralogism
(A 341/B 399–A 343/B 401)

Kant offers an initial description of transcendental paralogism: In this kind of inference "I conclude from the transcendental concept of the subject, which contains nothing manifold, to the absolute unity of this subject itself . . ." (A 340/B 397–8). Several questions are immediately provoked. What does "paralogism" mean, and what is the significance of Kant's use of it in the present context? What exactly is that "transcendental concept of the subject" from which the dialectical inference proceeds? What precisely is the "absolute unity" of the subject itself, and how does the dialectical inference lead to it? What is the basic fallacy that renders the inference dialectical? These four questions sketch the principal issues and provide an initial way of access to the complexities of Kant's own exposition. An index of this complexity is supplied by the fact that the chapter dealing with paralogism was the only section in the entire Transcendental Dialectic that Kant saw fit to revise for the second edition; the revision amounted to a complete rewriting and restructuring of most of the chapter.

The word "paralogism" is taken from formal logic, in which it is used to designate a specific type of formally fallacious syllogism: "Such a syllogism is a paralogism insofar as one deceives oneself by it." Kant distinguishes a paralogism, thus defined, from what he calls a "sophism"; the latter is a formally fallacious syllogism with which "one deliberately tries to deceive others."[1] So, even in its mere logical sense, paralogism is more radical than that mere sophistry which, directing others into error, still reserves the truth for itself. It is rather self-deception, inevitable illusion without reserve of truth. This character is still more prominent in Kant's definition of *transcendental* paralogism: "A transcendental paralogism is one in which there is a transcendental ground, constraining us to draw a formally invalid conclusion" (A 341/B 399). Transcendental paralogism involves a self-deception that is transcendentally motivated, that is "grounded in the nature of human reason." Such paralogism belongs, not to a sophistical art, but to the sophistry of reason itself. Reason entangles itself in paralogism in that sphere in which self-deception can assume its most radical form, the sphere of rational psychology; reason involves itself in self-deception regarding itself.

The second question concerns the premises on which such self-deceptively fallacious syllogisms are based. What exactly is that "transcendental concept of the subject" from which the dialectical inferences of rational psychology proceed? Kant identifies it as that expressed in the proposition "I think." This proposition provides "the sole text of rational psychology." This "mere apperception 'I think,'" this "universal representation of self-consciousness" from which all "empirical determination" is excluded, supplies the ground on which the entire metaphysics of the soul is erected (A 343/B 401). The critical task is to refer metaphysics back to this ground and to put in force the limitations which the bond to such a ground prescribes.

What is the mere apperception "I think"? It is a transcendental concept, and it belongs to the previously determined table of such concepts, not because it is a category, but because it is presupposed by all concepts, including the categories, because it "is the vehicle of all concepts." It is that transcendental concept which "serves only to introduce all our thought, as belonging to consciousness" (A 341/B 399–400).

Despite the brevity and apparent straightforwardness with which Kant here introduces it, the issue of apperception is one of the most complex in the *Critique of Pure Reason*—of notorious complexity. This issue stands at the center of the Transcendental Analytic, and the problems posed by its complexity were undoubtedly of primary concern to Kant when he rewrote most of the Transcendental Deduction for the second edition. On the other hand, one might well venture to suggest that the complexity of this issue does not stem from Kant at all but from the matter itself that would be put at issue under the title "apperception." One would then, perhaps, be prepared to insist both on the depth of Kant's insight into this matter and on the lucidity with which he expressed it; but Kant does not feign light where matters are intrinsically obscure, and the complexity which the issue involves is a gauge of the resultant wealth of this problematic. This wealth is testified by the range of interpretive appropriations which this issue has undergone since Kant, from Fichte's development of the concept of the absolute I, through the Neo-Kantian interpretation of the I as a logical subject, to Heidegger's rooting of the I in transcendental imagination or primordial temporality. Let me attempt—without betraying this wealth, yet in a preparatory, limited way—to sketch the main lines that compose the issue of apperception.

(b) Transcendental Apperception

In the delineation of the modes of gathering at the level of pure understanding (Ch. I, 3), it was shown how the possibility of experience requires that appearances be provided with an object. Also it was shown that such provision requires, in turn, that appearances be made to exhibit the unity that belongs to the concept of object in general. And it was shown that the institution of such unity in the manifold of intuition is accomplished through that *a priori* synthesis performed by pure imagination. The question now to be raised is: What is the transcendental ground of this unity and of the requirement for unity in the manifold? Kant answers: "This original and transcendental condition is no other than transcendental apperception" (A 106–7). The issue of apperception is thus introduced in connection with the gathering of the manifold of intuition into the unity of thought. It is of utmost significance that it is introduced in precisely this connection.

What is the character of this condition on which is grounded both the requirement of unity and the unity required for appearances? Kant writes: "There can take place in us no modes of knowledge, no connection or unity of one mode of knowledge with another, without that unity of consciousness which precedes all data of intuitions and by relation to which representation of objects is alone possible. This pure original unchangeable consciousness I shall name *transcendental apperception*" (A 107). Thus, transcendental apperception is the unity of consciousness—not unity in the sense of a property distinct from consciousness but rather that unity which consciousness fundamentally is. Transcendental apperception is that unitary consciousness, that "one consciousness" (A 116), to which all my representations must belong. It is "the thoroughgoing identity of the self in all possible representations" (A 116), the self-identical self which is the subject of all representations (of objects)—the subject of experience. It is *pure*: It is prior to everything empirical, it pertains primarily to pure synthesis. It is *original*: It is not dependent on sensibility, receptivity, and so is (again) prior to the empirical order. And it is unchangeable: It is prior to the order of intuition and time and is that unity to which even temporal manifoldness is referred back. Transcendental apperception is "the abiding and unchanging I" which "forms the correlate of all our representations" (A 123). It is that I to which reference is made when Kant writes of the "I think": "It must be possible for the 'I think' to accompany all my representations" (B 131).

But transcendental apperception is not merely an enduring I standing behind its manifold representations. The I does not possess its representations in the same way that a substance possesses its accidents, nor are they bound to it merely in the way that appearances are bound to the transcendental object. By virtue of its very character as an I, an enduring I is more than a mere enduring substratum, it is a subject (*subiectum*, ὑποκείμενον) in an exceptional sense, for the I not only possesses its representations but also is able to refer them to itself. It must be possible for the "I think" to accompany all my representations, that is, it must be possible to refer all representations back to an I to which they belong; but the referral is itself accomplished by the I, which thus represents itself as possessing certain representations. This is why Kant says that original apperception cannot be accompanied by any further representation (B 132): The referral of representations to the I of the "I think" (to transcendental apperception) is not accomplished by some further I to which a further referral would then be called for (in a manner reiterative *ad infinitum*), but rather the I itself refers representations to itself. This is also why Kant can identify transcendental apperception both as the I of the "I think" *and* as that which generates the representation "I think" (B 132). Apperception is both the I to which representations are referred *and* the I which thus refers them; it is both the I that is represented as the subject of representations *and* the I which thus represents it—and this I is one and the same. Apperception is the self-representing I. Original apperception is intrinsically also consciousness of oneself as original apperception (A 117 n), and this connection expresses the most fundamental sense in which apperception is original. The identity of the self is no mere passive persistence of a substratum for representations but is intrinsically also "consciousness of the identity of the self" (A 108); setting itself over against all the passivity, the receptivity, of intuition, apperception is "an act of spontaneity" (B 132). Consciousness is intrinsically also self-consciousness, and the unity of consciousness, instead of being mere static, passive oneness, is the spontaneous unification of self-consciousness. Transcendental apperception (as the word already suggests[2]) is transcendental "self-consciousness" (A 111, 113; B 132, 134–5)—or, more precisely, it is the possibility of self-consciousness, since it is required only that it be *possible* for the "I think" to accompany all my representations, not that it actually do so.[3]

We noted that the issue of transcendental apperception is introduced in response to a question of ground: transcendental apperception is posed as the ground of the requirement of unity and of the unity required for appearances. Granted its character as self-identical consciousness and, still more fundamentally, as self-consciousness, how does it serve as ground of unity and of the requirement of unity? How can its grounding function be made intelligible in terms of its own character? This problem is most directly addressed in the second edition: Here, Kant focuses on the way in which my representations are *mine*. In order that they be mine, they must all belong to one self-identical consciousness; in Kant's words, "the manifold representations, which are given in an intuition, would not be one and all *my* representations, if they did not all belong to one self-consciousness" (B 132). Only thus is the "I think" able to accompany all my representations—that is, the self-conscious referral of my representations to myself is possible only if my representations are already mine independently of any referral, only if they always already belong to one self-identical consciousness. In turn, if there are certain conditions to which representations must conform in order to belong to one self-identical consciousness, then all representations will stand under the demand so to conform. Thus, Kant continues: "As *my* representations (even if I am not conscious of them as such) they must conform to the condition under which alone they *can* stand together in one universal self-consciousness, because otherwise they would not all without exception belong to me" (B 132–3). Representations "can stand together in one universal self-consciousness" only if they are gathered into the unity of self-consciousness, only if they conform to that unity: "The original and necessary consciousness of the identity of the self is thus at the same time a consciousness of an equally necessary unity of the synthesis of all appearances according to concepts, that is, according to rules, which . . . determine an object for their intuition, that is, the concept of something wherein they are necessarily interconnected" (A 108). Representations can be mine, can stand in one self-consciousness, only if they are brought to unity—a unity which, on the side of representations, coincides with what, starting "from below," was previously thematized as the transcendental object. Representations can be mine only if they are given the forms of unity corresponding to apperception itself. Transcendental apperception, as that to which conformity is required, thereby grounds both the requirement of unity and the form of unity that is required.

Kant writes: "The principle of apperception is the highest principle in the whole sphere of human knowledge." Nevertheless, this principle, which expresses the demand for conformity and thus the grounding function of apperception, is "an identical, and therefore analytic, proposition" (B 135). Why is this highest principle analytic? Kant explains: "For it says no more than that all *my* representations in any given intuition must be subject to that condition under which alone I can ascribe them to the identical self as *my* representations and so can comprehend them as synthetically combined in one apperception through the general expression 'I think' " (B 138). This principle merely says: My representations must conform to the conditions required for them to be *my* representations (and thus to be capable of being referred in self-consciousness to the I of the "I think").

It is crucial, however, that this principle, itself merely analytic, is, on the other hand, linked up with the fundamental synthesis performed on the pure manifold by imagination; the latter is the ground of the possibility of all *synthetic* judgments, and thus Kant distinguishes between analytic unity (that of mere apperception) and synthetic unity (that instituted in the manifold). The question is: Precisely how are these two unities related? Already it has been shown that apperception (analytic unity) is the transcendental ground of the imaginative synthesis (synthetic unity). But now the point is that apperception *also* requires the imaginative synthesis, is dependent on it. This fundamental synthesis is required *even for the possibility of self-consciousness itself*: the analytic principle "reveals the necessity of a synthesis of the manifold given in intuition, without which the thoroughgoing identity of self-consciousness cannot be thought" (B 135). Several other passages express and elaborate this dependence of self-consciousness on that very synthesis the demand for which it grounds and the form of which it prescribes. One such passage: "Only insofar, therefore, as I can unite a manifold of given representations in *one consciousness*, is it possible for me to represent to myself the *identity of the consciousness in these representations* themselves, i.e., the *analytic* unity of apperception is possible only under the presupposition of a certain *synthetic* unity" (B 133). Still more decisive: "Synthetic unity of the manifold of intuitions, as generated *a priori*, is thus the ground of the identity of apperception itself, which precedes *a priori* all *my* determinate thought" (B 134).[4] Thus, in one sense transcendental apperception is the ground of the synthesis of the manifold of intuition, whereas, in another sense, as is now evident, the synthesis of the manifold grounds apperception. More precisely, transcendental apperception grounds the *requirement* of unity in the manifold and the *form* of unity thus *required*; but apperception does not perform the synthesis by which the manifold is brought to such unity and thus does not in the full sense ground the actually accomplished unity of the manifold. On the contrary, that unity is the accomplishment of transcendental imagination, and thus to the extent that apperception is dependent on the actual synthetic unification of the manifold, it is dependent on imagination; it is in this sense that the "synthesis of imagination [is] prior to apperception" (A 118). But this is only one side: Transcendental apperception is also prior to the synthesis of imagination; and it is original in a way that the synthesis is not, since it grounds both the requirement of unity and the form of unity which is actually realized in that synthesis.

From the outset Kant contrasts transcendental apperception with empirical apperception or inner sense. Such merely empirical consciousness of the self as given to itself intuitively in inner perception reveals "no fixed and abiding self" but only a "flux of inner appearances" (A 107). Even more decisive, the self as presented in inner sense is merely appearance, as is everything given in intuition, for we can thus intuit ourselves "only as we are inwardly affected": Inner sense "represents to consciousness even our own selves only as we appear to ourselves, not as we are in ourselves" (B 152–3; cf. 67–8). The contrast between transcendental apperception and inner sense is best clarified by considering exactly what kind of representation transcendental apperception is. That is, in what way am I conscious of myself in transcendental apperception? What mode of representation is such self-consciousness and under what aspect does it, accordingly, present the self? Kant answers: "On the other hand, in the transcendental synthesis of the manifold of representations in general and therefore in the synthetic original unity of apperception, I am conscious of myself, not as I appear to myself, nor as I am in myself, but only that I am. This representation is a thinking, not an intuiting" (B 157). In this crucial statement several points need to be noted. First, it should be observed that Kant here expresses the character of transcendental apperception within the full context of the problem of self-consciousness—that is, he considers it in its relation to that synthesis of the manifold on which it has its peculiar dependence, and it is thus that he terms it the *synthetic* original unity of apperception. Second, Kant declares that in transcendental apperception I am not conscious of myself as I am in myself; suddenly one is reminded of the operative distinction between human knowing and divine knowing and, accordingly, of the need to distinguish transcendental apperception from that divine "understanding which through its self-consciousness could supply to itself the manifold of intuition" (B 138–9), which, bringing itself forth, would in unity with its self-positing know itself as it is in itself. Third, Kant declares that in transcendental apperception I am not conscious of myself as I appear to myself; in transcendental self-consciousness there is no appearance to myself (as there is in inner sense), and, accordingly, Kant says that this representation is not an intuition. Thus, finally, Kant identifies this representation as a thinking in which I am conscious only that I am. How is this identification to be interpreted? What kind of thinking is transcendental self-consciousness? It is a thinking in connection with which the "I think" gets attached to my representations, that is, my representations get explicitly referred back to myself, to the I of the "I think" to which they always already belong. However, the dependence of transcendental apperception on the synthesis of the manifold is such that the actual referral can be accomplished, i.e., the I can posit itself, only on the basis already provided by the synthesis performed by imagination, the synthesis which takes place *as* the bringing of the manifold to the unity prescribed by apperception. What, then, is the function of that thinking which Kant identifies with transcendental self-consciousness? Its function can only be to posit that I to which the manifold of representations has already been attached by means of the synthesis by imagination. What kind of thinking is transcendental apperception? It is a *positing of itself*. This is why Kant says that in transcendental apperception I am conscious only that I am. A subsequent formulation expresses the same point more elegantly: "The consciousness of myself in the representation 'I' is not an intuition but rather a merely *intellectual* representation of the spontaneity [*Selbsttätigkeit*] of a thinking subject" (B 278).

In conclusion, two connections need to be established, both of them serving to assimilate the commentary on transcendental apperception, now completed, to the horizon for projective interpretation. First, transcendental apperception needs to be related to the general issue of gathering. This requires taking apperception in its structural connection with that synthesis on which it is dependent. On the one side, the I, which is one, posits itself and thus posits unity; in other words, there is a positing of the unity into which the relevant manifold is to be gathered, that is, a positing of a unity for the gathering. On the other side, there is the unification of the manifold of representations, the actual gathering of them into this unity through the synthesis accomplished by imagination. Thus, transcendental apperception, taken in its full structure, exemplifies the two-sidedness of gathering in general; and granted that transcendental apperception is "the highest principle in the whole sphere of human knowledge," one might well suppose that it is not only a matter of exemplification but also of grounding, even if only in a certain measure or regard. In any case, once apperception in its full structure is understood as gathering, then it becomes evident how the development of this issue deepens the sense of *a priori* knowledge sketched in the earlier survey: *A priori* knowing is not only a gathering of appearances into the unity of objectivity, into the transcendental object, but, as a gathering of them into the correlative yet original unity of transcendental apperception, it is, more fundamentally, the subject's gathering of appearances to itself.

The other connection is the positive counterpart of that contrast already drawn between human and divine self-consciousness. Transcendental apperception is a thinking, a self-positing, in which, however, the I is able to posit itself only as existing, not as having any determinate character. Yet, this suffices to make transcendental apperception an image of that divine self-knowing which is also intrinsically an absolute self-positing—that divine self-knowing in which God, as *causa sui*, would bring himself forth in his very knowing of himself.

(c) Transcendental Paralogism (A 343–4/B 401–2; A 396–A 405)

Two of the four directive questions that I posed regarding transcendental paralogism have now been treated. First, it has been noted that "paralogism" in its transcendental sense refers to a transcendentally motivated, formally fallacious syllogism in which, specifically, there is self-deception regarding the self. Second, that transcendental concept of the subject from which the dialectical inference proceeds has been identified as transcendental apperception. The remaining questions go directly to the heart of the issue of paralogism. The third asks about the conclusion and about the means by which it is reached. The fourth asks about the basic fallacy that renders the inference dialectical.

Kant does not proceed immediately to a definitive formulation of the answer to these two remaining questions. Instead, he begins with an introductory placing of the issues of these questions, that is, with a merely anticipatory sketch of the way in which they are to be worked out. This sketch is the only principal section of the critique of paralogism that Kant retained in the second edition. Though introductory, it broaches all the essential issues.

Kant addresses himself, first, to the conclusion that is drawn by transcendental paralogism and to the means by which rational psychology reaches this conclusion: As previously noted, such psychology has as its sole basis the "I think" of transcendental apperception. From this basis it proceeds to determine the I of the "I think," that is, to work out, to infer, the determinations that belong to the I. In this determining no empirical determinations can enter, for they would violate the purely rational character of such psychology. Consequently, rational psychology can determine the I only by means of "transcendental predicates" (A 343/B 401)—that is, through categories. In order to obtain the determinations which form the basis of rational psychology, it is thus merely required that "we follow the guidance of the categories" (A 344/B 402).[5] So, according to this introductory account, the inference itself consists merely in the determining of the I through the categories. The conclusions thereby reached are simply the judgments in which this determining is expressed. Corresponding to each major categorial heading, there is such a determining judgment:

1. Relation: The soul is *substance.*
2. Quality: The soul is *simple.*
3. Quantity: The soul is *unity* (i.e., numerically identical in the different times in which it exists).
4. Modality: The soul is in relation to *possible* objects in space.

From this basis all the other determinations that make up the conceptual content of rational psychology can, according to Kant, be derived—such determinations as immateriality, incorruptibility, spirituality, immortality. Thus, all of rational psychology would be generated from the categorial determining of the I. One should note, however, that this anticipatory sketch leaves several specific issues still to be clarified: What is the relation between the I of transcendental apperception and the soul of which the various determinations are predicated in the judgments of rational psychology? And what prescribes the specific category from each group that is to be applied as a determination to the self?

In the anticipatory sketch Kant addresses himself to the further question of the basic fallacy which renders the inferences of rational psychology paralogistic, primarily by reiterating the theory of transcendental apperception in such a way as to suggest that it offers too meager a basis for such knowledge as rational psychology would derive from it. The representation I is, he observes, "in itself completely empty." In the strict sense it is not even a concept—i.e., it is not a representation of some real determination that could belong to something—but rather is only "a bare consciousness which accompanies all concepts." Although it is indeed a thinking, it is not a thinking which determines but rather a thinking which posits, in this case a thinking which emptily posits itself. Through the I "nothing further is represented than a transcendental subject of the thoughts = x." It is the "unknown subject"[6] to which my thoughts belong as predicates—that is, it is "known" *only* in the sense that it is that to which my representations are referred in self-consciousness—that is, it is "known" *only as* that which thinks my thoughts. Apart from these thoughts we cannot, in the strict sense, have any concept of it at all but, as Kant explains, "can only revolve in a perpetual circle, since any judgment upon it has always already made use of its representation" (A 346/B 404). What, then, is the basic fallacy? It derives from the peculiar emptiness of the I of transcendental apperception or, in another formulation, from the way in which the inference of rational psychology is ultimately a movement in a perpetual circle. But neither of these formulations is more than introductory.

Following this introductory sketch Kant gives (in the first edition) detailed consideration to each of the four individual paralogisms. Only at the very end of the chapter does he return to the task of giving a general account of paralogism. At the point where he resumes this task he notes that it could not have been undertaken at the beginning, i.e., before consideration of the individual paralogisms, without risking obscurity and clumsy anticipation of the course of the argument. However, such postponement of the general account is probably unnecessary and perhaps produces even more obscurity and clumsy anticipation than would the opposite order. It is noteworthy in this regard that in the second edition the consideration of the individual paralogisms is so very brief that Kant does, in effect, go almost directly to the general account. Since, furthermore, the general account is so incisive, I shall reverse the order used by Kant and consider the general account first, basing my commentary on the more extended account given in the first edition (though supplementing it with some material from the second edition).

Kant begins at the level of the general problem of the Transcendental Dialectic—that is, he introduces again the general character of transcendental illusion and of the transcendental ideas in the origination of which such illusion arises, and he proceeds to show how transcendental paralogism arises as a specific form. Transcendental illusion, he recalls, consists in treating subjective conditions as though they were conditions of objects (A 396; cf. A 297/B 353, with I, 2). Such illusion arises in connection with transcendental ideas, which, as Kant says in accord with his earlier account, are concepts of "the totality of the synthesis of the conditions for a given conditioned" (A 396; cf. A 322/B 379, with II, 2). Kant specifies that, granted that the issue is transcendental and not empirical illusion, there are only three kinds of synthesis in relation to which can arise concepts of totality productive of transcendental illusion:

1. The synthesis of the conditions of a thought in general.
2. The synthesis of the conditions of empirical thinking.
3. The synthesis of the conditions of pure thinking.

It should be noted that these three kinds of synthesis correspond to those three kinds of relations in our representations on which Kant based the final step in the derivation of the ideas in Book I (cf. A 333–4/B 390–1, with Ch. II, 4).

In rational psychology pure reason concerns itself with the absolute totality of the first of these syntheses, that is, with the unconditioned condition of thought in general. But "thought in general" is, in contrast to the other two items, thought considered in abstraction from all relation to an object; and thus the relevant synthesis is that of thought with its subject. It is precisely this subjective condition, i.e., the synthesis of thought with its subject, which gets treated as though it were an objective condition in such a way that transcendental illusion, specifically, transcendental paralogism, arises.

In light of this reference of paralogism back to the general problems of the Transcendental Dialectic, Kant reiterates the answers to the first two directive questions, showing how they derive from the character of rational psychology as concerned with the unconditioned in the synthesis of the conditions of a thought in general. In the inference in which such psychology engages there can be no error as regards content, for it abstracts from all content or objects; it can be fallacious only in form, and as involving a formal fallacy such inference is appropriately termed "paralogism." Furthermore, since the relevant synthesis is that of thought with its subject, rational psychology will concern itself with the I insofar as it is unconditioned. But how is the I an unconditioned condition? In what sense? It is a condition in the sense that it must be possible for the "I think" to accompany all my representations; it is unconditioned in the sense that it cannot itself be accompanied by any further representation. In transcendental paralogism, however, the sense according to which the I of apperception is an unconditioned condition gets confounded with another sense; thereby the unconditionality of empty self-positing is replaced with a fullness of determination appropriate only to objects. The I gets "represented as an object which I think" (A 398)—rather than as a subject which thinks itself. It is precisely in terms of this transition that the distinction is to be understood between the I of apperception, which provides the basis for the dialectical inference, and the soul, which is the theme of the conclusions. The soul is the I represented as an object; since objects, if inner, are given in inner sense, the relevant unconditioned condition would be "the transcendental object of inner sense," and thus Kant identifies the latter as precisely what is designated by the word "soul" (A 361–2).

The inference which constitutes transcendental paralogism, the inferential movement itself, may thus be regarded as involving two distinguishable aspects, which, however, are unified in the actual inference. On the one hand, there is the movement from certain determinations of the I of apperception to the corresponding determinations of the soul. On the other hand, there is united with this movement the extension, or, more precisely, the transformation, of the concept of the I into that of the soul. In other words, it is not as though both concepts, that of the I and that of the soul, were had in advance such that the paralogistic inference would consist merely in the transference of the determinations of the former to the latter; on the contrary, it is precisely within the inference that the transcendental idea of the soul originates.

But what prescribes the relevant determinations that get ascribed to the soul? This is the other issue previously left unresolved. Now Kant offers some clarification: The soul gets determined "through those categories which in each type of category express absolute unity" (A 401). That just such determinations are appropriate is clear from the general character of dialectical inference as movement to the unconditioned condition or totality of the synthesis, i.e., to absolute unity in a sense that would be inclusive rather than exclusive of the entire relevant manifold. Kant adds that the specific categories which in transcendental paralogism get ascribed as determinations to the soul are those which "in each class form the basis of the unity of the others in a possible perception" (A 403). In both regards the connection between substance and unity and that between categorial unity and transcendental unity are, at least to an extent, clear; but in the case of the categories that fall under the heading of quality, neither the connection between reality and unity nor, as Kant admits (A 404 n), that between simplicity and reality is immediately evident; in the case of the modal categories it is not, on the surface of the matter, even clear which specific category is involved, since Kant formulates the determining judgment both in terms of the soul's relation to *possible* objects in space and in terms of its being conscious only of the *existence* of itself (A 404). But here the commentary is posed at the limit of the *general* account of the inference.

Already Kant has described in two distinct ways the basis of the fallacy which renders the inferences of rational psychology dialectical: It is constituted by the peculiar emptiness of the I of transcendental apperception or, alternatively, by the circularity into which such inference falls. Now he elaborates these two formulations. Such judgments as those at which rational psychology arrives, judgments which express determinations of the soul, must clearly be synthetic. But for synthetic judgments mere thought never suffices; rather, "intuition is always required" (A 398). Thus, the judgments at which rational psychology arrives would require some intuitive basis in order to be legitimate. But such an intuitive element is completely lacking in transcendental apperception, which, however, provides the *sole* basis for whatever conclusions are reached by rational psychology: In transcendental apperception I am not conscious of myself as I appear to myself, that is, I am not given intuitively to myself. However, the emptiness of transcendental apperception does not consist merely in its lacking the element of empirical intuition; nor is it this lack alone that undercuts the conclusions of rational psychology. In a sense this lack is even necessary for rational psychology which, in distinction from empirical psychology, is prohibited from being erected on any basis in which empirical elements are involved. As a *rational* doctrine of the soul, its judgments are never empirical (*a posteriori*) but rather synthetic *a priori*. What, then, is the decisive lack? What is the element required of the basis of such judgments yet lacking in transcendental apperception? It is precisely that element which virtually the entire Transcendental Analytic is devoted to establishing and exhibiting in its structure and function: Synthetic *a priori* judgments, in order to be legitimate, require as their basis a connection of pure thought, not directly to empirical intuition, but to pure intuition. Only insofar as pure thought provides rules for the forming of pure intuition, only insofar as it issues in transcendental determinations of time, i.e., transcendental schemata, does it gain the objectivity required of genuinely synthetic judgments. In short, the concepts of pure thought must be schematized. It is precisely this schematism, this connection to pure intuition, that is lacking in mere transcendental apperception and, hence, in that thought by which rational psychology seeks to establish the attributes of the soul:

> These attributes are nothing but pure categories, through which I never think a determinate object but only the unity of the representations, in order to determine an object for them. In the absence of an underlying intuition the category alone cannot yield a concept of an object; for by intuition alone is the object given, which thereupon is thought according to the category (A 399).

The categories as applied to the self in transcendental paralogism are merely pure, i.e., unschematized, categories—they are merely the forms of unity that are involved in the thought of anything whatsoever (cf. A 254/B 309), in distinction from the categories as rules for an *a priori* synthesis through which objects are determined. In terms of the distinction which Kant introduces in the second edition, the application of the categories to the I of transcendental apperception is a matter of mere thinking rather than knowing (B 406; cf. B xxvi). Transcendental apperception is self-positing thought, a thinking in which the I merely, emptily posits itself; it is not a determining thought, and any determinations for which it is taken as the basis are ultimately empty.

But how does it happen that one engages in such misapplication of the categories to the I of transcendental apperception? How is one led into such dialectical illusion? What is the character of the transcendental motivation operative in transcendental paralogism? Kant's second formulation of the basic fallacy exhibits this motivation. In rational psychology there is a decisive transition from the I of transcendental apperception to the soul, a transition in which the very idea of the soul originates. This transition amounts to a transition from the subject as merely thought (emptily posited) by itself *to* the subject as objectively known by itself. It is precisely in unity with this transition that the misapplication of the categories occurs, that is, that the categories get applied to the self in such a way that they are taken, not as mere forms of unity in thought, but as objective determinations of the self as it is in itself, i.e., of the soul. More precisely, what motivates the misapplication of the categories is a turning of the concept of the subject *as subject* into the concept of the subject *as object*—that is, a turning of the concept of the *determining* self into that of the *determinable* self (B 407). But this turning is a turning in a circle—in that circle to which Kant has already consigned rational psychology:

> We can thus say of the thinking "I" . . . that it does *not* know *itself through the categories* but knows the categories, and through them all objects, in the absolute unity of apperception, and so *through itself*. Now it is, indeed, very evident that I cannot know as an object that which I must presuppose in order to know any object and that the determining self (the thinking) is distinguished from the determinable self (the thinking subject) in the same way as knowledge is distinguished from its object. Nevertheless, there is nothing more natural and more misleading than the illusion which leads us to regard the unity in the synthesis of thoughts as a perceived unity in the subject of these thoughts (A 401–2).

In the second edition this circularity and its connection with the misapplication of the categories are expressed even more emphatically; also the peculiar involvement of the problem of time in this circularity is made explicit:

> The subject of the categories cannot by thinking the categories acquire a concept of itself as an object of the categories. For in order to think them, its pure self-consciousness, which is what was to be explained, must itself be presupposed. Similarly, the subject, in which the representation of time has its original ground, cannot thereby determine its own existence in time (B 422).

Thus, the general structure of transcendental paralogisms is evident. It involves two correlative aspects. On the one hand, there is the turning of the concept of the I into that of the soul, the turning in the circle. On the other hand, there is the movement from the determining of the I to that of the soul, that is, the peculiarly ambivalent application of the categories to the self. The turning motivates the peculiar determining of the self and, conversely, the determining fulfills the turning by letting the idea fully emerge. But the turning, however natural, embodies a confounding of a subjective condition with objective conditions—that is, it has the character of transcendental illusion.

2. THE FOUR PARALOGISMS (A 348–A 396)

(a) Substantiality (A 348–A 351)

Kant presents the first paralogism, that of substantiality, in syllogistic form. The major premise reads: "That, the representation of which is the *absolute subject* of our judgments and cannot therefore be employed as determination of another thing, is *substance*." This premise expresses the character of transcendental apperception: The I is represented as (i.e., thinks itself as) the absolute subject to which all judgments and, hence, all representations belong in such fashion that the "I think" must be able to accompany all my representations; but, as self-consciousness, this subject is thought by itself, so that no further representation can accompany it. All representations belong to the I, are "accidents" of the I, but the I is not, in turn, an accident belonging to something else. The I is substance.

The minor premise reads: "I, as a thinking being, am the *absolute subject* of all my possible judgments, and this representation of myself cannot be employed as predicate of any other thing." This premise identifies the subject with the Cartesian *res cogitans*.[7] In the conclusion the *res cogitans*, identified as the soul, is then declared to be substance: "Therefore I, as thinking being (soul), am *substance*. In outline form the syllogism is:

Absolute subject is substance.
Thinking being (soul) is absolute subject.
∴Thinking being (soul) is substance.

In terms of the general structure of transcendental paralogism, the major premise expresses the basis (transcendental apperception), the minor premise expresses the turning from the I of apperception (absolute subject) to the soul, and the conclusion expresses the corresponding misapplication of the category to the determination of the soul.

The major premise, merely expressing transcendental apperception, is unobjectionable. With respect to the entire syllogism, what is decisive about this premise is that it fixes the sense which "substance" would need to have in the conclusion in order genuinely to follow. On this premise "substance" designates a pure, i.e., unschematized, concept; it has here only a logical and not an objective sense, since categories can have objective validity only through connection with the element of intuition, which is totally lacking in transcendental apperception. Indeed, it can be said quite legitimately that the I is substance. But this amounts simply to making a formal distinction between determinations and that of which they are determinations, a distinction which can be made with regard to any and every thing: "I can say of any and every thing that it is a substance, in the sense that I distinguish it from mere predicates and determinations of things" (A 349). To say that the I is a substance is thus to say virtually nothing. Kant asks: What use can be made of this concept of a substance? And he observes, in particular, that it cannot be used to prove the *persistence* of the I—i.e., to prove that the I neither arises nor perishes but is immortal. Yet, this is precisely the use to which rational psychology wants to put its concept of substance and indeed the entire paralogism of substantiality.

The minor premise expresses the turning of the I into the soul, and it is precisely through this turning that the inference is rendered dialectical. In different terms, the identification which this premise makes between the soul and the subject is possible only if the I (absolute subject) has already been turned into the soul. But in that case the sense of "absolute subject" is not the same in the two premises of the syllogism. Referring to this middle term of the syllogism as the condition, Kant expresses both the formal fallacy committed as well as the correlative ambiguity which would be required in the term "substance" in order to grant the intended conclusion of the syllogism: "Whereas the major premise, in dealing with the condition, makes a merely transcendental use of the category, the minor premise and the conclusion, in dealing with the soul which has been subsumed under this condition, use the same category empirically" (A 402). Here it is clear exactly how a transcendental paralogism, if formulated syllogistically, proves to be formally fallacious: It commits the fallacy of using the middle term in two different senses. The paralogism is a *sophisma figurae dictionis*.[8]

(b) Simplicity (A 351–A 361)

The structure of the second paralogism is basically the same as that of the first. Instead of the relational category of substance, it is qualitative unity, i.e., simplicity, that is here ascribed as a determination to the self.[9] And in place of the character of the I as absolute subject, there is here substituted its character as one. The second paralogism may thus be outlined:

> That which is one (=I) is simple.
> Thinking being (soul) is one.
> ∴Thinking being (soul) is simple.

Here again the major premise expresses the basis: "The proposition, 'I am simple,' must be regarded as an immediate expression of apperception" (A 354–5); the minor premise expresses the turning from the I of apperception to the soul; and the conclusion expresses the corresponding misapplication of the category to the determination of the soul.

Likewise, the major premise here establishes the sense which "simple" has in the conclusion—or, alternatively, the sense which must be violated in order to reach the intended conclusion. The violation is effected by the turning that is expressed in the minor premise. What is the sense of "simple" in the major premise? Kant explains:

> "I am simple" means nothing more than that this representation, "I," does not contain in itself the least manifoldness and that it is absolute (although merely logical) unity. . . . It is obvious that in attaching "I" to our thoughts we designate the subject of inherence only transcendentally, without noting in it any quality whatsoever—in fact, without being acquainted with [*kennen*] or knowing [*wissen*] anything of it. It means a something in general (transcendental subject), the representation of which must, no doubt, be simple, if only for the reason that there is nothing determinate in it. . . . But the simplicity of the representation of a subject is not *eo ipso* knowledge of the simplicity of the subject itself (A 355).

The I of transcendental apperception "is simple solely because its representation has no content" (A 381). In other words, its simplicity is merely formal, merely conceptual, not that objective simplicity which in the conclusion is ascribed to the subject *as* object (soul) to which the syllogism is turned by the minor premise.

In the proper sense determined by the major premise, it can indeed be said that the I is simple. But this is to say practically nothing and is to serve in no way whatsoever the real intent behind this paralogism, that of showing that, unlike matter, the soul is not corruptible.[10] The simplicity of the I is mere emptiness and contributes nothing to the solution of the problem that is really at issue here, the problem of immortality. Indeed, Kant goes even further and shows that the very approach to the problem of immortality in terms of the simplicity of the soul is basically faulty. Even if it could be proved that the soul is simple, this would not suffice to distinguish it from matter and, hence, from what is corruptible, for of matter as it is in itself we know nothing: "Accordingly, even granting the human soul to be simple in nature, such simplicity by no means suffices to distinguish it from matter, in respect of the substratum of the latter—if, that is to say, we consider matter, as indeed we ought to, as mere appearance" (A 359). This approach is completely undermined by Kant's already established transcendental idealism.

(c) Personality (A 361–A 366)

The third paralogism exhibits the same general structure as the first two. Instead of the category of substance or the qualitative concept of simplicity, this paralogism ascribes to the self quantitative or extensive unity, i.e., personality. And in place of the character of the I as absolute subject and as one, there is here substituted its character as being "conscious of the numerical identity of itself at different times" (A 361). The paralogism may thus be outlined:

> That which is conscious of its identity (=I) is person.
> Soul is conscious of its identity.
> ∴Soul is person.

Again, the major premise expresses the apperceptive basis, in this case focusing especially on the character of transcendental apperception as self-consciousness; again, the minor premise expresses the turning by which the sense of "person" established in the major premise gets violated; again, the conclusion expresses the corresponding misapplication of the categorial concept to the determination of the soul.

What is the sense of "person" or of "personal identity" that is established in the major premise? In the sphere of inner sense there is an analogue to that experience of external objects in which we attend to the permanent element that remains identical throughout all change of determinations: "I refer each and all of my successive determinations to the numerically identical self and do so throughout time, that is, in the form of the inner intuition of myself" (A 362). But the analogy is just as much a contrast: In the case of external objects, the determinations that are referred to the permanent element serve genuinely to determine the object, in such a way that there is intuitively filled experience (i.e., knowledge) of permanent objects, even though the permanence experienced is merely that proper to the domain of appearances; by contrast, the determinations (e.g., representations) that are referred to the numerically identical I do not, in the strict sense, serve to determine it, that is, they belong to it, not as accidents, but rather in the manner proper to the subject *as* subject, the manner expressed in the "I think." Thus, the I does not know itself as numerically identical but only thinks itself as such—that is, the I posits itself as the numerically identical, but indeterminate, term to which the manifold of inner sense is referred. Therefore, Kant declares: "The identity of the consciousness of myself at different times is therefore only a formal condition of my thoughts and their coherence and in no way proves the numerical identity of my subject" (A 363).[11] Rational psychology can take the former as proving the latter only because in the minor premise of the paralogism it turns the I of apperception into the soul. Kant makes this turning manifest by drawing the contrast between my personal identity *for myself* and my personal identity (permanence) *for an outside observer*. This contrast simply presents more vividly that which obtains between the subject *as* subject and the subject *as* object. Regardless of the specific formulation, the issue is that turning in which subjective conditions are confounded with objective conditions, that turning in which originates all dialectical illusion regarding the self.

The transcendental concept of personality, as expressed in the major premise, is thoroughly unobjectionable if taken apart from its paralogistic extension—as unobjectionable as the corresponding concepts of substance and simplicity expressed in the major premises of the previous two paralogisms. Clearly this concept of personality contributes nothing to the resolution of that issue to which rational psychology would address itself by means of this paralogism—namely, that of immortality. But Kant insists, without yet elaborating, that "taken in this way, the concept is necessary for practical employment and is sufficient for such use" (A 365).

(d) Ideality (A 366–A 396)

The structure of the fourth paralogism is more complex than that of the other three. This complexity results primarily from the peculiar character of the modal categories, namely, "that they do not in the least enlarge the concept to which they are attached as predicates" but rather "only express the relation of the concept to the faculty of knowledge." In the case of the modal categories, "no additional determinations are thereby thought in the object itself" (A 219), and, as a result, transcendental paralogism with respect to a modal category cannot generate a claim to a real determining of the soul; transcendental paralogism cannot in this case simply be constructed through a turning from the I of transcendental apperception to the soul. Because of the character of the modal categories, the claim must rather concern the relation to the faculty of knowledge, to the knower. In general there are two such kinds of relations, that of outer objects to the knower and that of the knower to himself. The fourth paralogism, involving both these kinds of relations, thus has two sides, an "outward" side and an "inward" side. Yet it is not a matter of mere doubling—that is, the two sides are not simply parallel. How, then, are they related, and how do they enter into the paralogism?

The specific category involved in the fourth paralogism is existence (*Dasein*). How is it involved, granted that it cannot be a matter of turning transcendental determinations into real determinations? The fourth paralogism treats the self "as the correlate of all existence, from which all other existence must be inferred" (A 402). In other words, this paralogism poses the self's knowledge of its own existence as the standard, and then by reference to this standard it assigns merely derivative status to the self's knowledge of the existence of other things. The outward side of the paralogism expresses this assigning; the inward side expresses the standard. Kant's initial formulation gives only the outward side; an abbreviated version might read:

> That the existence of which is only inferred has doubtful existence.
> Outer appearances are such that their existence is only inferred.
> ∴Outer appearances have doubtful existence.

Kant proceeds immediately, however, to refer these premises back to the inward side involved in the paralogism.

The reference takes the form of a regress from the minor premise—that is, the standard which constitutes the inward side of the paralogism is involved as that from which the minor premise follows. Kant says: "We can with justification maintain that only what is in ourselves can be perceived immediately and that my own existence is the sole object of a mere perception" (A 367). With what justification can this be maintained? The justification is that, if taken in a purely transcendental way, this standard merely expresses the character of transcendental apperception from a specific perspective. That I have immediate perception only of what is within myself simply expresses the demand that the "I think" must be able to accompany all my representations—that is, that all experience be referred back to the I, gathered into the sphere of that I. That I have an immediate awareness of only my own existence means that the I posits itself as existing, that transcendental apperception is the thought that I am. It is in this connection that it becomes clear why existence is the specific modal category that gets involved in the paralogism: It is that modal category which is involved in absolute unity, in this case the unity of the I with itself. The category of existence pertains to the I's self-positing: In self-consciousness the I posits itself neither as merely possible nor as necessary but simply as existing.

Kant shifts toward the outward side: "The existence, therefore, of an actual object outside me (if this word 'me' be taken in the intellectual sense) is never given directly in perception" (A 367). What is beyond the sphere of my self-consciousness, i.e., beyond that which is gathered into the unity of the I, is not immediately perceived as existing, that is, its existence is inferred: I "can only infer their existence from my inner perception, taking the inner perception as the effect of which something external is the proximate cause" (A 368). In this connection Kant mentions Descartes. But he does not yet mention explicitly that there is a basic ambiguity in the phrase "outside me," hence, in the concept "outer appearance"—an ambiguity through which Kant's radical divergence from Descartes is to emerge, an ambiguity on which the fourth antinomy will prove to turn.

Kant continues: "Now the inference from a given effect to a determinate cause is always uncertain, since the effect may be due to more than one cause." This observation yields the major premise of the paralogism as formulated: That the existence of which is only inferred has doubtful existence. The position which, accepting these premises, concludes that outer appearances have doubtful existence Kant calls "idealism." But there are two types of idealism, and it is in the contrast between them that Kant decisively brings to light the basic ambiguity that informs the fourth paralogism. One type of idealism is that which Kant himself has undertaken to establish in the Transcendental Aesthetic, namely, transcendental idealism; the other type is empirical idealism, the Cartesian position expressed by this paralogism of ideality. Kant describes transcendental idealism as "the doctrine that appearances are to be regarded as being, one and all, representations only, not things in themselves, and that time and space are therefore only sensible forms of our intuition." He then *opposes* to such transcendental idealism the position of transcendental realism, which "regards time and space as something given in themselves, independently of our sensibility" and which, consequently, "interprets outer appearances . . . as things-in-themselves which exist independently of us and of our sensibility and which are therefore outside us—the phrase 'outside us' being interpreted in conformity with pure concepts of understanding" (A 369). The decisive point is that the transcendental realist, when he tries to come to terms with the problem of outer appearances, turns into that other kind of idealist, the empirical idealist: Having supposed that outer appearances are things-in-themselves existing independently of our senses, he rightly concludes that their mere effect on us is insufficient to establish their existence. The fallacy lies, however, in the supposition that outer appearances are things-in-themselves. It is precisely this fallacy that is exposed by transcendental idealism, as established by Kant in the Transcendental Aesthetic. Referring to the transcendental idealist, Kant observes: "Matter is with him, therefore, only a species of representations (intuition) which are called external, not as standing in relation to objects *in themselves external*, but because they relate perceptions to the space in which all things are external to one another, while yet the space itself is in us" (A 370). Thus, for the transcendental idealist external objects prove to be no less certain than inner appearances: "For in both cases alike the objects are nothing but representations, the immediate perception (consciousness) of which is at the same time a sufficient proof of their reality" (A 371). The transcendental idealist proves to be an empirical realist.

What is the basic fallacy in the fourth paralogism, and what is the dialectical movement with which it is connected? One way of diagnosing this paralogism would be merely to declare the minor premise false: As transcendental idealism shows, outer appearances are *not* such that their existence is only inferred. However, this approach fails to bring out the affinity between this paralogism and the other three; it fails even to indicate how this inference could be termed a paralogism, since, by definition, a paralogism involves a formal fallacy. The issue is clear if we focus on the basic ambiguity at work in the paralogism. This ambiguity, on which the entire paralogism turns, lies in the word "outer," which may refer either to objects of outer sense or to objects which are completely outside the sphere of self-consciousness, i.e., things-in-themselves. In order for the paralogism in its Cartesian orientation to be binding, the term "outer appearances" would in the conclusion have to be taken in the sense of objects of outer sense, whereas in the minor premise it would have to have the sense of things-in-themselves (in order that this premise be true). Thus, formally regarded, the syllogism commits the fallacy of using one and the same term in two different senses; hence, the fallacy which the fourth paralogism involves differs from that committed by the other three only by the fact that the operative ambiguity has its primary locus in the minor term rather than in the middle term. From another perspective the minor premise may be regarded as expressing the turning between the poles of this ambiguity. It is this turning that constitutes the fundamental dialectical movement of the paralogism, the turning of objects of outer sense (outer appearances in the strict, transcendental sense) into things-in-themselves.

Kant says that there are three dialectical questions which constitute the real goal of rational psychology: the question of the possibility of the communion of the soul with the body, that of the beginning of this communion (i.e., of the soul in and before birth), and that of the end of this communion (i.e., of the soul in and after death). The fourth paralogism is meant to serve for settling the questions of birth and death—that is, of immortality in the broader sense—by supporting the contention that the soul has a kind of absolute existence independent of the merely possible existence of external things. The paralogism is intended to answer affirmatively the question "whether this consciousness of myself would be even possible apart from things outside me . . . and whether, therefore, I could exist merely as thinking being (i.e., without existing in human form)" (B 409). Critique of the paralogism serves, however, to undercut the alleged contributions to resolving these questions; on the other hand, transcendental idealism proves to be in service to precisely the same negative purpose that motivates rational psychology in this regard, the purpose of securing "our thinking self against the danger of materialism," for it shows that "if I remove the thinking subject the whole corporeal world must at once vanish," that matter "is nothing but an appearance in the sensibility of our subject and a mode of its representations" (A 383). Furthermore, transcendental critique shows that the basic turning which generates the paralogism is what determines the very way in which is posed the problem of the communion between soul and body, between mind and matter—at least, the way in which this problem was posed by Descartes and developed by his successors. The notorious Cartesian problem was to explain how extended things can act on thinking beings (and conversely); because of the difficulty of accounting for such communion between these radically different domains in terms of physical influence, other types of explanation arose, such as the theory of pre-established harmony (Leibniz) and that of divine intervention (Occasionalism) (cf. A 390). However, this problem was from the outset a false problem: It arose merely as a result of regarding external (extended) things as things-in-themselves. What Kant's transcendental idealism shows is that there is no such breach as that which generates this problem of communion: Extended things are nothing but appearances in the form of outer sense and as such exist only in the subject.

Kant says that all the difficulties that arise when rational psychology takes up its central questions "rest on a mere delusion by which it hypostatizes what exists merely in thought and takes it as an actual object existing, in the same character, outside the thinking subject" (A 384). This hypostatizing is the basic turning that animates the fourth paralogism. More generally, such a hypostatizing constitutes the decisive turning involved in all the paralogisms. In each case it is a matter of "treating our thoughts as things and hypostatizing them" (A 395). But this hypostatizing, this objectifying, can take place in two different connections. It can take place with regard to the subject, as in the first three paralogisms: Then it takes the form of a turning of the subject *as* subject (transcendental apperception) into the subject *as* object (soul). Or, as in the fourth paralogism, it can occur with respect to the object, in which case it becomes a turning of the object *as* subjective into the object *as* objective, more precisely, a turning of outer appearances into things-in-themselves. Such turning from subjective to objective is the movement of dialectical illusion.

3. PROJECTIVE INTERPRETATION OF THE PARALOGISMS

Shifting to the level of projective interpretation, the task becomes that of projecting the issues of transcendental paralogism (as thematized in the commentary now completed) upon the horizon that was assembled for such interpretation—of projecting these issues in such a way that they get understood from that horizon, mirrored back, reflected, from it. The horizon is constituted by the conception of human knowing as a movement of gathering, a movement in which the fragmentary beginnings are gathered up into a unity akin to that of divine knowing, in such a way that the fragmentation of the beginnings is repaired, surpassed. Reason comes into play as the final phase of this movement, as the highest mode of gathering. Through reason even that fragmentation which persists after the synthetic accomplishments of pure understanding (in conjunction with pure imagination) would be overcome. Reason would take over the manifold and bring it under a higher unity, specifically under those unities which Kant calls transcendental ideas.

The gathering of reason involves three modes, the first of which is transcendental paralogism. To project the issues of transcendental paralogism upon this horizon means, then, to take the paralogistic movement *as* a movement of gathering. It is a matter of showing how the various moments within paralogism are specific forms of the general elements previously identified as pertaining to that movement which human knowing is.

Kant summarizes the basic issue of the paralogisms in these words: "Thus all controversy in regard to the nature of the thinking being and its connection with the corporeal world is merely a result of filling the gap where knowledge is wholly lacking to us with paralogisms of reason, treating our thoughts as things and hypostatizing them" (A 395). So, the basic issue is that of filling a gap in our knowledge with a substitute knowledge; in other words, the central movement of paralogism, that hypostatizing which takes the form of a turning from subjective to objective, is linked to the provision of a surrogate. Projective interpretation needs to focus on this surrogate character of transcendental paralogism.

Paralogism would fill a gap; it would overcome a certain state of separation, a condition of fragmentation. What is the gap to be filled, the fragmentation to be overcome? It is the gap in our knowledge of ourselves, the gap of self-ignorance. It is the fragmentation constituted by man's being condemned to know himself only as appearance and not as he is in himself—man's condition of not being one with himself, of being separated from himself by ignorance. More precisely, the relevant fragmentation is constituted by the separation between the self *as* subject of knowing and the self *as* object of knowing; in other words, the gap is simply a disunity between subject and object *within* the sphere of self-knowing; it is simply a specification of the first of the four general forms of fragmentation that belong to the beginning of human knowing. Transcendental paralogism would fill this gap, would overcome this fragmentation within man, this fragmentation of self-ignorance. However, Kant's critique of paralogism shows that paralogism cannot succeed in filling the gap, that reason's alleged gathering of man into unity with himself fails. It shows that the very dialectical inference that would overcome ignorance of self is itself a fallacious turning from subjective to objective, a turning away from self, a self-forgetting, the result of a profound and almost self-concealing ignorance of self. The critique of paralogism thus serves, in effect, to set man back knowingly within the limits of his self-ignorance. It issues in a recollection of self which, structurally distinct from that self-knowledge to which paralogistic metaphysics aspires, grants and incorporates the fragmentation of self-ignorance. One might venture to suggest that this is Kant's most profound affinity with Socrates.

The relevant fragmentation is thus a specific form of the fragmentation between subject and object. However, this specific fragmentation—hence, the gap to be filled by paralogism—is, in turn, grounded in the fragmentation of intuition, i.e., in the second major form of fragmentation as it takes shape within the sphere of self-knowledge. In other words, the gap, the lack, in self-knowledge is grounded in the fact that the intuition of self is not original—that is, by the fact that I am given to myself *only* as I am affected by myself, only through self-affection. Given to myself in this radically fragmentary way, I know myself only as appearance.

Transcendental paralogism would provide a surrogate for this impoverished knowledge of self, this knowledge impoverished by the fragmentary character of the intuition of self. However, the surrogate knowledge is not to be based on intuition. Rather, for the impoverished knowledge of self based on intuition, paralogism would substitute a purely rational knowledge of self, a knowledge based solely on thought. In other words, the gap in self-knowledge would be filled by a rational self-knowledge, a determining of the self solely through thought.

This provision of rational self-knowledge takes the form of a gathering of reason. In general, the structure of gathering is two-sided: On the one side, there is the positing of the idea as unity for the gathering, a positing which takes the form of an extending of a categorial unity up to the level of absolute unity; on the other side, there is the actual gathering of the relevant manifold into this unity. This general two-sidedness is exemplified by the movement of paralogism, which, as the commentary has shown, involves two distinct aspects. On the one side, paralogism involves a transformation of the concept of the I (of transcendental apperception) into that of the soul, a turning of the I into the soul; in general terms, this turning amounts precisely to a positing of the transcendental idea (soul) by means of an extending of a categorial unity, namely, of the fundamental categorial unity, transcendental apperception. Thus, the turning constitutes one side of the gathering: It is the positing of the unity for the gathering. On the other side, paralogism involves a determining of the concept of soul—more precisely, a movement from the transcendental determinations of the I of apperception to corresponding real determinations of the soul.

But how does this second aspect of paralogism exemplify the actual gathering into the posited unity? How does the attribution of certain determinations to the soul constitute a gathering into the unity of the self? It does so at two levels. Insofar as such attribution amounts to the attainment of knowledge of self, it constitutes an overcoming of that ignorance of self to which man is condemned at the level of intuitively-based knowledge, that is, an overcoming of man's separation from himself in ignorance, of the separation between the self *as* subject of knowing and the self *as* object of knowing. Paralogism, insofar as it is an attainment of knowledge of the self, constitutes a gathering of this manifold, i.e., this twofold, into unity. The specific dependence which the second aspect has in this regard on the prior turning is especially significant: The determining of the soul can constitute a gathering of the self as object of knowing into unity with the self as subject of knowing only on the basis provided by the turning of the subject as subject into the subject as object.

In addition to such overcoming of self-ignorance in deed, there is also another level of gathering constituted by the attribution of determinations to the soul. This other level becomes evident if it is carefully noted just how the self determines itself in this alleged self-knowledge. It determines itself *as* simple, unitary, absolutely existing substance—that is, it determines itself *as* excluding qualitative differentiation, *as* excluding dispersal in time, *as* excluding essential connection with the body. In other words, it determines itself as excluding various fundamental types of fragmentation (qualitative, temporal, bodily)—types of fragmentation which bear not so much on the limits of objective knowledge as on the destiny of the soul. In the paralogisms the soul is determined as held in unity with itself in these various regards. Furthermore, behind all these self-determinations, the real task at issue is to prove the immortality of the soul, that is, to determine the soul as immortal, that is, to determine the soul as escaping the most radical of all kinds of fragmentation, that utter separation from self that would take place in *death*, were the soul not immortal.

Therefore, transcendental paralogism is a gathering of reason. And Kant's syllogistic presentations of the individual paralogisms constitute sketches of the four modes of this specific gathering of reason. What is especially remarkable is that in each such sketch the principal elements of the gathering are clearly delineated: The major premise expresses the categorial unity that gets extended by reason; the minor premise expresses the turning of the I into the soul, that is, the positing of the unity for the gathering; and the conclusion expresses the attribution of a determination to the soul, that is, the actual gathering into unity.

However, transcendental paralogism is dialectical—that is, the gathering fails. Aimed at overcoming a specific fragmentation between subject and object that is grounded, in turn, in a fragmentation of intuition, the gathering runs aground on the other basic forms of fragmentation, those pertaining to thought. How does this failure show itself to the critique of paralogism? How is it manifest? It is manifest at three levels, corresponding to the three constituent judgments of a transcendentally paralogistic syllogism.

At the level of the attribution of determinations to the soul, the level expressed by the conclusion, the failure is manifest in the fact that the alleged determinations prove to be merely pure, i.e., unschematized, categories—that is, merely forms of unity involved in the thought of anything whatsoever, not objective determinations. More precisely, the critique of paralogism shows that the alleged determinations can be attributed to the soul *with justification* only if they are taken as empty forms of thought rather than as real determinations. In other words, the attribution of determinations to the soul is referred critically back to that basis which prescribes the limits within which such attribution is justified. But the basis on which paralogism is built is transcendental apperception, which in the syllogistic presentation is expressed in the major premise.

How is the failure of the gathering manifest at the level of apperception? In other words, how is the emptiness of the alleged determinations of the soul grounded in the character of apperception as the basis on which the attribution of those determinations would be built? In this regard apperception serves as basis simply in the sense that a certain determining of the I of apperception is transferred to the level of the soul, is extended into a determining of the soul. Thus, the emptiness of the alleged determinations of the soul is grounded simply in the emptiness of the determining of the I in apperception. The emptiness of apperception consists in the fact that in apperception the I merely posits itself as existing—that is, it does not posit itself as determined in any definite ways, does not posit itself in its determinacy. As posited by itself in apperception the I is completely indeterminate, the mere X to which all representations can be referred; and the alleged determinations, substantiality, unity, and simplicity, merely express the formal structure of the self-positing. Why, in pure human thought, does the I think itself emptily? Why does it not posit itself in its determinacy? Because of the fragmentation of human thought—that is, because human thought can establish determinacy only in relation to something given, because its content must be supplied from elsewhere, lacking which it remains empty. In different terms, human thought is incapable of that absolute unity with intuition that would enable it, as thought, to bring itself forth with intuitive fullness and determinacy; on the contrary, human self-knowing is condemned to the fragmentation, the disunity, between thought and intuition.

There is still a third level at which the failure of paralogism is manifest, the level expressed in the minor premise of each paralogistic syllogism. This is the level of the turning of the subject as subject into the subject as object, the turning which constitutes the most fundamental constituent in the movement of paralogism, since, by Kant's own account (A 401–2), it is what first motivates the extension of the empty self-positing of the I up to the level of a determining of the soul. But this turning, from which the entire gathering movement of paralogism originates, must itself be referred back to the I, to a self-positing I. What, then, is the character of the turning as referred back to the I which carries it out, the I which goes on to construct paralogisms? The turning is a fundamental modification of the I's own self-positing: It is a diversion of the positing of itself *as* subject into a positing of itself *as* object. It is from this primordial self-objectification that paralogism originates. And it is here too, in this confounding of subjective and objective, that the failure of the paralogistic gathering is prepared.

Kant says that rational psychology legitimately exists "not as doctrine furnishing an addition to our knowledge of the self, but only as discipline" (B 421). The projective interpretation allows it to be regarded as the discipline which constrains man within that condition of fragmentation to which his self-knowing is bound, which constrains him within the limits of his proper self-ignorance; and this requires especially that it restrain man from that primordial diversion of his own self-positing, that self-objectification, which constitutes the origin of paralogism. Kant suggests, in turn, that such restraining constraint ought ultimately to serve to prepare reason for a more fitting employment: "But though it furnishes no positive doctrine, it reminds us that we should regard this refusal of reason to give satisfactory response to our inquisitive probings into what is beyond the limits of this present life as reason's hint to divert our self-knowledge from fruitless and extravagant speculation to fruitful practical employment" (B 421).

CHAPTER IV

THE GATHERING OF REASON IN THE ANTINOMIES

The antinomy of pure reason, which constitutes the second type of dialectical inference, is the most significant from a genetic point of view. Indeed, there are grounds for regarding the problem of the antinomies as "the cradle of the critical philosophy";[1] and Kant himself testifies in a letter to Garve that this problem was what awoke him from his dogmatic slumbers and drove him to a critique of reason.[2]

The antinomy of pure reason is the topic of the second chapter of the critical investigation of the dialectical inferences of pure reason. In a brief introductory passage leading up to Section 1 of this chapter Kant sketches the general character of such inference. The characterization involves three items.

First, Kant notes that, in terms of the general analogy between pure (dialectical) reason and logical reason, this type of dialectical inference corresponds to the hypothetical syllogism. The point of the correspondence is simply that, just as hypothetical syllogism involves regression or progression in a simple linear series of conditions (most notably if extended through prosyllogisms or episyllogisms), so in the antinomy of pure reason the concept of a linear series of conditions is central.

Second, Kant observes that the content involved in such dialectical inferences is "the unconditioned unity of the objective conditions in the [field of] appearance" (A 406/B 433), that is, "absolute totality of the synthesis of appearances" (A 407/B 434). Such content, taken in various regards, constitutes transcendental ideas of a distinctive kind; Kant calls them "cosmological ideas" or "cosmical concepts" (*Weltbegriffe*).

They are the concepts that belong to rational cosmology. It is especially to be noted that such concepts, and, hence, the inferences in which they are involved, are related *only to appearances*. In the antinomies reason surpasses the limits of possible experience, not by leaping from appearances to things-in-themselves, but rather by passing from the synthesis of appearances in experience to the absolute totality of that synthesis.

Finally, Kant calls attention to a special point of contrast between the antinomies and the paralogisms. In the case of the paralogisms the illusion that is produced is purely one-sided: There is not also produced an illusion in support of the opposing assertion. By contrast, in the case of the antinomies both an assertion *and* its opposite find support, and this means that reason falls into contradictions. As with all results of dialectical inference, these contradictions are no mere products of an artificial sophistry that could be corrected by logical criticism. Rather, they are unavoidable; they constitute "an entirely natural antithetic . . . into which reason of itself quite unavoidably falls" (A 407/B 433–4)—an antithetic belonging to the sophistry of pure reason itself. As Kant elaborates subsequently, this antithetic involves "a natural and unavoidable illusion, which even after it has ceased to beguile still continues to delude though not to deceive us and which though thus capable of being rendered harmless can never be eradicated" (A 422/B 449–50).

1. THE COSMOLOGICAL IDEAS (A 408/B 435–A 425/B 453)

Kant's first major task is to derive the system of cosmological ideas and the antinomies linked to them. As a basis for undertaking this task, he resumes his earlier considerations of the relation between reason and understanding. Previously (A 326–7/B 383–4, with Ch. II, 4) Kant focused on the parallel between reason and understanding: Just as understanding brings to unity the manifold given in intuition, so reason brings to unity the manifold knowledge supplied by understanding. Thus, concepts of reason, i.e., transcendental ideas, are unities for the unification of what remains manifold at the level of understanding. In a sense such ideas may be regarded as originating from reason; they constitute the pure content originated by reason, corresponding to the categories originated by understanding. Yet, the two cases do not wholly correspond: The ideas are themselves derivative from the categories in a way that prevents their being regarded as simply generated by reason.

In the more precise account which Kant now offers, this derivativeness is unequivocally expressed:

> In the first place we must recognize that pure and transcendental concepts can arise only from the understanding. Reason does not really generate any concept, but rather, at most, it *frees* a concept of *understanding* from the unavoidable limitations of possible experience and so endeavors to extend it beyond the limits of the empirical, though still in connection with the empirical. This is achieved in the following manner. For a given conditioned, reason demands on the side of the conditions—to which as the conditions of synthetic unity the understanding subjects all appearances—absolute totality and in so doing converts the category into a transcendental idea (A 408–9/B 435–6).

So, reason does not generate any concepts simply from itself; specifically, it does not simply generate the transcendental ideas, though, of course, it is involved in their origination. The point is that ideas are not merely generated *ex nihilo* but rather arise from the categories. Reason frees a category from its limitation to possible experience and extends it beyond the empirical, beyond the domain of possible experience: "The transcendental ideas are thus, in the first place, simply categories extended to the unconditioned." However, this extension beyond the empirical is not simply a leap from appearances to things-in-themselves. In the case of those transcendental ideas that are cosmological, the extension has nothing whatsoever to do with things-in-themselves. Even where, as in the paralogisms, there is an extension to things-in-themselves, that extension still has essential connection with the domain of the empirical or, more precisely, with the domain of understanding; thus the basic turning that grounds the paralogisms proved to be a modification of that self-positing which, as transcendental apperception, is the fundamental condition of understanding.

The cosmological ideas originate through an extension from certain categories up to absolute totality in the synthesis of appearances, or, more precisely, in the *regressive* synthesis of appearances (cf. A 411/B 438). It is a matter of transforming certain categories into concepts of the absolute totality of the series of conditions of appearances. Which categories are capable of such extension? Only those in which the prescribed synthesis has a series character. In Kant's words, "not all categories are fitted for such employment but only those in which the synthesis constitutes a *series* of conditions subordinated to, not coordinated with, one another and generative of a [given] conditioned" (A 409/B 436). The categories capable of being transformed by reason into cosmical concepts are precisely those in relation to which a regressive series is possible, those which permit generation of a series through regression from conditioned to condition. The task of deriving the cosmological ideas amounts to determining which categories meet this condition and then exhibiting the corresponding extension into transcendental ideas.

Kant considers, in turn, each of the four general types of categories, showing how in each case there is possible a specific extension up to the level of absolute totality in the synthesis of appearance. In the case of quantity the character and result of the relevant extension can be seen most clearly in reference to the principle corresponding to this category, the principle that "all intuitions are extensive magnitudes"—or, more precisely, that "all appearances are, in their intuition, extensive magnitudes" (A 162/B 202). Appearances can be extensive magnitudes in two respects: with respect to time and with respect to space. Thus, quantity, embodied in appearances as extensive magnitude, can be extended to the level of absolute totality in these same two respects. In the case of time the extension is straightforward: Time is a series (in fact, the formal condition of all series), and the regressive extension simply moves from the presently given appearance back through the series. The absolute totality is simply the series of appearances throughout all past time, and the corresponding transcendental idea is simply the concept of such an absolute totality.

The case of space is more complicated, for space is not in itself serial nor is there in space any distinction between progression and regression. Considered *in itself*, space is such that its parts are coexistent; it is an aggregate, not a series. However, space is not something in itself but rather is a form of intuition; even more important, determinate space (*quantitas* as opposed to mere *quantum*) presupposes synthesis (cf. A 162/B 202–A 166/B 207). Thus, Kant focuses on the character of space, not as in itself nor even just as mere intuition, but rather in terms of that synthesis which pertains to its constitution: "Nevertheless, the synthesis of the manifold parts of space, by means of which we apprehend space, is successive, taking place in time and containing a series" (A 412/B 439). The synthetic activity by which space is apprehended takes place in time, so that the serial character of time is thus carried over to space. But what sense does this seriality have with regard to space? Kant continues:

> And since in this series of the aggregated spaces . . . of the given space, those which are thought in extension of the given space are always *the condition of the limits* of the given space, the *measuring* of a space is also to be regarded as a synthesis of a series of the conditions of a given conditioned, only with this difference that the side of the conditions is not in itself distinct from that of the conditioned and that in space *regressus* and *progressus* would therefore seem to be one and the same (A 412–13/ B 439–40).

So, the seriality carried over from time takes the form of a series of limits in the sense that a given space is limited by another space and it, in turn, by another, etc. Thus, Kant says: "In respect of limitation the advance in space is thus also a regress, and the transcendental idea of the absolute totality of the synthesis in the series of conditions likewise applies to space" (A 413/B 440). Therefore, the category of quantity provides reason with the basis for forming transcendental ideas of the totality of appearances both in all past time and in space. These are the two forms taken by the first of the four cosmological ideas. In its general formulation it is the concept of "absolute completeness of the *composition* of the given whole of all appearances" (A 415/B 443).

The derivation of the second cosmological idea is quite brief. Kant simply names the relevant category, indicates the kind of conditioning involved in it, and then points to the extension of that conditioning up to the level of absolute totality. The categorial heading is quality, the specific category that of reality. In accordance with the cosmological context, this category is considered primarily with respect to *outer* appearances; and so Kant focuses on reality in space. But, reality in space is simply the material (nonformal) element in outer appearances—that is, matter (understood transcendentally). Hence, the question is: What kind of conditioning is involved in matter? Kant answers that it is the conditioning of a whole by its parts:

> Its internal conditions are its parts, and the parts of these parts its remote conditions. There thus occurs a regressive synthesis, the absolute

> totality of which is demanded by reason. This can be completed only by a completed division in virtue of which the reality of matter vanishes either into nothing or into what is no longer matter—namely, the simple (A 413/B 440).

The cosmological idea that results is that of "absolute completeness in the *division* of a given whole in the [field of] appearance" (A 415/B 443).

With regard to the categories of relation Kant stresses that the category of substance is not suitable for being extended into a cosmological idea: "in it reason finds no ground for moving regressively to conditions" (A 414/B 441). The point is that in the case of substance the necessary serial character is lacking, that the accidents of a substance do not form a series either in relation to one another or in relation to the substance itself. Among the categories of relation the requisite serial character is found only in the case of causality. In this connection the extension moves regressively through the entire series of causes and effects, and the resulting cosmological idea is that of "absolute completeness in the *origination* of an appearance" (A 415/B 443).

The final derivation is briefest of all:

> Fourthly, the concepts of the possible, the actual, and the necessary do not lead to any series, except insofar as the *accidental* in existence must always be regarded as conditioned and as pointing in conformity with the rule of the understanding to a condition under which it is necessary, and this latter in turn to a higher condition, until reason finally attains unconditioned necessity only in the totality of the series (A 415/B 442).

The resulting cosmological idea is that of "absolute completeness as regards *dependence* of *existence* of the alterable in the [field of] appearance" (A 415/B 443).

Within the full structure of the inferential movement pertaining to the cosmological ideas, it is necessary to distinguish two moments. The first is that movement, just traced, by which the cosmological ideas themselves originate: the extension of the relevant category up to the level of absolute totality of the series of conditions. The second moment is that by which the first is brought to its genuine completion; it is the movement in which the antinomies are generated.

Kant observes that in the extension up to the level of absolute totality what is really sought is the unconditioned: "What reason is really seeking in this serial, regressively continued, synthesis of conditions is solely the unconditioned" (A 416/B 443–4). So, reason moves to the absolute totality of conditions in order thereby to arrive at the unconditioned. This requires that the unconditioned somehow be contained in the absolute totality of conditions: "This *unconditioned* is always contained in the absolute totality of the series as represented in imagination" (A 416/B 444)—that is, the absolute totality of conditions *must* contain the unconditioned, for otherwise there would be some further condition beyond this totality which would, then, render it less than the absolute totality. The second movement within the full structure of the inferential movement is simply the way in which, by reaching the absolute totality of conditions, reason attains the unconditioned.

The crucial point is that the unconditioned can be contained in the absolute totality in two radically different ways:

> This unconditioned may be conceived in either of two ways. It may be viewed as consisting of the entire series in which all the members without exception are conditioned and only the totality of them is absolutely unconditioned. This regress is to be entitled infinite. Or alternatively, the absolutely unconditioned is only a part of the series—a part to which the other members are subordinated and which does not itself stand under any other condition (A 417/B 445).

Thus, by moving to the absolute totality of the series, reason can arrive at the unconditioned in two different ways, that is, it can arrive at two different forms of the unconditioned: the unconditioned as the entire infinite series (no member of which is unconditioned) or the unconditioned as a first member in the series to which all other members are subordinate. Reason's involvement in antinomies results from this duality—from the fact that there are two radically opposed (contradictory) forms of the unconditioned.

Thus, for each of the general cosmological ideas there are two opposed forms to which the inferential movement can lead. And so, corresponding to each of the four ideas there is an antinomy: The thesis results from the inference in which the unconditioned takes the form of a first member of the series; the antithesis results where it takes the form of the entire infinite series.

The impending conflict that is to be unleashed by the cosmological ideas is foreshadowed within the structure of the first moment of the inferential movement, that moment in which the ideas originate. In its simplest form the conflict lies in the fact that the extension of the categories *beyond* the limits of experience is, on the other hand, carried out *in connection with* the empirical. Kant describes it as a conflict between reason and understanding:

> Since this unity of reason involves a synthesis according to rules, it must conform to the understanding; and yet as demanding absolute unity of synthesis it must at the same time harmonize with reason. But the conditions of this unity are such that when it is adequate to reason it is too great for understanding; and when suited to the understanding, too small for reason. There thus arises a conflict which cannot be avoided, do what we will (A 422/B 450).

On the one hand, the extension is carried out in terms of the synthesis prescribed by the category in its relation to experience, i.e., as a category of understanding, and, consequently, must conform to *understanding*; on the other hand, it is an extension beyond experience, beyond the domain of understanding, up to the level of absolute unity demanded by reason and, hence, must harmonize with *reason*. The extension, the inferential movement in which the cosmological ideas originate, incorporates by its very nature the conflict between reason and understanding. The critical task is to resolve this conflict—that is, to institute "a lasting and peaceful reign of reason over understanding and the senses" (A 465/B 493). The task is decidedly *not* to eliminate reason and its demand for unity but rather to transform the demand in such a way as to grant reason its legitimate rule over understanding. The task is not to eliminate *metaphysica specialis* but to reform it, to bring it into conformity with the finitude of human knowing.

2. THE FOUR ANTINOMIES (A 426/B 454–A 461/B 489)

Before setting about the genuine critical task of resolution, Kant first lets the conflict unfold to its full extent. In relation to each cosmological idea he opposes a thesis to an antithesis. He then enforces that opposition by constructing proofs for both of the conflicting assertions. Granted the posing of the cosmological ideas, the oppositions are in all cases irresolvable, and what at first took the form of a conflict between reason and understanding becomes also a conflict within reason itself.

At the level of the antinomies, reason, having demanded absolute unity, is no longer even one with itself.

For the most part I shall limit myself to a mere presentation of the opposed assertions constituting the antinomies, considering these in relation to the corresponding idea.[3]

The cosmological idea in relation to which the first antinomy is generated is that of absolute totality with regard to composition. In other words, the idea is that of the world as a whole in regard to time, i.e., of the world in its temporal totality, in its complete temporal extension; and of the world as a whole in regard to space, i.e., the world in its spatial totality, in its complete spatial extension. The issue in the antinomy is: whether the world in these two respects is limited or unlimited,[4] that is, whether the unconditioned takes the form of a first (limiting) term or of the entire unlimited series. Hence, Kant's statements:

> *Thesis*: The world has a beginning in time and is also limited as regards space.
> *Antithesis*: The world has no beginning and no limits in space; it is infinite as regards both time and space.

The cosmological idea in relation to which the second antinomy is generated is that of absolute completeness with regard to division. It is the idea of complete division of a whole, an appearance, into parts. More precisely, it is the idea of the total series of divisions of a whole, of the totality of the series which begins: whole, parts, parts of parts . . . . The issue in the corresponding antinomy is: whether or not the regress through this series arrives at a final member, at absolutely simple parts which would allow no further division and which would thus be unconditioned as regards division. But this, again, is simply to ask whether the unconditioned takes the form of an ultimate member of the series or of the entire (infinite) series. Kant's statement reads:

> *Thesis*: Every composite substance in the world is made up of simple parts, and nothing anywhere exists except the simple or what is composed of the simple.
> *Antithesis*: No composite thing in the world is made up of simple parts, and there nowhere exists in the world anything simple.

It should be observed that this antinomy relates not only to the issue of the infinite divisibility of matter[5] but also to another issue.[6] This other issue can be seen in connection with the antithesis, which, it should be noted, not only affirms the infinite divisibility of composite things but also asserts that "there nowhere exists in the world anything simple." Kant explains that, within the context of the position represented by the antithesis, this assertion means "that the existence of the absolutely simple cannot be established by an experience or perception, either outer or inner" (A 437/B 465). The point is that in its denial of simple parts the antithesis (and so the antinomy as a whole) refers not only to simple parts of the appearances of outer sense (material atoms) but also to simple parts of appearances of *inner* sense. In the latter regard, the issue is that of the soul as a simple thinking substance. The issue is Leibniz's monadology. It is the issue of transcendental paralogism. The second antinomy thus provides a point of contact between rational cosmology and rational psychology.

The cosmological idea in relation to which the third antinomy is generated is that of absolute completeness (totality) with regard to the origination of appearances. It is the idea of the complete regressive series of causes of an appearance, the idea of the totality of the series that regresses from a given appearance to its cause, to the cause of the cause, etc. The issue in the corresponding antinomy is: whether this series is limited or unlimited, that is, whether it has a first (unconditioned) member or whether, on the contrary, the only thing that is unconditioned is the entire series of causes. A first member, a causality that would itself be uncaused, an absolutely spontaneous action from which a whole series would follow, would be an act of *freedom*. Hence, Kant's statement:

> *Thesis*: Causality in accordance with laws of nature is not the causality from which the appearances of the world can one and all be derived. To explain these appearances it is necessary to assume that there is also another causality, that of freedom.
>
> *Antithesis*: There is no freedom; everything in the world takes place solely in accordance with laws of nature.

Mention should be made of Kant's reference, in connection with the thesis, to the fact that the ancients posited a prime mover beyond nature, a freely acting cause capable of initiating a causal series; but, he says, "They made no attempt to render a first beginning conceivable through nature's own resources" (A 450/B 478). The reference serves to indicate that the denial of freedom in the antithesis coincides with that kind of denial that was linked to the development of modern science, a denial of freedom on the ground that its affirmation would introduce into nature a lawlessness inimical to science.

The cosmological idea in relation to which the fourth antinomy is generated is that of absolute completeness (totality) as regards dependence of existence. It is the idea of the complete regressive series in the order of existential dependence, that is, of the totality of the series which runs from an accidentally existing being to the being on which its existence depends, then from the second being (which itself exists accidentally) to the further being on which its existence depends, etc. The issue in the corresponding antinomy is: whether this series is limited or unlimited, that is, whether it has a first (unconditioned) member or whether, on the contrary, the only thing that is unconditioned is the entire series of accidentally existing beings. A first member would be a being whose existence is not accidental (dependent), i.e., a being that necessarily exists. Hence, Kant's statement:

> *Thesis*: There belongs to the world, either as its part or as its cause, a being that is absolutely necessary.
> *Antithesis:* An absolutely necessary being nowhere exists in the world, nor does it exist outside the world as its cause.

The absolutely necessary being whose existence is here disputed is of course God. In fact, Kant identifies the argument given in support of the thesis with the traditional cosmological argument (cf. A 456/B 484). Thus, the fourth antinomy is the principal point of contact between rational cosmology and the rational theology to be taken up in the final main part of the Dialectic. It should, however, be observed that cosmology can deal with the idea of God only by appropriating this idea to its own perspective, only by regarding God as a being which belongs to the world either as its part or as its cause—that is, only by refusing to distinguish radically between God and the world.

3. THE INTEREST OF REASON (A 462/B 490–A 476/B 504)

The questions at issue in the antinomies are of ultimate import. They have to do with "those highest ends that most closely concern humanity" (A 463–4/B 491–2). The question whether the soul is an indivisible unity, whether there is freedom, whether a supreme cause of the world exists—these are questions of ultimate human concern. Thus, how these questions are answered can never be a matter of indifference. One has a stake in them, and various human interests are differently served by different answers to these questions. In order to indicate the full human import of the antinomies, Kant considers in some detail "how we should proceed if we consulted only our interest and not the logical criterion of truth" (A 465/B 493). In other words, he sets about indicating how the two positions that are in conflict in the antinomies relate to various interests.

First, he names the two positions. That position represented by the antithesis in each antinomy is pure *empiricism*. The position represented by the thesis is *dogmatism*. The latter is distinguished by the fact that, in addition to the empirical mode of explanation, it presupposes intelligible beginnings. Kant proceeds then to relate each position to various interests.

He considers dogmatism first. He insists that this position serves "a certain *practical interest* in which every well-disposed man, if he has understanding of what truly concerns him, heartily shares" (A 466/B 494). The point is that the assertions on the side of the thesis—such assertions as that of the indestructibility and freedom of the soul, of the existence of a supreme being—are the "foundation stones of morals and religion." Dogmatism serves also a *speculative interest*: "When the transcendental ideas are postulated and employed in the manner prescribed by the thesis, the entire chain of conditions and the derivation of the conditioned can be grasped completely *a priori*" (A 466–7/B 494–5). The point is that the assertions on the side of the thesis, i.e., which arrive at the unconditioned in the form of a first, unconditioned member, i.e., which arrive at an intelligible beginning, bring the regress (from conditioned to condition) to a genuine conclusion, so that one really grasps the entire series. Dogmatism also has the advantage of *popularity*. Common sense does not find anything puzzling in the concept of a first member or intelligible beginning; it even finds comfort and direction in such concepts. By contrast, "In the restless ascent from the conditioned to the condition, always with one foot in the air, there can be no satisfaction" (A 467/B 495).

On the other side stands empiricism. It does not have the advantage of serving *practical interest*. In contrast to dogmatism, it appears to destroy all support for and all the power of morals and religion. On the other hand, empiricism serves *speculative interest* in a way that far surpasses the service done this interest by dogmatism. Empiricism constrains understanding to its proper domain, that of possible experience, and insists that there is no need to leave this domain and resort to ideas; empiricism prohibits understanding from passing over into the sphere of transcendent concepts where it would no longer be bound by any evidence. Thus, empiricism serves to subdue rashness and presumption; and Kant says that, if the empiricist remained at this level, "his principle would be a maxim urging moderation in our pretentions, modesty in our assertions, and yet at the same time the greatest possible extension of our understanding through the teacher fittingly assigned to us, namely, through experience" (A 470/B 498). However, the problem is that empiricism tends to become itself dogmatic. It becomes a dogmatic denial of what is affirmed by dogmatism, a denial of everything that would lie beyond empirical knowledge. In this tendency "it betrays the same lack of modesty; and this is all the more reprehensible owing to the irreparable injury which is thereby caused to the practical interests of reason" (A 471/B 499). In this regard it is clear how in the opposition between dogmatism and empiricism the conflict between reason and understanding is embodied. Finally, empiricism is universally *unpopular* because of the support which the indolence and vanity of common sense lend to dogmatism.

Kant appends a consideration of still another interest, the architectonic interest of reason. It is especially in this interest that reference can be seen to the character of reason as gathering. Kant says that "Human reason is by nature architectonic" and explains this as meaning that "it regards all our knowledge as belonging to a possible system" (A 474/B 502). For knowledge to belong to a system is tantamount to its items belonging together in a unity. Thus, Kant links the architectonic interest of reason to "the demand not for empirical but for pure *a priori* unity of reason" (A 475/B 503). In its beginning knowledge lacks unity; it still involves fragmentation even at the level at which it is already fully authenticated as knowledge, the level of understanding. Reason demands that this fragmentation be abolished and strives to gather knowledge into final unity. This architectonic interest is served by the theses of the various antinomies, by dogmatism. In terms of the issue of gathering, this means that the thesis represents in each case the upward thrust which, if unimpeded, would bring to completion the gathering of fragmentary knowledge into unity. On the other hand, the empiricist position embodied in the antitheses of the antinomies hinders this interest, it is such as to "render the completion of the edifice of knowledge quite impossible" (A 474/B 502). This means that the antithesis represents in each case the downward force which, if unimpeded, would constrain human knowledge to the level of understanding with its attendant fragmentation. Hence, in the conflict between thesis and antithesis is enacted the conflict between the upward-moving gathering of reason and the downward-moving force of understanding, that advocacy of mere understanding that would shatter the unity of reason's gathering. One may suppose that to resolve the antinomies, to resolve the conflict between reason and understanding, would amount to establishing human knowing at a point of equilibrium between the upward thrust of reason and the downward force of understanding.

4. THE CRITICAL SOLUTION OF THE ANTINOMIES (A 476/B 504—A 507/B 535)

Kant has shown how the cosmological ideas originate. He has traced out the structure of that inferential movement by which the serial categories are transformed into cosmological ideas, and he has indicated how the conflict between reason and understanding intrinsic to this movement, or, alternatively, how the conflict between the two forms which the unconditioned can take, serves to force reason, in its very quest for unity, into disunity with itself. This disunity Kant has then exhibited in his presentation of the four antinomies. His reference to the involvement of the issues of the antinomies in various human interests has suggested, finally, both the urgency and the difficulty of a critical solution of the antinomies.

In order to prepare for such a solution Kant proceeds to show that the questions at issue in the antinomies are of such a kind that they can be fully and finally settled. He seeks, in other words, to establish that rational cosmology is one of those sciences in which, as he says, "the answer must issue from the same sources from which the question proceeds" (A 476/B 504), so that one is prohibited from pleading unavoidable ignorance of the matters at issue in these questions. How must these matters be in order for this to be the case? How must they be in order that there be no finally unanswerable questions, in order that the very means needed to ask the question suffice for answering it?

The questions being contested in the antinomies make use of the general cosmological idea of *world.* They are questions *about* the idea—or, more precisely, about the *object of* this idea, the object corresponding to it, the world itself. The questions, by making use of this idea, ask whether the world itself has a beginning in time, limits in space, etc. How would one ordinarily proceed if he wanted to answer such questions? He would go beyond the mere concept as it occurs in the question and would investigate the object of that concept. Such investigation might suffice to settle the question; but it might, on the other hand, fail to answer it *if* the object were such as to remain in certain regards concealed. In the latter case one would be forced to leave the question unanswered, and one could, as it were, blame the unknown object for one's ignorance. Now Kant wants to show that this kind of situation does not obtain in the case of the antinomies. Here one cannot just leave the questions open and blame his ignorance on an unknown object, because in the case of the cosmological ideas there is and can be *no corresponding object outside the idea.* Hence, beyond the question and the idea it involves, there would be nothing else to which an appeal would need to be made in order to answer the question; there would be nothing which, by remaining concealed, could render the question unanswerable. It is a matter of showing that "that very concept which puts us in a position to ask the question must also qualify us to answer it, since . . . the object is not to be met with outside the concept" (A 477/B 505).

Kant's proof that there can be no object corresponding to the cosmological idea involves two steps. First, it is to be observed that the cosmological idea cannot have for its object a thing-in-itself, which would be intrinsically concealed so as to render the questions unanswerable. That the idea can have no such object is clear from the very character of the inferential movement in which this idea originates: The movement is no leap from appearances to things-in-themselves but rather remains within the order of appearances. The cosmological ideas (i.e., the fundamental idea, that of world, determined in the various categorial regards) are ideas of totality in the synthesis of *appearances*; this is what distinguishes them from all other transcendental ideas and what is ultimately responsible for the fact that they alone are such that no question can remain unanswerable.

The second part of the proof involves showing that in the order of appearances there can be no object corresponding to the cosmological idea. To an extent this follows from its very character as an idea: There are no objects in experience corresponding to the idea of world. However, what has to be shown is not just that there is no such object but that there *can be no such object*, that such an object is impossible. In this connection possibility is to be understood in accord with the first postulate of empirical thought: It means agreement with the formal conditions of experience. Thus, Kant proceeds by showing that what is thought in the cosmological ideas lacks such agreement, specifically, that it lacks agreement with the conditions of understanding:

> If, therefore, in dealing with a cosmological idea, I were able to appreciate beforehand that whatever view may be taken of the unconditioned in the successive synthesis of appearances, it must either be *too large* or *too small* for any *concept of the understanding*, I should be in a position to understand that, since the cosmological idea has no bearing except upon an object of experience which has to be in conformity with a possible concept of the understanding, it must be entirely empty and without meaning; for its object, view it as we may, cannot be made to agree with it (A 486/B 514).

For example, in the case of the first antinomy, the view of the unconditioned expressed in the antithesis, that the world has no beginning, makes it *too large*; for understanding involves a successive regress, which can never reach the whole eternity that would have elapsed. On the other hand, the view expressed in the thesis, that the world has a beginning, makes the unconditioned *too small*; for understanding always demands further regress from any such alleged beginning. Kant shows that this situation prevails in all the antinomies, so that in no case is an appearance even possible corresponding to the idea. Kant concludes that the cosmological idea has no relation to any object. Consequently, "If from our concepts we are unable to assert and determine anything certain, we must not throw the blame upon the object as concealing itself from us. Since such an object is nowhere to be met with outside our idea, it is not possible for it to be given. The cause of failure we must seek in our idea itself" (A 481–2/B 510–11). Kant is now prepared to carry out such a search.

In fact, the critical solution involves little more than simply applying the result just established. The idea of the world as a whole has no object. In other words, the world does not exist *as a whole*, and anything which does exist as an object outside the concept is conditioned, is less than the world as a whole, is partial, fragmentary. Thus, in reference to the first antinomy, for example, it may be said: The world is neither an infinite whole nor a finite whole, because it is not a whole at all. In Kant's words, "If, then, this series is always conditioned and therefore can never be given as complete, the world is not an unconditioned whole and does not exist as such a whole either of infinite or of finite magnitude" (A 505/B 533). Likewise in the case of the other antinomies: the relevant series do not exist as wholes but are always conditioned, partial, fragmentary, and in each case the assertion regarding the character of the whole has no objective reference whatsoever.

This solution poses a further question: How is it possible for the world (in the sense of a conditioned series of appearances) to exist as a part without also existing as a whole? Does a part not always presuppose the whole in reference to which it is a part? This would be so *if* appearances were things-in-themselves: The part which one could gather in a serial regression would have to be part of a pre-existing whole. But appearances are not things-in-themselves, and the partial, conditioned character of the series is determined, not by reference to some pre-existing objective whole, but by reference to the subject, to the specific character of synthesis that belongs to finite knowing. This is why, as the title of one section expresses it, transcendental idealism is "the key to the solution of the cosmological dialectic."

Another formulation of the critical solution, which points to more fundamental matters, can be given by expressing as a syllogism that inference from which the cosmological ideas originate. The syllogism is (A 497/B 525):

> If the conditioned is given, the entire series of all its conditions is likewise given.
> Objects of the senses are given as conditioned.
> ∴ The entire series of conditions of objects of the senses is given.

This syllogism expresses the extension of the serial categories up to the level of absolute totality, i.e., the inference by which those categories are transformed into cosmological ideas. If the syllogism were correct (i.e., the premises true and the inference valid), then the generation of the cosmological ideas would be objectively legitimate; and in that case the antinomies would be unavoidable. Reason's conflict with itself could not, then, be resolved. However, the inference is not valid: "The major premise of the cosmological inference takes the conditioned in the transcendental sense of a pure category, while the minor premise takes it in the empirical sense of a concept of the understanding applied to mere appearances. The argument thus commits that dialectical fallacy which is entitled *sophisma figurae dictionis*" (A 499/B 527–8). So, the fallacy lies in the use of the term "conditioned" in two different senses in the two premises. In the major premise it is used "in the transcendental sense of a pure category." Here its sense is that which corresponds to pure thought, a sense in which there is no consideration of the way in which *objective* thought must be bound to intuition and its forms. From this point of view it may indeed be said that with a conditioned there is also given all its conditions, because for pure thought "given" means simply "presupposed" in the sense in which a conclusion presupposes its premises. In other words, it may be said that for pure thought the totality of conditions is given, precisely because pure thought, by virtue of its very character as pure, as unschematized, has *no connection whatsoever to givenness* in the sense that this has for a finite subject (with its sensible intuition and the corresponding requirement by which its thought can be objective only by being bound to intuition). On the other hand, in the minor premise "conditioned" is used in the sense appropriate to finite subjectivity, "in the empirical sense of a concept of the understanding applied to mere appearances." According to this sense, it cannot be said that the totality of conditions is given.

In the first case, that of the major premise, the regress from conditioned to condition is a regress in *pure* thought and, hence, is essentially independent of time-conditions: "There is no reference to a time-order in the connection of the conditioned with its condition; they are presupposed as given *together* with it" (A 500/B 528). In other words, the totality of conditions may be thought *all together*, i.e., as totality, because they are not "spread out" in time, because the thinking of them is not required to subordinate itself to any objective temporal order. But, the situation is radically different in the case of empirical thought, of thought as linked to intuition and to objects as given in intuition. Kant is explicit about the contrast: He says that the synthesis in the major premise is such as not to involve "any limitations through time or any concept of succession." He continues: "The empirical synthesis, on the other hand, that is, the series of the conditions in appearance, as subsumed in the minor premise, is necessarily successive, the members of the series being given only as following upon one another in time; and I have therefore, in this case, no right to assume the absolute *totality* of the synthesis and of the series thereby represented" (A 500/B 528–9). The point is that, insofar as thought maintains its bond to intuition, it must subordinate itself to the objective temporal order that belongs to appearances; and this prevents thinking the totality of conditions *all together*, i.e., as a given totality.

In reference to the critical solution of the antinomies there are three conclusions that need to be drawn out as pointing to the level of our projective interpretation.

According to the results of the Transcendental Analytic, thought can have objectivity only by means of its bond to intuition, only insofar as it provides rules for the ruling of the manifold of intuition. It follows that the pure thought for which the totality of conditions can be given lacks objectivity. But to say that a non-objective totality of conditions is given to pure thought amounts to saying that pure thought *posits* the totality, since this totality is nothing beyond the thought such that it could in any empirical sense be given. We conclude: the pure thought expressed in the major premise *posits the cosmological ideas*.

Kant's syllogistic presentation serves to make clear that the conflict underlying the antinomies is that between pure thought and a thought bound to intuition (and, hence, to appearances and their time-order). It is a conflict regarding the bond of thought to time. We conclude: The conflict of reason with itself is a conflict over reason's bond to time.

In farther-reaching terms, the basic conflict is between the pure thought which posits the unity (the idea) into which the series would be gathered *and*, on the other side, the thought which is bound to the fragmentation wrought by time, to the "spreading-out" of appearances in time, the thought which, rather than positing unity, would build it up from the fragmentation, would *gather* the manifold of appearances into the unity. What happens is that these two functions of thought, these two sides of the gathering, fall apart—eventually into the opposed positions of the antinomies. The gathering up of the manifold cannot match the unity into which the manifold would be gathered, and the gathering movement of cosmological reason culminates in a radical breach.

5. THE REGULATIVE EMPLOYMENT OF REASON (A 508/B 536–A 515/B 543)

Up to this point Kant's detailed considerations of reason have dealt almost exclusively with reason's capacity to generate dialectical illusion. Now he proceeds to develop within the context of his detailed considerations that other kind of employment that was already introduced before these considerations began, namely, regulative employment. The placing of reason in such employment is not a matter of eliminating the illusion-laden cosmological ideas. On the contrary, reason by its very nature demands unity, posits the ideas, and this is why the illusion into which these ideas can lead is a "*natural* illusion." The ideas are always already granted, and the problem is to determine how they are to be employed.

In those inferences that terminate in the antinomies the ideas are given a "constitutive employment." The absolute totality of conditions, which is thought in the idea, is regarded as being actually present as an object, the idea is regarded as having a corresponding object outside it, so that the inferences involving this idea, the logically valid inferences by which the theses and antitheses of the antinomies can be proved, would yield a means for attaining a knowledge transcending all limits of possible experience. However, reason comes thereby into conflict with itself. By examining that conflict Kant has shown that no constitutive employment of the cosmological ideas is legitimate, since there can be no object corresponding to them. Constitutive employment confounds subjective and objective, turns ideas into objects, and thus has the character of dialectical illusion (cf. A 297/B 353, with Ch. II, 1). But even if reason holds back from this turning, the ideas remain, and it is a matter of indicating their proper employment as mere ideas.

Their proper employment is regulative—that is, to regulate, to direct, the regress of empirical thought from conditioned to condition:

> The principle of reason is thus properly only a *rule*, prescribing a regress in the series of the conditions of given appearances and forbidding it to bring the regress to a close by treating anything at which it may arrive as absolutely unconditioned. . . . It is rather a principle of the greatest possible continuation and extension of experience, allowing no empirical limit

> to hold as absolute. Thus it is a principle of reason which serves as a *rule*, postulating what we ought to do in the regress, but *not anticipating* what is present *in the object as it is in itself*, prior to all regress (A 508–9/B 536–7).

So, in its regulative employment the idea is used as a *rule* rather than as an idea *of* an object. As a rule, it prescribes the greatest possible extension of the regress from conditioned to condition—without, however, positing that regress as accomplished by objective thought or as realized on the side of the object. Employed as a rule, the idea "cannot tell us what the object is but only how the empirical regress is to be carried out so as to arrive at the complete concept of this object" (A 510/B 538).

6. FREEDOM AND NECESSITY (A 515/B 544–A567/B 595)

Having worked out the general critical solution of the antinomies, Kant turns, finally, to the application of this solution to the particulars of the individual antinomies. In the case of the first two antinomies little is added beyond what was already indicated in the general solution. As regards these antinomies both thesis and antithesis must be declared false; for example, the world is neither a finite spatial whole nor an infinite spatial whole, because it is not a whole at all. However, beginning with the transition to the third antinomy a new issue arises. It is introduced by means of an elaboration of the distinction between mathematical ideas and dynamical ideas, corresponding to the distinction made in the Analytic between mathematical categories and dynamical categories. The eventual outcome is that in the case of the third and fourth antinomies it proves not to be necessary to declare both thesis and antithesis false. On the contrary, it proves possible to think both together as true. The detailed considerations in which this result is established and elaborated require special attention.

Kant refers back to the distinction between mathematical and dynamical categories in order to introduce the analogous distinction with respect to the cosmological ideas. The relevant point of the earlier distinction is that mathematical categories (those of quantity and quality) prescribe a synthesis of *homogeneous* terms, whereas dynamical categories (those of relation and modality) prescribe a synthesis of *heterogeneous* terms. For example, a cause and its effect are not necessarily of the same kind in the way that two spaces must be. If the distinction is, now, applied to the cosmological ideas in relation to the dialectical inference in which they arise, it means that in the regress from conditioned to condition, which is carried out according to the relevant serial category, the condition will be homogeneous *or* heterogeneous with the conditioned, depending on whether the category being extended is mathematical or dynamical. Specifically, in the case of the cosmological ideas involved in the third and fourth antinomies the unconditioned condition demanded by reason can be thought as heterogeneous with the conditioned in a very crucial sense, namely, as *outside* the entire series of appearances, as purely intelligible: "In the dynamical series of sensible conditions, a heterogeneous condition, not itself a part of the series but *purely intelligible* and as such outside the series, can be allowed" (A 530/B 558). One crucial consequence of allowing such a purely intelligible condition is that both reason and understanding then have their demands satisfied: Reason's demand for the unconditioned is satisfied by this intelligible condition, without violence being done to the nature of understanding, to its bond to the objective time-order and its insistence that no appearance can be an unconditioned condition. To say that both reason and understanding are satisfied is to say that their respective demands cease to conflict—that the conflict between reason and understanding is resolved.

Kant turns to the third antinomy in order to show how the general resolution just traced applies to this specific conflict. In this antinomy the conflict is between two kinds of causality, that by nature and that by freedom. In order to clarify the conflict Kant defines more precisely the meaning of freedom: "By freedom . . . in its cosmological meaning I understand the power of beginning a state spontaneously" (A 533/B 561). According to this transcendental idea of freedom, causality by freedom is such that the cause is not itself, in turn, the effect of another cause. Kant notes that freedom in the practical sense, "the will's independence of coercion through sensuous impulses," is based on the transcendental idea of freedom, so that "the denial of transcendental freedom must, therefore, involve the elimination of all practical freedom" (A 534/B 562). How, then, does the general solution apply to the conflict in this antinomy? The solution in this case lies simply in the possibility that causality both by nature and by freedom can in different regards be found in one and the same event, specifically in that instance in which the causality by freedom is related to an intelligible condition outside the entire series of appearances: "While the effects are to be found in the series of empirical conditions, the intelligible cause, together with its causality, is outside the series. Thus the effect may be regarded as free in respect of its intelligible cause and at the same time in respect of appearances as resulting from them according to the necessity of nature" (A 537/B 565). With respect to such an instance both thesis and antithesis of the third antinomy can be retained.

Kant introduces a further development: Not only can a single effect be referred both to causality by nature and to causality by freedom but also a single *agent* can be regarded as embodying both kinds of causality. This is possible because the intelligible condition that is posited outside the entire series of appearances may belong to an agent that is also an appearance. In other words, the agent may have both an intelligible character, by which it exercises causality by freedom, and an empirical character, by which it exercises causality by nature. Ultimately, this duality is based on that of noumenon and phenomenon: one and the same agent may be both noumenon (intelligible) and phenomenon (appearance).

It should especially be noted how Kant identifies this intelligible character *in man*. He refers to transcendental apperception and then says of man: "He is thus to himself, on the one hand, phenomenon, and on the other hand, in respect of certain faculties the action of which cannot be ascribed to the receptivity of sensibility, a purely intelligible object. We entitle these faculties understanding and reason" (A 546–7/B 574–5). Kant is suggesting that the intelligible character in man is his character as transcendental I, as a purely spontaneous power that demands and prescribes unity, as reason and understanding, as thinking subject. Essentially Kant is indicating that it is *as rational* that man has an intelligible character, that it is *as rational* that he can be an agent of intelligible causality, of causality by freedom. However, Kant is only pointing to this intelligible character and this causality by freedom, not yet establishing it, not yet showing that and how it is. Indeed, he cannot really establish it within the framework of the *Critique of Pure Reason*, for what testifies to it is the "ought," i.e., practical imperatives: "That our reason has causality, or that we at least represent it to ourselves as having causality, is evident from the *imperatives* which in all matters of conduct we impose as rules upon our active powers" (A 547/B 575). Here Kant is merely preparing for the consideration of freedom in relation to the moral law in the *Critique of Practical Reason*.

One additional point should be noted with regard to this intelligible character. As outside the entire series of appearances, this character is not subject to the form of appearances, i.e., time. In fact, it could not be subject to time without violating its very character as intelligible causality, for, if it were subject to time, it would be subject to what is required for time-determination, i.e., categories, hence, specifically, would be subject to the category of natural causality. Thus, Kant writes: "Pure reason, as a purely intelligible faculty, is not subject to the form of time, nor consequently to the conditions of succession in time. The causality of reason in its intelligible character does not, in producing an effect, *arise* or begin to be at a certain time" (A 551–2/B 579–80).

Kant concludes his considerations of the third antinomy by stating quite precisely what he has shown and distinguishing it from what he has not intended to show. What has he *not* proved? He has not proved the actuality of freedom, that it actually exists. He has not even proved the possibility of freedom in that material sense of possibility defined in the postulates of empirical thought. Rather, "what we have alone been able to show, and what we have alone been concerned to show, is that this antinomy rests on a sheer illusion and that causality through freedom is at least *not incompatible with* nature" (A 558/B 586). Kant has shown that there is no necessary contradiction between the thesis and antithesis of this antinomy, that it is logically possible for both to be true, that both can be thought together.

The application of the general solution to the fourth antinomy follows basically the same line as with the third. An absolutely necessary being may be thought *as* outside the entire series of contingent appearances. Thus, it is logically possible that in the intelligible order there is such a being (in which case the thesis, hence, reason, is satisfied) but that in the order of appearances there is only contingency (in which case the antithesis, hence understanding, is satisfied). Kant explains:

> A way of escape from this apparent antinomy thus lies open to us. Both of the conflicting propositions may be true, if taken in different connections. All things in the world of sense may be contingent, and so have only an empirically conditioned existence, while yet there may be a nonempirical condition of the whole series; that is, there may exist an unconditionally necessary being. This necessary being, as the intelligible condition of the series, would not belong to it as a member . . . (A 560/B 588).

There is only one basic difference between the solution of the third and that of the fourth antinomy. In the case of causality, only the causality of the agent was thought as intelligible, and thus the agent could be regarded as also appearance. Kant draws the contrast: "Here, on the other hand, the necessary being must be thought as entirely outside the series of the sensible world (as *ens extramundanum*) and as purely intelligible" (A 561/B 589). The absolutely necessary being must be thought, not as being also appearance, but as being in every respect outside all appearances.

What consequences does the critique of the antinomy of pure reason have for rational cosmology?

It has been noted that the antinomies encompass the entire range of transcendental ideas, not only the idea of the world but also that of the soul (in the second antinomy) and of God (in the fourth antinomy); cosmology thus tends to extend its scope to such a degree that it comes virtually to coincide with *metaphysica specialis* as a whole. The solutions to the third and fourth antinomies serve in effect to check this cosmological extension, to restrain cosmological reason—that is, to secure the other disciplines of metaphysics from encroachment by rational cosmology. With regard at least to logical possibility, causality by freedom is posited outside the series of appearances; this means that the problem of freedom is withdrawn from cosmology and preparation is made for the assignment of this problem to the domain of the critique of practical reason. One might suppose, further, that the problem of freedom is just the problem of the self in its most genuine form, the problem definitive of psychology; this supposition is supported by the manner in which Kant relates freedom to apperception and reason, i.e., to the concept of the self as it remains after the purging carried out through the critique of paralogism. Likewise, in the fourth antinomy an absolutely necessary being is posited outside appearances and the problem of God thus withdrawn from cosmology.

Thus, the critical solution breaks up the domination which cosmological reason tends to assume. In other words, the unity which cosmological reason would institute between all the transcendental ideas by relating them all to appearances (to the world) gets broken up. The critical solution is such as to reassert the fragmentation that holds these highest unities apart. It thus testifies that reason's unities, those ideas into which reason would gather all manifoldness, cannot themselves be brought to unity but remain a threefold.

7. PROJECTIVE INTERPRETATION OF THE ANTINOMIES

What is the character of the gathering in the antinomies? It has been thematized already in connection with Kant's syllogistic presentation of the relevant inferential movement. The major and minor premises, respectively, express the two sides of the gathering. On the one side, pure thought posits the cosmological idea as the unity for the gathering; on the other side, empirical (time-bound) thought would gather the manifold (i.e., the series of conditions) into this unity.

How is the issue of fragmentation involved in this gathering and in its outcome? As in every case, it is directed toward overcoming a certain fragmentation; it would gather a certain fragmented manifold into unity and completeness. What, then, is the fragmentation that would be overcome in the antinomies? Most generally, it is the fragmentation *of world*, i.e., the fragmentation involved in the fact that the world is always *partial* in each of the four possible ways of regarding it (in terms of spatio-temporal extension, division, causality, and dependence of existence). The fragmentation is that constituted by the incompleteness of the various categorial series pertaining to world. This should be contrasted with the fragmentation that was at issue in the paralogisms, in which case it was a matter of man's lack of self-knowledge, of his being separated from himself by ignorance. In the paralogisms it was a fragmentation within man; in the antinomies it is a fragmentation within appearances.

The fragmentation that would be overcome in the antinomies belongs to the level of understanding; it is an incompleteness that remains after the gathering that is directed by pure understanding. What is its basis? Why does fragmentation still remain even after the gathering of pure understanding? Why is there still framentation even after the *a priori* synthesis? In general, the basis for this fragmentation lies in the fragmentation of thought. More specifically, fragmentation remains because understanding cannot simply posit its object in its entirety but rather merely posits an object *for* appearances, posits objectivity, posits the transcendental object; consequently, knowing remains dependent on the givenness of appearances and thus subject to the form of their givenness, time; and time fragments the appearances, spreads them out so that they are never more than partially given. The basis of the fragmentation is the fact that understanding is subject to the sensible condition expressed in the schematism, that the unities which it posits (the categories) are unities into which appearances are gathered by the mediation of time, hence *partially*.

What happens in the inferential movement is that thought (as reason) posits these unities at a level at which they would be free of such reference to time and appearances. Reason posits them as *pure* unities rather than as schematized unities, rather than as unities capable of prescribing time-determination and thereby fitted for the gathering of appearances. And thus, when the gathering of reason actually commences, time-bound thought cannot succeed in gathering the series of appearances into these unities. The unities are not fit for appearances, and, regardless of the form in which they are posited, whether as a first member or as the entire series, there is *discord* with appearances as gathered by time-bound thought. The gathering fails, and, in place of the unity that reason would institute (if the gathering could succeed), reason is led into contradictions, into the utter disunity of opposed assertions, of thesis and antithesis. Reason is thrown into contradiction, into radical disunity, with itself.

In the wake of this failure and the resultant conflict of reason with itself, there are two alternatives open to reason, i.e., two possible directions in which the gathering may be diverted so as to resolve reason's conflict with itself.

The gathering may be diverted in the direction of regulative employment. Already it has been seen how in its regulative employment reason is brought back into an essential relation with understanding, in contrast to that constitutive employment in which it goes beyond the realm of experience and understanding. Specifically, reason comes, in its regulative employment, to provide directive unities for the empirical employment of understanding, and thus is brought into *service* to understanding. Nevertheless, its service to understanding consists in its *ruling* over understanding, in the sense of providing understanding with the rules for its empirical regress. Through this constraining of reason to its regulative function there is established what Kant celebrates as "a lasting and peaceful reign of reason over understanding and the senses." But, what is important in the present context is that the constraining of reason to its regulative employment not only establishes reason in its proper service to understanding but also does so in such a way as to *resolve* reason's conflict with itself (as exhibited in the antinomies). How? In that conflict the basic issue is the disparity between the unity posited by pure thought *and* the gathering of appearances by empirically bound thought. A genuine *constitutive* employment of reason would require that this disparity be overcome, and this conflict on which reason runs aground results from the fact that it cannot be overcome. By contrast, in regulative employment the disparity and its inevitability are granted: What is required is not that the gathering of appearances measure up to that unity posited by pure thought but only that the gathering be directed toward such unity, that the idea be regulative, directive, for the gathering. Thus, in place of the conflict that results from the demand for overcoming this disparity, there is a relation established between the two sides (pure and empirical thought) which harmonizes the disparity (and its inevitability) with the demand for its overcoming. On the one hand, the disparity remains: The empirical regress never achieves absolute totality, never matches up to the idea posited by pure thought. On the other hand, the demand for overcoming the disparity remains in force *as* the ruling of reason over understanding, as the demand that understanding proceed *toward* absolute totality, strive for it. Thus, in being diverted into its regulative employment, reason is brought into agreement with itself, freed of the conflict, the disunity, with itself.

There is also another direction in which reason may be diverted, that of practical reason. This direction is indicated especially in the solution of the third antinomy. Reason posits a first member *outside* the causal series, "outside" in the sense of being noumenal; this positing serves to resolve the conflict expressed in the antinomy. But there is something curious about this positing. What is that first member that reason posits outside the causal series? It is just *itself*. Furthermore, it is able really to be a first member because, as noumenal, its causality is intelligible, i.e., is not bound to time. And, as a genuine first member, it succeeds in actually effecting a gathering of the series. Thus, by positing itself as freedom, i.e., as practical reason, reason can accomplish that gathering which it cannot accomplish as cosmological (speculative) reason. At this point the primacy of practical reason begins to announce itself. However, Kant has shown only that reason *can* posit itself as free, i.e., that in doing so it does not again fall into contradiction, into disunity with itself. The question is: How is a ground for this positing, something that requires of reason that it posit itself, to be exhibited? A central issue of Kant's practical philosophy is to exhibit the moral law as such a ground.

CHAPTER V

THE GATHERING OF REASON IN THE IDEAL

The third of the three types of dialectical inference is entitled the ideal of pure reason. This is the theme of the third chapter of Kant's critical investigation of the dialectical inferences of pure reason.

The brief introductory section is devoted primarily to explaining what in general is meant by an "ideal." The crux of the explanation lies in this statement: "By the ideal I understand the idea, not merely *in concreto*, but *in individuo*, that is, as an individual thing, determinable or even determined by the idea alone" (A 568/B 596). Here Kant is saying that an ideal is an idea *in* an individual thing, or, more precisely, that the ideal is an individual thing in which the idea is *present*. But this presence must be of a special kind. It is not merely a matter of the idea being exemplified by the individual; the individual is not merely an instance of what is represented in general in the idea. Rather, the sense is that the idea is present in such a way as to determine the individual completely. An ideal is an individual that is completely determined by the idea, an individual every determination of which is prescribed by the idea. An ideal is an idea in the form of an individual thing—though still within the domain of concepts, not of existing things. In strict terms, an ideal is a concept of an individual that is completely determined by a general concept having the special character of an idea.

Kant notes that ideals have the character of standards or archetypes. Since an ideal is a (concept of an) individual thing completely determined by an idea, it can serve as the standard by which actually to measure the approximation of other things to the complex of determinations expressed in the idea. Kant refers to the example of the Stoic ideal of the wise man. Although this ideal, which accords with the idea of wisdom, exists only in thought, it can appropriately serve as an archetype or standard by which to measure individual men as regards wisdom.

Kant insists that human reason contains ideals. Just as in the case of ideas, they are not arbitrarily invented but rather arise from the very nature of reason; and, as providing standards, they perform an indispensible service to reason. Yet, they are clearly beyond the limits of possible experience and so lack all objective reality. They cannot be realized in an example, and, in fact, the attempt to do so even works against their proper practical function.

1. THE TRANSCENDENTAL IDEAL (A 571/B 599–A 583/B 611)

Kant proceeds to focus on a particular ideal, the transcendental ideal. This is not, however, just one ideal among others; it will prove to be the only genuine ideal of reason. Kant's presentation of this exceptional ideal is quite condensed, and accordingly I shall undertake, though within the space of duplex interpretation, to fill out the context which informs Kant's development of this issue.

The general character of reason is such that reason posits unity by which the manifoldness that remains at the level of the objects of experience, at the level of understanding, would be overcome. Such positing, taken in its full extent and structure, constitutes dialectical inference. In each type of dialectical inference the unity is posited in relation to objects *considered in a certain respect*. For example, in the antinomies objects are considered with respect to their specific character as appearances, with respect to their seriality as appearances; and the unity posited is a unity of the objects as appearances, an absolute totality of a series of appearances. In connection with the transcendental ideal, objects are considered with respect to their character as objects of thought in general (cf. A 334/B 391, with Ch. II, 4). This means that they are considered *as* subject to determination or predication in empirical thought, that is, they are considered with respect to their determinations or predicates. What, then, is the totality, the unity, that reason posits in this regard? At the simplest level, what it posits is the total (complete) determination of the object, i.e., its determination with respect to every possible predicate. In Kant's terms, what reason posits is that every thing is "subject to the principle of *complete* determination." This means that for each thing "if all the possible predicates of things be taken together with their contradictory opposites, then one of each pair of contradictory opposites must belong to it" (A 571–2/B 599–600). In other words, in positing the *complete* determinations of things, reason is positing their determination with respect to the totality of possible predicates. Therefore, in positing the complete determination of things, reason *must also posit that idea of totality* with respect to which completeness of determination is defined. Consequently, reason posits the idea of the *totality of all possible predicates*. This is the idea that arises in the third major type of dialectical inference, and it is from this idea that the transcendental ideal is generated.

Kant proceeds to indicate in some detail the exact character of this totality of all possible predicates. At the simplest level, it can be regarded as a totality of pairs, each pair consisting of contradictory opposites. In each case one member will be affirmative and the other negative. At the transcendental level, at which, in contrast to the merely logical level, the difference between affirmative and negative cannot be relativized, one member of each pair (the transcendental affirmation) "expresses in itself a being," while the other member (the transcendental negation) "signifies in itself not-being" (A 574/B 602). In fully transcendental-critical terms, one member will be a *reality*, the other a *negation*. In this context, just as in the consideration of the categories, "reality" (*Realität*) does not mean "actuality" (*Wirklichkeit*) or "existence" (*Dasein*); rather, it designates that which belongs to *what* a thing is, to its whatness, its essence, its "material" content.[1] Thus understood, reality has priority. Negation is derivative, is mere lack of being, mere lack of the corresponding reality: "All concepts of negation are thus derivative; it is the realities which contain the data and, so to speak, the material or transcendental content for the possibility of complete determination of things" (A 575/B 603). The result is that the idea which must be posited in reason's positing the complete determination of things, the idea of the totality of possible predicates, is simply the idea of the totality of realities; it is the idea of the "*All der Realität* (*omnitudo realitatis*)" (A 575–6/B 603–4).[2]

How is this idea related to an ideal? How in general is a concept related to an individual thing? What is the character of the distinction? It may be regarded as constituted by the fact that a thing is determinate whereas a concept is indeterminate in various degrees, depending on its level of generality. For example, the concept of house is indeterminate as regards color; a house may be white or brown or yellow, etc. But, an individual house is determinate in this regard; it must be some definite color. It is clear, then, what would be required in order for there to be an ideal corresponding to an idea, in order for an individual to be determined by the concept alone. An exception to this distinction would be required: a concept not indeterminate, a completely determinate concept. The idea of the totality of realities is precisely such a concept: It is not itself indeterminate with respect to any pair of opposite predicates; but rather, with respect to every such pair, one member belongs to it, namely, "that which belongs to Being [*Sein*] absolutely," the reality (A 576/B 604). Therefore, this idea is a concept of an individual being, in that strong sense by which the individual receives its complete determination from the idea. To the idea of the totality of realities there corresponds an ideal. This ideal, the transcendental ideal, is the only genuine ideal of human reason:

> This ideal is the supreme and complete material condition of the possibility of all that exists—the condition to which all thought of objects, so far as their content is concerned, has to be traced back. It is also the only genuine ideal of which human reason is capable. For only in this one case is a concept of a thing—a concept which is in itself universal—completely determined in and through itself and known as the representation of an individual (A 576/B 604).

Kant proceeds to elaborate the character of this totality of realities, understood as ideal, as an individual being determined by the idea alone. Since it contains no negation but only realities and since, furthermore, it contains all realities, it can be termed the *most real being*—*ens realissimum*. In positing the corresponding transcendental idea, reason does not suppose that the ideal, this *ens realissimum*, actually exists but rather only posits it as the *archetype* for the complete determination of all other beings. Specifically, all other beings, as objects of thought in general, i.e., with respect to their determinations, are merely results of *limitation* of the ideal (by means of negation): "All manifoldness of things is only a correspondingly varied mode of limiting the concept of the highest reality which forms their common substratum" (A 578/B 606). This means that, whereas in the ideal every determination is a reality, in every other thing only some determinations are realities, while others are negations, lacks, of the corresponding realities. Hence, all other things are derivative by negation (limitation) from the ideal, which may thus be appropriately called the *primordial being* (*Urwesen*)—*ens originarium*. Furthermore, since this being has nothing above it, it being most real, it may also be called the *highest being*—*ens summum*. And since everything else is subject to it, it may be called the being of all beings (*das Wesen aller Wesen*)—*ens entium*—in the sense of *ground*, not of sum (from which beings would be derived by division). This being is *God* in the transcendental sense, and thus the ideal of pure reason is the object of transcendental theology, the third of the disciplines of *metaphysica specialis*.

2. THE EXISTENCE OF GOD (A 583/B 611–A 642/B 670)

Although reason posits the transcendental ideal as standard for the complete determination of things, it posits it *only as ideal*. Merely on the basis of the positing, it would never be presumed that such a being actually exists. One would never come to suppose its existence, were he not impelled to do so by still another factor. What is this other factor? It is that factor that was presented in the fourth antimony, namely, reason's demand for the completion of the regress from conditioned to unconditioned, specifically, reason's dialectical inference from contingent existence to the existence of a necessary being. It is this inference which effectively drives the advance beyond experience to an existing primordial being.

More specifically, what happens is this: Having been led by the argument of the fourth antinomy to the existence of a necessary being, reason then searches for a concept of this being that would be suitable to its character as absolutely necessary, as unconditionally existing; the concept which it finds is precisely that of the ideal, of the *ens realissimum*, which, since it contains the conditions (realities) of all beings, is unconditioned and, hence, is in accord with the concept of a necessarily existing being. Kant sums up this natural procedure of reason:

> Such, then, is the natural procedure of human reason. It begins by persuading itself of the existence of *some* necessary being. This being it

> apprehends as having an existence that is unconditioned. It then looks around for the concept of that which is independent of any condition and finds it in that which is itself the sufficient condition of all else, that is, in that which contains all reality (A 586–7/B 614–15).

Immediately, however, Kant points out the defectiveness of this procedure. The most serious defect lies in the argument that the necessarily existing being must be conceived as an *ens realissimum*. The argument is simply not valid: "It by no means follows that the concept of a limited being which does not have the highest reality is for that reason incompatible with absolute necessity" (A 588/B 616). In other words, there is no contradiction involved in the concept of a necessary being which is limited in respects other than existence and is thus not the highest reality.

Is it, then, possible to prove by some other means the existence of that *ens realissimum* whose existence one is led to suppose, even if without sufficient grounds, by consideration of contingent existence? In general, Kant points out, there are three distinct ways in which such proof can be attempted. There is *physico-theological proof*, which proceeds from determinate experience and the specific constitution of the world of sense; there is *cosmological proof*, which proceeds from indeterminate experience, from the experience of existence in general; and there is *ontological proof*, which proceeds by *a priori* argument from mere concepts. Kant's intent is to show that all of these attempted proofs fail.

Kant considers first the ontological proof, which he explicitly attributes to Descartes. In this regard he also mentions Leibniz, referring specifically to the latter's attempt at a "comprehension *a priori* of the possibility of this sublime ideal being" (A 602/B 630). So, Kant's criticism is to be taken as directed in general at the form which the ontological proof assumed in Descartes' Fifth Meditation; on the other hand, it is necessary to distinguish from the Cartesian form of the proof the more refined form which it assumed in Leibniz and to refer Kant's more exacting criticism to the latter version.[3] In the Cartesian form of the proof it is simply argued that the existence of God cannot be separated from the essence of God. In other words, the argument is that the concept of God as a supremely perfect being is that of a being to whose essence existence belongs; thus God must exist, since it would be contradictory to conceive of a God who lacks existence.[4] The refinement brought by the Leibnizian version of the proof lies in the demand that it be shown that the concept of God is the concept of a *possible* being, that the concept itself involves no self-nullifying contradiction.[5] Thus, in its Leibnizian form the proof is given by the following syllogism:

> If God is possible, he exists.
> God is possible.
> ∴ God exists.

Kant's criticism involves two principle stages, corresponding to these two forms of the proof.

At the outset Kant states his critical position, of which all the further criticisms are merely elaborations and applications. The position is that no inference can be made from the order of concepts to that of existing beings, from the mere concept of God to his existence. Kant grants that we can of course give a merely verbal definition (*eine Namenerklärung*) of God as that the nonexistence of which is impossible. But, he insists, "This yields us no insight into the conditions which make it necessary to regard the nonexistence of a *thing* as absolutely unthinkable. It is precisely these conditions that we desire to know, in order that we may determine whether or not, in resorting to this concept, we are thinking anything at all" (A 592–3/B 620–1). In such a case we have simply framed our concept in a certain way, and this allows absolutely no inference regarding the order of existing things.

Kant develops his position by criticizing the way in which certain examples have in effect been used to conceal the fallaciousness of the inference. For example, in the Fifth Meditation Descartes argues that the proposition "God exists" has the same status as the proposition "A triangle contains three angles"—that neither can be denied without contradiction resulting.[6] However, Kant insists that the two cases are not at all analogous. Whereas the proposition "God exists" is an assertion about a being, the proposition "A triangle contains three angles" does not asset that anything exists but only that *if* a triangle exists, if it is given, it must have three angles. In the case of such a proposition there would be contradiction only if the subject were accepted and the predicate rejected; whereas, on the other hand, if the subject were also rejected, there would be no contradiction:

> If, in an identical proposition, I reject the predicate while retaining the subject, contradiction results; and I therefore say that the former

> belongs necessarily to the latter. But if we reject subject and predicate alike, there is no contradiction; for nothing is then left that can be contradicted. To posit a triangle, and yet to reject its three angles, is self-contradictory; but there is no contradiction in rejecting the triangle together with its three angles (A 594/B 622).

The decisive point is that in the case of the proposition "God exists" it is impossible to reject the predicate and retain the subject, that is, the rejection of the predicate is already a rejection of the subject. In this case contradiction is impossible: "If its existence is rejected, we reject the thing itself with all its predicates; and no question of contradiction can then arise" (A 595/B 623). Thus, the denial of the existence of God does not result in contradiction, and so the ontological proof collapses.

Kant begins the second stage of criticism by introducing the ontological proof in its Leibnizian form and in explicit connection with the transcendental ideal as *ens realissimum:* "It is declared that it possesses all reality and that we are justified in assuming that such a being is possible. . . . Now, 'all reality' includes existence; existence is therefore contained in the concept of a thing that is possible. If, then, this thing is rejected, the internal possibility of the thing is rejected—which is self-contradictory" (A 596–7/B 624–5). This statement serves to reconstruct the syllogism (stated above) in terms of the concept of God as transcendental ideal, as totality of realities. The minor premise is reconstructed first. The implicit argument is that, as *ens realissimum*, God contains *only* realities, no negations, and, consequently, no contradictorily opposed predicates, no contradictions; thus, it is concluded, the concept of God contains no internal contradictions that could nullify the concept—that is, God is possible. The major premise is likewise reconstructed. As *ens realissimum*, God possesses all realities; among these realities is existence; thus existence is contained in the concept of God, and, unless this concept is self-nullifying, i.e., internally self-contradictory, it must be concluded that God exists. In other words, if God is possible, he exists.

Kant addresses himself critically to each premise in turn. His criticism of the major premise begins with the accusation that this premise, which would be based on the principle of noncontradiction, is itself caught up in a contradiction: "My answer is as follows. There is already a contradiction in introducing the concept of existence—no matter under what title it may be disguised—into the concept of a thing which we profess to be thinking solely in reference to its possibility"

(A 597/ B 625). He is saying that there is contradiction involved when we think something as merely possible and yet introduce into it the concept of existence. Why? Because there is a fundamental difference between possibility (especially as mere noncontradiction) and existence. That difference lies in the fact that existence is determined by a factor that goes beyond the domain of mere thought; something can be genuinely thought *as* existing only by going beyond mere thought, only through reference to sensibility, to the material conditions of experience, only by reference beyond the realm of mere formal possibility. Kant formulates this issue in terms of the distinction between analytic judgments, which remain within the domain of mere thought, mere formal possibility, and synthetic judgments, which require reference beyond mere formality. He asks: Is the proposition that something exists an analytic or a synthetic proposition? He argues that, if the proposition is analytic, then by definition the predicate adds nothing to the subject, i.e., the assertion of existence adds nothing to the mere thought. But in that case one of two alternatives must follow: Either the existence affirmed is merely that of the thought itself, in which case the very distinction between thought and thing collapses, *or* the existence affirmed in the predicate has simply been presupposed in the subject, in which case the alleged proof is just a "miserable tautology." The upshot is, as Kant insists, that all existential propositions must be synthetic. If so, then they cannot be based on the principle of noncontradiction. God's existence cannot be proved from the mere concept.

Kant brings his criticism still closer to the heart of the matter, proceeding to show just how it is that existence does not belong to the concept of God. He draws a distinction between two kinds of predicates: Whereas anything whatsoever can be made to serve as a *logical predicate*, logic abstracting from all content, *a real predicate* is one which determines a thing, a determining predicate in the sense that it "is added to the concept of the subject and enlarges it" (A 598/B 626). A real predicate expresses a *reality*, the totality of which makes up the transcendental ideal. The crux of Kant's criticism is his thesis that existence is *not a real predicate*. He introduces this thesis through the more comprehensive thesis regarding Being as such: "*Being* [*Sein*] is manifestly not a real predicate; that is, it is not a concept of something which could be added to the concept of a thing. It is merely the positing [*Position*] of a thing, or of certain determinations, in themselves"

(A 598/B 626). Being is not a reality, does not belong to the totality of realities, thus does not belong to the concept of God as *ens realissimum.*

Kant develops the issue by considering the senses of the word "is." On the one hand, it serves as copula—for example, in the proposition "God is omnipotent." In this case the "is" does not add, express, a real predicate, but rather posits the predicate in its relation to the subject; the "is" expresses a positing rather than a reality. On the other hand, "is" may be used without any predicate following it—for example, in the proposition "God is" or "There is a God." It is in this case that Being takes the form of the modality "existence." The decisive point is that here too the word "is" expresses a positing rather than a reality: "If, now, we take the subject (God) with all its predicates (among which is omnipotence), and say "God is" or "There is a God," we attach no new predicate to the concept of God, but only posit the subject in itself with all its predicates, and indeed posit it as being an *object* that stands in relation to my *concept*" (A 599/B 627). So, existence is not a reality, and when one says that something exists he does not add any determination to the concept of it. In fact, if something were added through the existential "is," a most curious result would follow: What exists would not be the same as the thing thought in the concept but something more, something with an additional determination.

Existence is not a reality. Hence, it does not belong to the concept of God. Therefore, the existence of God cannot be inferred from the concept of God. The major premise of the ontological proof collapses. And in making it collapse, Kant has, at the same time, thematized the concept of Being with rare incisiveness. Being is "merely the positing of a thing"—that is, Being means being posited as object by and for a subject. This concept can be extended to the modalities of Being; it has, in effect, already been so extended in the *postulates* of empirical thought. An object can be posited in different types of fundamental relations to the subject—namely, as in agreement with the formal conditions of experience, or as bound up with the material conditions of experience, or as connected with the actual by certain universal conditions. To these three modes of being-posited correspond the three modalities of Being: being-possible, being-actual, and being-necessary (cf. A 218/ B 265–6).

Kant adds a brief criticism of the minor premise ("God is possible"). In this premise "possibility" is taken to mean merely noncontradiction, and it is only on this assumption that the possibility of God can be derived from the concept of God as *ens realissimum*. But, this is merely *logical* possibility, not the possibility of a being, not *real* possibility. The latter can be determined only in relation to the formal conditions of experience. Clearly the Leibnizian attempt to prove that God is possible remains oblivious to this requirement.

Kant turns next to a consideration of the cosmological proof. This proof involves two distinct parts. The first part may be presented syllogistically as follows:

> If anything exists, an absolutely necessary
> being must also exist.
> I, at least, exist.
> ∴ An absolutely necessary being exists.

This syllogism corresponds to the thesis of the fourth antinomy. The second part of the proof consists then in the identification of the concept of *ens realissimum* as the only concept appropriate to the necessary being whose existence has been proved in the first step. In this identification the inference is that the absolutely necessary being is the *ens realissimum*.

Kant says that in this proof "there lies hidden a whole nest of dialectical assumptions" (A 609/B 637). However, he focuses primarily on just one central fallacy, merely enumerating most of the other issues raised by this proof. He observes that although the proof claims, in contrast to the ontological proof, to proceed from experience, it actually makes use of this experiential basis only for the first step, by which the existence of an absolutely necessary being is inferred. Its empirical basis provides no means whatsoever for determining the concept of this being, and thus the second part of the proof becomes necessary. However, this second part completely abandons the empirical basis and ends up proceeding entirely by means of concepts. Furthermore, the second part logically entails the inference that constitutes the ontological proof. It claims: Every absolutely necessary being is a most real being, which, applying conversion by limitation, yields: Some most real beings are absolutely necessary beings. But one most real being is in no way different from another (any most real being is simply the totality of realities), and so whatever is true of some must be true for all. Hence, we get: All most real beings are absolutely necessary beings. But this is simply the inference from the transcendental concept of God to his existence—that is, it is the ontological proof. Kant concludes that the cosmological proof is dependent on the ontological proof and that the refutation of the latter constitutes already the refutation of the former.

Kant considers, finally, the physico-theological proof, which proceeds from determinate experience (i.e., order, regularity, purposiveness, beauty in nature) to a supreme being as cause of such order, regularity, etc. Kant's commendation of this proof is striking:

> This proof always deserves to be mentioned with respect. It is the oldest, the clearest, and the most accordant with the common reason of mankind. It enlivens the study of nature, just as it itself derives its existence and gains ever new vigor from that source. It suggests ends and purposes, where our observation would not have detected them by itself, and extends our knowledge of nature by means of the guiding-concept of a special unity, the principle of which is outside nature (A 623/B 651).

Nevertheless, Kant does not accept the proof as valid. He observes that it proceeds by means of an analogy between natural productions and human art, a mode of reasoning which is questionable to say the least. But even if it were accepted, the proof still could establish the existence *only of an architect* of the world, who impresses purpose and order on the material of the world but who is limited by that material; it could not prove the existence of a creator or ultimate cause of the world. In order to proceed beyond establishing a mere architect, it would be necessary to have recourse to the argument from the contingency of matter (to which the mere architect would be subject) to the existence of a necessary being. In other words it would be necessary to have recourse to the cosmological proof and thus, ultimately, to the ontological proof. In the end, all the proofs depend on the ontological proof, the refutation of which constitutes, therefore, a refutation of all attempts by speculative reason to prove that God exists.

Despite his devastating attack on rational theology, Kant concludes his considerations by assigning to it two rather important functions. These functions he assigns, respectively, to *transcendental theology*, which, linked to the ontological and cosmological proofs, conceives God as *ens realissimum*, and to *natural theology*, which, linked to the physico-theological proof, conceives God through concepts taken from nature. With reference to the first, he writes: "For if, in some other relation, perhaps on practical grounds, the *presupposition* of a supreme and all-sufficient being, as highest intelligence, established its validity beyond all question, it would be of the greatest importance accurately to determine this concept on its transcendental side" (A 640/B 668). Kant proposes also that in such event it would also fall to transcendental theology to free the concept of God from all anthropomorphism and "to dispose of all counterassertions, whether *atheistic*, *deistic*, or *anthropomorphic*." Thus, Kant is proposing, though still hypothetically, that transcendental theology could have a genuine function if subordinated to moral theology, if placed in service to the development of the problem of God in relation to the moral law, in the sphere of practical reason. He is more explicit about the second function. He asserts (though as something still to be shown) that only a *moral* theology is possible in the full sense—that, more specifically, the moral law is what justifies postulating the existence of God (though still only from a practical point of view). In this connection he then indicates the function of natural theology: "The physico-theological proof, as combining speculation and intuition, might therefore perhaps give additional weight to other proofs (if such there be); but taken alone, it serves only to prepare the understanding for theological knowledge and to give it a natural leaning in this direction, not to complete the work in and by itself" (A 637/B 665). Natural theology is preparatory for moral theology. We recall Kant's famous statement from the end of the *Critique of Practical Reason*: "Two things fill the mind with ever new and increasing admiration and awe, the more often and more steadily we reflect on them: the starry heavens above me and the moral law within me."[7]

3. PROJECTIVE INTERPRETATION OF THE IDEAL

The proofs for the existence of God, taken together with the positing of the transcendental ideal, constitute in its full structure the third of reason's dialectical inferences. This is the last of those movements of gathering by which reason seeks to bring to unity the fragmentation that remains at the level of understanding. Each such movement has proved to be correlative to a specific kind of fragmentation. In the case of the paralogisms, the relevant fragmentation is that constituted by man's ignorance of himself, by his separation from himself; it is a fragmentation within man. In the case of the antinomies, it is a fragmentation of world, i.e., incompleteness of the various categorial series in the order of appearances. Finally, in the case of the ideal of pure reason, the fragmentation is one pertaining to the determination of things by human knowing; the fragmentation is precisely the incompleteness of such knowing, of such determination at the empirical level. The fragmentation is a separation between man and things. Thus, the unity which reason seeks in its final gathering movement is the greatest unity of all. It is not a unity merely on the side of man, as in the paralogisms, nor merely on the side of appearances, as in the antinomies. Rather, it is a unity which would contain the determinations of all things; and, since all things, including the soul, appearances, and the world, would be grounded in this unity (in God), it would serve to establish the unity of all things. In Kant's words, "it would prove an affinity of all possible things through the identity of the ground of their complete determination" (A 572/B 600).

What is the character of this gathering in the ideal of pure reason? As in every case, the gathering involves two sides, the positing of unity and the actual gathering of the relevant manifold into that unity. What specific form do each of these sides take in the case of the ideal of pure reason?

The unity which reason posits is the transcendental ideal, i.e., the concept of God in the transcendental sense, God as the *ens realissimum*, as totality of realities. What does this positing involve? How does reason accomplish it? Repeatedly it has been observed that reason does not simply generate any concepts; rather, it takes the concepts of understanding, the categories, and extends them beyond the limits of possible experience, thereby converting them into transcendental ideas. So, in the case of reason's positing of the ideal, it needs to be asked: What is the category that gets extended? And what is the character of the extension? Kant's way of designating the idea, as the totality of realities, indicates clearly enough what the relevant category is: The category that gets converted into the transcendental ideal is that of *reality*. But what is the character of the extension?

One of the results of the Transcendental Analytic is that all empirical thought, all determination of objects, presupposes the operation of that pure (though schematized) thought by which the objects to be determined are first constituted as such. This operation of pure thought, the *a priori* synthesis, is most fully expressed in the principles of pure understanding. In this sense it may, then, be said that all empirical thought, all determination of objects, takes place on the basis provided by the principles. What reason does in positing the transcendental ideal is to transpose this basis in a certain decisive way. In what way?

Among the principles the one which corresponds to the categories of quality is that of the anticipations of perception (cf. A 166/B 207–A 176/B 218). In effect, the operation, the ruling, expressed in this principle is such as to constitute an anticipation of all realities. Specifically, realities are anticipated with regard to their degree-character, i.e., as *all* having intensive magnitude, as *all* filling time to some degree. Thus, within the structure of the anticipation there is involved a determination of time: Realities are anticipated as filling time, as determinations of time with regard to content. What reason does is to free the category (hence, its operation as expressed in the principle) from the link to time-determination. Thus, the extension is from the category, by the operation of which all realities are *anticipated*, to an ideal in which all realities are *contained* (and thus are thought).

Granted this positing of the unity for the gathering, what form, then, is assumed by the other side? How would the manifold, i.e., all things in general, be gathered into this unity? What form does the actual gathering take? In a sense it may be said that the unity itself gathers the manifold to itself; it is the *ground* of all things, and, as the ground to which they are all related, it unifies them, gathers them to itself of itself. However, this gathering is actually accomplished *only if* the unity, to which and by which the manifold would be gathered, is an *existing* ground and not merely something posited by thought. Thus, whereas the positing of the ideal poses the *possibility* of the gathering of the manifold, the *actuality* of that gathering requires, i.e., is accomplished by, proving that the ideal exists, i.e., by the proofs for the existence of God. This actual gathering-character of the proofs is most evident in the cosmological and physico-theological proofs: In both cases, things (either determinate or in general) are gathered in the sense of being brought back to their ground (God). Yet, only as transcendental ideal is God a fit unity for the gathering; neither as absolutely necessary being nor as architect of the world is God adequate to the gathering. Thus, what must be proved is the existence of God as transcendental ideal. Consequently, the decisive phase in the actual gathering into the unity, i.e., the fundamental moment constitutive of this side of the gathering as such, is simply the *ontological proof*.

How is the issue of fragmentation involved in this gathering and in its outcome? As in every case, the gathering is directed toward overcoming a certain fragmentation. The general character of this fragmentation has already been noted: It is a fragmentation pertaining to the determination of things by human knowing. It is that incompleteness which belongs to such determination. It is the fragmentation constituted by the fact that in the determining of things (in empirical thought) there is always also an indeterminacy, that the determining is never brought to completion.

What is the basis of this fragmentation? Clearly the basis is to be found in the fragmentation of human thought, which consists in the fact that human thought, in contrast to divine thought, cannot simply posit its object but rather is always a positing relative to a "given," i.e., a positing dependent on what is given through intuition, i.e., a positing of determination (a determining) in relation to what is given. Now, in order to see how such fragmentation of thought forms the basis of the fragmentation at issue in the ideal, it is necessary to consider more closely the peculiar dependence on the given that lies at the core of the fragmentation of thought.

This dependence, this relation to the given, involves two distinct moments. The first moment may be roughly stated: Human thought must apply itself to the given, must be a determining of the given. However, this statement requires two refinements. First, it must be asked: Under what condition is it required that human thought apply itself to the given? The answer is that it must do so *if* it is to have any kind of objectivity—i.e., *if* it is to be a thought *of* something, and not a mere play of concepts—i.e., *if* it is to be a thought *of being*. The second refinement is that thought need not apply itself *immediately* to the given but may do so indirectly; for example, in thinking something merely possible, thought is applied to something which *could* be given, which is in accord with the formal conditions of experience. Thus, incorporating these refinements, one could express the first moment of the dependence in this statement: In order to be thought *of being*, human thought must be a determining related to the intuitively given. It is clear what this moment of the dependence entails: Human thought is not immediately a thought *of* being. Hence, at the core of the fragmentation of thought there is a fragmentation, a separation, *between thought and being*.

There is a second moment of dependence. Human thought determines a thing always *in terms of* something, that is, thought determines it by positing its determination, by attaching certain determinations to it. These determinations have the form of *concepts*; thought, one may say, determines a thing by bringing it under various concepts. But, what is the origin of these concepts, these determinations? They are derived from experience, *from the given* (by abstractive reflection). So, the second moment of the dependence may be expressed thus: Human thought must draw its determinations from the given.[8] Now, because of this dependence on the given, which is itself fragmentary, human thought does not have all determinations at its disposal. There is a radical incompleteness, fragmentation, as regards the determinations available to human thought for determining things.

In positing the transcendental ideal, reason posits that unity (totality) by which this second moment in the fragmentation of thought would be overcome, namely, the absolute totality of all determinations. Furthermore, the gathering of things into this unity, i.e., the grounding of things on this ground, would amount to letting this store of determinations become effective as determinations of things. In other words, to ground things on this totality of determinations would amount to determining things (objectively) through these determinations.

However, consider what kind of determining this would be if it were possible: It would be an objective determining of things *by mere thought*. It would be a thought *of being* which, however, would *not* be related to the given. Hence, it would be a determining that would violate the fragmentation (separation) between being and thought. And thus it is precisely this fragmentation that breaks out at the center of the attempted gathering. It is on this fragmentation that the ontological proof runs aground. The proof fails because it cannot bridge the gap between thought and being (specifically, being-actual, existence). It fails because being is not a real predicate but rather a positing which thought alone can never accomplish.

The gathering fails. In the wake of this failure reason has, as in the other instances, two alternatives, two directions in which it can be legitimately employed. One is its employment in service to the practical sphere, to which Kant refers in his discussion of the positive functions of theology. The other is regulative employment, in which reason's positing of unity is brought into positive service to understanding, in which reason's positing of unity becomes a positing of systematic connection which can serve as directive for understanding, which can thus promote the utmost extension of the empirical employment of the understanding. In regulative employment the conflict over the disparity between the two sides of the gathering is, in effect, replaced by a directedness of the manifold *toward* the unity. Conflict is resolved by being transformed into a striving.

CHAPTER VI

REASON, IMAGINATION, MADNESS

1. INVERSION

A new space is now to be prepared: the space of inversion. Eventually, I shall undertake to unleash within this space a play of inverse imaging by which a concealed stratum of the Transcendental Dialectic can be exposed. But, first of all, the phases of the projective interpretation need to be consolidated in such a way as to bring clearly into focus the structures that will be at issue once the play of inversion is unleashed.

By assembling the horizon from Kant's text and especially by projecting the textual commentary upon that horizon, I have sought in the projective interpretation to recover the issue of gathering in the Transcendental Dialectic. It is a matter of the gathering of reason, of the movement in which reason would gather into unity the manifoldness that remains at the level of understanding. This gathering of reason forms the final phase of that movement of gathering that constitutes the inner dynamics of human knowing as such, the movement by which the fragmentary beginnings of human knowing would be gathered into a unity akin to that of divine knowing.

But the Transcendental Dialectic puts this matter at issue: It is a critical re-enactment of the gathering[1]—that is, it unfolds the structures of that gathering in order to undertake a critical determination of its very possibility. Or rather, since the fact of such gathering (i.e., the history of metaphysics) establishes the possibility of its being in some sense carried out, critique determines whether this sense fulfills what metaphysics intends; in short, it determines whether the metaphysical gathering of reason succeeds or fails.

The determination is that the gathering of reason fails, that it cannot be fulfilled. The fragmentation which it would repair thus proves irreparable.

Consider the paralogisms. As in all cases, reason posits an unconditioned unity: By extending the concept of the apperceptive I up to the level of the unconditioned, reason posits the idea of the soul. The other moment within the structure of the paralogistic gathering is, then, the determination of the soul (as substance, as simple, etc.)—or, more precisely, the transposition of these determinations from their basis, transcendental apperception, to the idea of the soul. With this second moment the actual gathering would be accomplished, the gathering would be fulfilled. The fragmentation within man, the separation from self constituted by self-ignorance, by nonpresence to self, would be repaired—not by installing an impossible presence to self (original self-intuition), but by providing a surrogate: rational knowledge of self, conceptually mediated, rationally reconstructed presence to self. But the gathering fails: Because of the emptiness of the basis from which they are detached, the determinations remain empty and thus fail to measure up to, to fulfill, that unity posited for the gathering.

The gathering structure of the antinomies lies almost on the surface of Kant's text, and little more than an allusion to the assembled horizon was required in order to draw it to the surface. Again, reason posits the unity for the gathering: Extending the appropriate categories up to the level of absolute totality of the series of conditions for a given conditioned, reason posits the cosmological idea. The other moment within the structure of the cosmological gathering is, then, the actual gathering of the manifold, of the series of conditions, into this unity—a gathering executed by time-bound thought, by a thought which, linked to appearances and their mode of givenness, would build up from the fragmented appearances that unity merely posited by reason, thus gathering them into that unity. Unlike the other gatherings of reason, the cosmological moves within the domain of appearances, of the intuitively present, and thus would provide something more than a mere surrogate for the presence that is lacking. It would repair the fragmentation within appearances—repair it through reason yet without completely transcending the domain of appearances. This very ambivalence makes conflict, antinomy, inevitable: The thought that would gather the series of appearances into the idea posited by reason is intrinsically bound to the fragmentation wrought by time, to the "spreading-out" of appearances in time, to *articulation* in a fundamental sense, to *articulated presence*. The gathering of the articulated manifold into presence cannot measure up to the unity posited by reason; between the two sides of the gathering there ensues a radical breach which, setting reason in utter conflict with itself, ultimately generates those antinomies on which rational cosmology runs aground.

The transcendental ideal is the highest unity posited by reason. This ideal, as ground, essentially gathers to itself the manifold of all things, and thus for the actual gathering the only requirement is that the ideal be established as *existing* ground; the second moment in the structure of the gathering lies in the proof that the ideal exists—pre-eminently in the ontological proof. This gathering of reason in the ideal would repair the fragmentation that haunts all determination of things in human knowing, the fragmentation between man and things. But the proof fails, and all actual determining of things retains its bond to the intuitively given; it remains this side of that total determination which would be grounded by the transcendental ideal.

Thus, in each of the gatherings of reason, critique exhibits a radical non-correspondence between the two moments that belong to the structure of the gathering, between the unity posited by reason and the actual gathering of the manifold into this unity. It shows that in every case the actual gathering of the manifold falls short of the unity into which reason would gather that manifold. An inversion is thus prepared: With respect to its outcome the gathering of reason is precisely the inverse of that gathering of pure understanding that is measured in the Transcendental Analytic. Whereas the gathering of reason culminates in the installation of radical difference between its moments, the gathering of understanding issues in identity, unity, fulfillment. Into the unities (the categories) posited by understanding the manifold of intuition is gathered; thus gathered into the unity of objectivity, appearances are, furthermore, gathered by the subject to itself, to its positing of itself as that transcendental apperception to which the unity of objectivity, the transcendental object, is correlative. This gathering is limited, and the Transcendental Analytic rigorously establishes those limits; but within them the gathering is unreservedly fulfilled.

On what does the inversion turn? On imagination. In the gathering of pure understanding it is transcendental imagination which actually gathers the manifold in such a way that the gathering is fulfilled, in such a way that the unity of unity and diversity is established. Imagination gathers the manifold of intuition into the unity of the categories, and this gathering is, correlatively, a gathering into the unity of objectivity, a gathering of the object into presence—that is, the *gathering by imagination* is *both a gathering into unity and a gathering into presence*. It is the latter that is most obtrusively lacking throughout most of the gathering of reason. In the paralogisms the self is not gathered into presence to itself; on the contrary, reason would provide only a surrogate—the merely posited, merely rational determinations of the idea of the (substantial) self. To an even greater degree rational theology, undertaking to prove the existence of God from the mere concept, remains aloof from all gathering into presence. Only in the case of the cosmological ideas, which remain within the domain of appearances, is the gathering of reason linked to a gathering into presence; and one might venture to suggest that this is why the only reference to imagination in the entire Transcendental Dialectic (other than some merely referring back to the Analytic) occurs in the critique of rational cosmology—specifically, in the tracing of that movement of inference from the absolute totality of the series of conditions *to* the unconditioned: "This *unconditioned* is always contained in the *absolute totality of the series* as represented in imagination [*Einbildung*]" (A 416/B 444). But its very link to a gathering into presence by a thought bound to the temporal "spreading-out" of appearances, bound to articulated presence, is what destines the gathering of cosmological reason to failure.

The inversion serves to broach several questions. Is the inversion between the two gatherings merely a matter of the involvement or noninvolvement of imagination? In that case how would one account for the reference to imagination just cited from the critique of cosmological reason? And what is that power of imagination that can gather not only into unity but also into presence? The inversion, the inverse imaging, brings to the fore the *problem of imagination*.

2. IMAGINATION

In the major Kantian texts the problem of imagination is not often taken up directly and for its own sake but rather is usually introduced in connection with other problems and without explicit elaboration. The one exception is the text based on a course of popular lectures that Kant gave for some thirty years and finally published (after his age forced him to discontinue the course) under the title *Anthropology from a Pragmatic Point of View*. The style of this text, adapted to a general audience, lacks much of the rigor and precision that is characteristic of most of those texts that Kant prepared solely for publication; yet what the text lacks in this regard is more than compensated for by the more venturesome, freer, occasionally almost exotic mode of exposition—to say nothing of its being the only text in which certain topics, among them imagination, are explicitly developed.

Imagination is first introduced in a section (§15) entitled: "On the Five Senses"[2]—that is, it is introduced within the framework of a consideration of sensibility. Kant begins: "The sensibility in the faculty of knowledge (the faculty of representation in intuition) contains two components: sense and imagination."[3] Thus, imagination is introduced not only within the framework of sensibility but *as* one of the two forms assumed by sensibility. Immediately Kant differentiates the two forms by introducing the opposition between presence and absence: "Sense is the power of intuiting in the presence of the object, imagination without its presence." The differentiation is especially curious because the very concept of sensibility, of intuition, is tied to that of presence: Intuition is understood to mean being in immediate relation to the object, having it *present* to one's seeing, to one's receptive capacities. Consequently, imagination as the power of intuiting an object without its presence, of intuiting an absent object, involves *making present* something which is and remains in another regard *absent*. Even at this elementary level imagination inaugurates a certain play of presence and absence, a gathering into presence. And because it *makes* something present, imagination cannot be merely passive (as sense is); it is an active stem within sensibility, within passivity in general. Inaugurating a play of presence and absence, imagination installs itself as a play of activity and passivity, as activity within passivity.

The elaboration of the problem of imagination is given in §28, which falls under the heading "On Imagination."[4] Kant begins: "Imagination (*facultas imaginandi*), as a power of intuiting even without the presence of the object, is either *productive*, i.e., a power of exhibiting the object originally (*exhibitio originaria*), which thus precedes experience;

or *reproductive*, derived (*exhibitio derivativa*), which brings back to mind a previously had empirical intuition." Thus dividing imagination into two kinds, Kant correlates the two oppositions, productive-reproductive and original-derivative. A few sentences later he adds another: "Imagination is (in other words) either inventive [*dichtend*] (productive) or merely recollective [*zurückrufend*] (reproductive)." So, imagination is either productive-original-inventive or reproductive-derivative-recollective. If one focuses especially on the opposition original-derivative, referring it to the opposition between original and derivative intuition in the *Critique of Pure Reason*, the crux of the difference becomes evident: Productive imagination is such as to give itself its object rather than merely bringing back to mind some previously had empirical intuition. This is why Kant adds the clarification: In productive imagination there is an exhibiting "which thus precedes experience."

But then the problem is to distinguish such productive imagination (which belongs to a finite subject, dependent on affection) from that original intuition (which could be had only by an infinite knower). In order to deal with this problem, the character of the object that productive imagination gives itself needs to be more closely delimited. What precisely is the object that productive imagination exhibits (intuits) in such original exhibition? The receptivity intrinsic to human knowing, its dependence on affection, is such that this object could not be an empirical object; the latter can be intuited only if it affects the subject, hence, not originally. The only kind of object that productive imagination could give itself would be one capable of being intuited independently of affection, i.e., intuited *a priori*. But only space and time, the mere forms of intuited objects, satisfy this condition: "Pure intuitions of space and time are original exhibitions; all others presuppose empirical intuition." Thus, productive imagination brings forth originally the forms space and time, i.e., spatial and temporal form.

Kant refers, in effect, to the distinction between finite productive imagination and infinite original intuition by distinguishing between "productive" and "creative": "However, productive imagination is not thereby exactly *creative*; it cannot bring forth a sense representation that was *never* given to the power of sense, but rather one can always trace the material back to this [i.e., to sense]." He adds: "So, no matter how great an artist, and even enchantress, imagination may be, it is still not creative, but must get the *material* for its images from the *senses*." The point is: Productive imagination gives itself, creates, only the form of its object (the spatial and temporal form); the material, the sense-content, it must get by reproducing a content once given to sense. Consequently, productive imagination is built on reproductive imagination and must always include the latter as that component which provides the content. What distinguishes productive from mere reproductive imagination is that it produces, invents, the form of the object rather than merely reproducing a previous form.[5] Productive imagination *forms* images, brings sense-content together into the spatio-temporal form of an image.

The previously identified involvement of the oppositions presence-absence and passive-active in the concept of imagination can now be thematized. The moment of absence is constituted by the fact that the content of the image is not given: It was previously given (was present) but is not given (is absent) now. Thus, the absence is essentially opposed to a past presence; it is a present absence correlative to a past presence—that is, the play of presence and absence in imagination connects up with the temporal opposition between present and past.

In the opposition passive-active as it is in play in imagination, the moment of passivity is constituted by the fact that the content must have been given (passively received) through the senses. The moment of activity lies in the reproducing of that content and, in the case of productive imagination, the forming of it. Here too a connection with temporal opposition is obtrusive: The passivity of imagination is not immediate but is rather a mediated passivity, mediated by the opposition between past and present.

The *Critique of Pure Reason* does not diverge from the general concept of imagination elaborated in the *Anthropology*. Though it does not at all reproduce that elaboration, it takes over the delimitation of imagination from which the elaboration proceeds, takes it over explicitly: "*Imagination* is the faculty of representing in intuition, an object that is *not itself present*" (B 151). But attaching the issue of imagination to the problem of the conditions of the possibility of experience, ultimately to the problem of synthesis, the *Critique of Pure Reason* brings into focus a new distinction: Corresponding to the distinction between the synthesis of the pure manifold and that of the empirical manifold, Kant distinguishes between two functions of imagination (as agent of synthesis), hence between empirical imagination and transcendental imagination. This distinction is located outside the framework of the *Anthropology*: It does not correspond to the distinction between productive and reproductive imagination, for both empirical and transcendental imagination, giving form to a manifold, fall on the side of productive imagination.

More precisely, empirical imagination, producing synthesis in the empirical manifold, forming sensible content into an image, corresponds to productive imagination as distinguished in the *Anthropology*: It involves both a reproductive moment by which its content is provided *and* a productive moment by which that content is formed into an image. Its difference from productive imagination is chiefly a function of the difference of its context: Empirical imagination is a "necessary ingredient of perception itself" (A 120 n), whereas productive imagination, at least as thematized in the *Anthropology*, is accidental and superadded to perceptual experience rather than pertaining to the conditions of its possibility.

On the other hand, transcendental imagination produces synthesis in the pure (*a priori*) manifold. In this regard Kant is emphatic: "But only the *productive* synthesis of the imagination can take place *a priori*; the reproductive rests upon empirical conditions" (A 118). Consequently, transcendental imagination can involve no reproductive moment but is purely productive (in contrast to the productive imagination distinguished in the *Anthropology*, which intrinsically involves a reproductive moment). But even without Kant's emphatic statement one could arrive at the same result: Whereas transcendental imagination, through transcendental schematism, forms the manifold of pure intuition, thus forms time, reproductive imagination presupposes formed time (with its serial, ordered character) and so is possible only on the basis provided by the function of transcendental imagination. Nothing in the *Anthropology* corresponds even structurally to the transcendental imagination. And yet a connection remains, a connection through that general conception common to the two texts, that imagination is the power of making present something which (in another regard) is absent, that imagination inaugurates a play of presence and absence: Transcendental imagination, though it does not make present any absent object, makes possible objectivity as such and is thus the condition of the very possibility of presence and absence.

3. IMAGINATION AND DIALECTICAL ILLUSION

In a sense the failure of the gatherings of reason is in each case attributable to the second of the two moments belonging to the full structure of gathering. This moment, the actual gathering into the unity posited, fails to measure up to the unity of the idea, and the gathering collapses as a result of the breach thus installed between its moments. Even in that one case in which the second moment of the gathering retains a bond to appearances, time, and articulated presence, that case in which consequently the gathering power of imagination, attested by the gathering of understanding, could come into play—even here (indeed, most notably here) the actual gathering falls disastrously short of the idea posited by reason.[6]

On the other hand, there is nothing to prevent shifting one's perspective in such fashion as to attribute the failure to the first moment in the gathering of reason; one may with equal right regard the failure as following from the way in which reason posits the unity for the gathering utterly beyond the reach of any actual gathering. Indeed, with respect to two of the three types of gatherings, Kant tends to establish the locus of the failure in the first moment, to exhibit reason's positing of the idea as that which renders the inference dialectical. In the case of the paralogisms this positing is unmasked as an illicit turning of the determining self into the determinable self, a turning of the subject *as* subject (transcendental apperception) into the subject *as* object (*res cogitans*), a diverting of its positing of itself *as* subject into a positing of itself *as* object, a primordial self-objectification, a self-forgetting. It is, more generally, a matter of "treating our thoughts as things and hypostatizing them" (A 395), of confounding a subjective condition with something objective—a turning from subjective to objective. Such turning, it will be recalled, was identified at the very beginning of the Transcendental Dialectic as the way in which dialectical illusion originates (cf. A 297/B 353—with Ch. II, 1). And it is no less at the root of the cosmological gathering. Especially in the critical solution of the antinomies it becomes clear that the basic fallacy which generates the conflicts expressed in the antinomies lies in taking the idea of the world (in its various categorical respects) to have a corresponding object outside it—that is, in confounding the subjective (the idea of the world) with the objective (the world itself), in turning from subjective to objective. Only in the case of the gathering of reason in the ideal is the shift to the first moment lacking—not, however, because the dialectical illusion in this case originates in some way other than by the turn from subjective to objective. On the contrary, this final, most purely rational gathering is from its outset so aloof from all articulated presence that it consists of virtually nothing but such a turning, culminating in what one might well consider the archetype of such turning, the inference from the idea of God to the existence of God, the ontological proof.

Once this shift to the first moment of gathering has been made, more importantly, once the origination of dialectical illusion has been located in the positing of the idea, specifically in the character of that positing as a turning from subjective to objective, then an archaic re-reading of certain texts is called for. What would this re-reading expose? A number of textual indications of *imagination's complicity in the origination of dialectical illusion*. Let me merely assemble some of these indicative texts:

1. In the Introduction to the *Prolegomena*[7] Kant refers to the decisiveness of the Humean attack on metaphysics: "Since the *Essays* of Locke and Leibniz, or rather since the beginning of metaphysics so far as we know its history, nothing has ever happened which could have been more decisive to its fate than the attack made upon it by David Hume." Having established this context, that of the attack on traditional metaphysics, then summarizing Hume's attack on the concept of causality, Kant concludes: "Hence he inferred that reason was altogether deluded with reference to this concept, which she erroneously considered as one of her own children, whereas it was nothing but a *bastard of imagination*, impregnated by experience, which subsumed certain representations under the law of association and mistook a *subjective necessity* (habit) for an *objective necessity* arising from insight" (italics added). This text establishes the following schema (easily detached from the concept of causality, which Kant himself detached from it in the Transcendental Analytic): an (illicit) turning from subjective to objective, though it may seem (even to reason itself) to originate from reason, actually originates from imagination—not, however, in a lawful way but illegitimately.

2. A remarkable passage in the *Anthropology* begins after Kant, referring through several examples to the reproductive moment intrinsic to productive imagination, remarks that imagination "is not so creative as we pretend." As if to compensate for its weakness in this respect by exhibiting its exceptional strength in another dimension, he continues: "The deception caused by the *strength* of man's imagination often goes so far that he thinks he sees and feels outside himself what is only in his mind." Mentioning the vertigo experienced by some of the "mentally ill," Kant then concludes with an exotic example: "The sight of others eating loathsome things (as when the Tunguse rhythmically suck out and swallow the mucus from their children's noses) moves the spectator to vomit, just as if he himself were forced to eat it."[8] The same schema as before—only supplemented now with a reference of the lawlessness of imagination to strength, madness, and exotic spectacles.
3. The one passage (cited already) in which Kant inscribes imagination within the problematic of the Transcendental Dialectic can now be re-read: "This *unconditioned* is always contained in the *absolute totality of the series* as represented in imagination [*Einbildung*]" (A 416/B 444). This passage disrupts the simplicity of origin previously attributed to dialectical illusion—attributed to it, for instance, in that provisional title that Kant employed in the Introduction to the Transcendental Dialectic: "Pure Reason as the Seat of Transcendental Illusion." The idea does not originate merely through a positing by reason but requires also imagination for its origination. Especially for the idea as that of an unconditioned first member or totality, the origin is mixed—reason *and* imagination.
4. It is now appropriate also to re-read that passage in the very first paragraph of the Transcendental Dialectic in which Kant explicitly connects metaphysical turning from subjective to objective with the influence of sensibility: "Now since we have no source of knowledge besides these two [understanding and sense], it follows that error is brought about solely by the unobserved influence of sensibility on the understanding, through which it happens that the subjective grounds of the judgment enter into union with the objective grounds and make these latter deviate from their true function,—just as a body in motion would always of itself continue in a straight line in the same direction, but if influenced by another force acting

> in another direction starts off into curvilinear motion" (A 294/ B 350 f.).[9] One need only recall (for instance, from the *Anthropology*) that imagination falls on the side of sensibility, that it is one of the two forms assumed by sensibility; it is the active stem within sensibility and precisely on that account is the element of sensibility capable of exercising an "unobserved influence," capable of assuming the role of "another force acting in another direction."

This is, then, the stratum of the Transcendental Dialectic that I wanted to expose by the strategy of inversion: Dialectical illusion, constituted by the turning from subjective to objective, has as its origin not only the positing power of reason but also the (intuitively) representing power of imagination. Indeed, one might venture to suppose that even transcendental imagination belongs to this origin, perhaps even pre-eminently, since it is in this capacity, this function, that imagination becomes the condition of the very possibility of objectivity, of articulated presence. One might well wonder whether the ingression of imagination into the origin of the gathering of reason is not necessary if there is ever to occur that transition from mere thought to the positing of the soul, the world, and God as (presumed) objectively present. One might well wonder whether it is not primarily imagination that, impelling man beyond himself, incites him to such inevitable illusion, rendering it something forever distinct from mere errors of judgment.

But imagination, giving birth to metaphysics, does so illegitimately, outside the law, lawlessly. That turning which it inscribes at the origin of metaphysics is akin to certain vertiginous turnings of madmen as well as to the nausea experienced by a Westerner before certain exotic, savage spectacles. Can one, then, merely pass over as curiosities of a past era those extended passages in the *Anthropology*[10] in which Kant connects mental derangement, i.e., madness, "this most profound degradation of humanity," with imagination and its characteristic power of turning subjective into objective—for example, dementia (*Wahnsinn*), in which the madman "is led, by his falsely inventive imagination, to take the ideas he has himself made up for perceptions?" Is there a theoretical confinement capable of isolating such madness? Can (Western) rational man effectively isolate himself from the threat of its strength, from revulsion in the face of its savagery? Or, has madness, ecstasy of imagination, always already encroached upon the very origin of reason and its gathering, of metaphysics? Has it always already infused itself, irrepressibly, in this "natural disposition" of man? Has it, in a past absolutely irretrievable, already installed itself at "the point at which the common root of our power of knowledge divides and throws out two stems, one of which is *reason*?"

CHAPTER VII

METAPHYSICAL SECURITY AND THE PLAY OF IMAGINATION

1. THE PLAY OF ABSENCE

The beginning of metaphysics cannot remain simply intact. On the contrary, the archaic reflection, still only partial, has already adumbrated the issue of crisis, the crisis of metaphysics, of its beginning. For that beginning is marked by that "point at which the common root of our power of knowledge divides and throws out two stems, one of which is *reason*": Metaphysics begins in a retracing of this division, a retracing in which, turning away from the immediately present, one comes to have recourse to reason. And the schema defined by this beginning, the structure constitutive of metaphysics, cannot simply accommodate that encroachment upon reason that I have sought to release by bringing into play the manifoldness, the insecurity, the openness, of the new beginning traced in Kant's texts.

Two severe shocks have been absorbed by this structure, at considerable cost to its security. The first was brought by the projective interpretation: Here the strategy aimed at recovering what remained only subliminally in that concept of reason by which the traditional structure is largely determined, at interpreting reason as gathering (into presence), so as, in effect, to open up within the Kantian text itself the difference between the traditional structure and its Greek origin, so as to unsettle the traditional structure by confronting it with its forgotten origin, to unsettle it by the return to its beginning. To the concept of reason, thus unsettled, the inversive interpretation (or rather that phase of it that remains within the limits of the first *Critique*) brings a still more violent shock by installing imagination at the very origin of reason and its gathering. The autonomy of theoretical reason is thus undermined, its autonomy even as dialectical, as agency of illusion; and in place of autonomous reason thinking the absolute in utter aloofness from articulated, intuitive presence, there is inscribed the dyad, reason/imagination, imaging in the mirror of perversion, of madness, the dyad by which the fulfillment of the gathering of understanding was secured.

Both the traditional structure and the Kantian retracing of it, both metaphysics and critique, are thrown out of joint by the encroachment of imagination upon reason. For imagination is intrinsically connected with absence, with a play of presence and absence, a play for which a principal condition is the irreducibility of the difference between presence and absence. Imagination makes present something which is in another regard absent and which remains in that other regard absent with a necessity of the same order as that of the passing of time. This absence is not such that, turning away, one would eventually annul and surpass it by having recourse to a more primordial presence, but rather it is such as to be sustained in all making-present, sustained as a condition of the possibility of making-present. Even that paradigmatic gathering into presence that is retraced in the Transcendental Analytic is inscribed ineffaceably in the arc of such absence: Kant's text, almost contradictorily, turns in this arc through a series of positions. At one extreme is the gesture with which the Transcendental Aesthetic opens: Though one can experience objects only if affected by them, though even then thought also is required to supplement the intuition, nevertheless when these conditions are met, one does actually have experience of the objects; they are actually present to one's knowing, even if only partially, from a limited perspective, merely as they appear. Without entirely suppressing this gesture, the Transcendental Analytic adds another: Since knowledge is built up entirely from mere sensations within the subject that informs them, there remains no identity, no continuity whatsoever, between the object by which, precritically speaking, one would be affected and the object actually experienced by being reconstructed from the sheer fragments. This gesture invokes the irreducible absence of the object; and it is of utmost significance that the arc joining these gestures, the circling between them, proves to be insuppressible, short of destroying the entire Kantian project.[1] Jacobi's well-known declaration retraces this circle: Without the thing-in-itself one cannot enter the *Critique of Pure Reason*, but with the thing-in-itself one cannot remain within it.[2] Even Fichte's strategy, extending the arc by incorporating even affection into the constructive power of the subject—even this strategy, rather than erasing the circle, served instead to engrave it and its connection with imagination still more deeply.[3]

The connection with irreducible absence is what renders imagination ecstatic: Imagination extends one beyond himself, opening him to what, as intrinsic complement of that opening, is itself closed. Imagination is dispossession of presence to self, displacement not only from the self-presence of inner intuition but also from that self-presence that would be its surrogate, rational knowledge of self, rational self-presence, reason's presence to itself. It is at this level especially that the critical project is unsettled, thrown irreparably out of joint: The encroachment of imagination upon reason, the installation of radical non-self-presence within the very upsurge of reason, deprives reason, beyond appeal, of its title to serve unquestioningly as its own tribunal. The very conditions of critical self-possession are decisively withdrawn, and the space is thus prepared for turning metaphysics back into crisis, for subverting both critical and metaphysical security.

2. THE PLAY OF CRITICAL METAPHYSICS

This turning (into crisis) is not merely something exterior that would limit or terminate the critical project but is already broached within it, broached within the Kantian revolution, the turning around, the reversal, of traditional metaphysics, broached in such a way as eventually to issue in a turning out of metaphysics, back from it, a turning which thus revokes the very intention of that revolution in which it is born. In order to aid in this birth, there is need to stage the play of critical metaphysics, to unfold those scenes in which the Kantian revolution was applied to that established distinction by which metaphysics was inaugurated, the distinction between intelligible and sensible. It will be a matter of resuming at a different level the movement of certain already familiar texts and of extending the textual basis to include all three Critiques, elaborating this extended basis only to the extent required for reinstalling the critical texts within the history of metaphysics. Especially in touching upon the *Critique of Judgment* a new dimension of inversive interpretation will be broached: the inversion in creative imagination of that perverse blending of reason and imagination on which the Transcendental Dialectic runs aground. My primary intention, however, is to stage this play of critical metaphysics as preparation for re-entering, from within the critical project as a whole, that space of subversive interpretation which that perversion has already served to open up.

Let me date the three scenes that are to be staged. The first occurs at the end of Kant's so-called precritical period, the time of the *Inaugural Dissertation*; in this scene one can delineate the form in which Kant took over the metaphysical distinction between intelligible and sensible. The second scene occurs during the time of transition to the critical philosophy; here one can observe a Kantian occlusion of the distinction. The third scene presents the unfolding of the critical system in its character as a reconstituting of the distinction.

Scene 1 Eleven years of public silence separate Kant's final precritical work, the *Inaugural Dissertation* of 1770, from the *Critique of Pure Reason*. Measured by the standards of the critical writings, the *Dissertation* is, in a decisive sense, a traditional work, even though one can quite easily isolate in this text certain major conceptions which mark an open break with the tradition and which are carried over unchanged into the *Critique of Pure Reason*. Most notable in this regard is the conception of sensibility put forth in the *Dissertation*; according to this conception, objects as they affect the senses are invested with form by the mind, a kind of form for which Kant already uses the term "pure intuition" and which he identifies with space and time. With this conception Kant has clearly initiated the break that he will announce again in the Transcendental Aesthetic; and yet, at the same time, he suppresses what is radical and unsettling in this conception of sensibility by inscribing it within a general framework that remains thoroughly traditional, the framework of the traditional distinction between intelligible and sensible. In fact, this distinction gives the work its name; the *Dissertation* is entitled "On the Form and Principles of the Sensible and Intelligible World."[4] Yet, if the traditional distinction serves to suppress the unsettling conception of sensibility, that distinction is itself, by the same stroke, threatened from within.

But, however threatened, the traditional distinction remains intact in the *Dissertation*, and it is in this text that one can discern most clearly how Kant took over the distinction from the tradition. What tradition? Most immediately, the metaphysical tradition as reshaped by Leibniz and systematized during the eighteenth century by Wolff and Baumgarten. Thus, the distinction as Kant takes it corresponds in general to the Leibnizian distinction between the realm of grace and the realm of nature—the intelligible world comprising things as they are, in distinction from the sensible world of things as they affect our senses. With this distinction on the side of things there is correlated a distinction on the side of the subject: Just as the sensible is presented to sensibility, so the intelligible is presented to the intellect. And although intuitive knowledge of the intelligible, i.e., intellectual intuition, is denied to man, there is nonetheless reserved a "real use" of the intellect by which are given, in total independence of sensibility, concepts of things as they are; through the real use of the intellect man is thus granted knowledge of the intelligible.

Here a very old schema is retained, a schema that one can easily trace in Book 5 of the *Republic*: That which truly is, is known through the pure intellect; that which appears, is known through sensible experience.

Scene 2 takes place during that long period of public silence leading up to the *Critique of Pure Reason*. Its main script is the well-known letter which Kant wrote to Marcus Herz on February 21, 1772—the letter in which Kant reproaches himself for having maintained a certain silence in the *Dissertation*, for having, as he says, "silently passed over the further question."[5] What question? The question of the concepts given in the real use of the intellect, the concepts through which one would know the intelligible, the concepts which now, in the letter to Herz, Kant terms "pure concepts of the understanding." How are these concepts questionable? What is the question regarding them? What is the question which Kant now reproaches himself for having "silently passed over"? It reads: "What is the ground of the relation of that in us which we call 'representation' to the object?" The structure within which this question is posed is perfectly symmetrical: If a representation in the subject is caused by the object, this causality is then sufficient ground for the relation; if, on the other hand, the object is caused by the subject in which the representation inheres, if the subject brings the object into being in the very act of representing it, this causality likewise sufficiently grounds the relation. The aporia is that neither type of grounding suffices for the pure concepts of understanding: They are neither caused by the object (since any such causality would involve sensibility, of which the real use of the intellect is totally independent) nor are they generated in the very creation of the object (since they are representations "in us," i.e., in a finite subject). Kant's letter to Herz testifies that this aporia remained untouched in the *Dissertation*, passed over in silence—that is, the relation of pure concepts to objects remained simply ungrounded, merely posited. In the long interval, the years of public silence, the emptying of this relation is played out. By the time of the *Critique of Pure Reason* Kant is prepared to deny man any knowledge of the intelligible; and those pure concepts, previously taken as supplying such knowledge, now serve only for knowledge of objects of experience. Intellect, understanding, is placed in service to sensibility; it becomes a moment within the full structure that belongs to sensible experience, to knowledge of appearances. Thereby the metaphysical schema that was still intact in the *Dissertation* is disrupted in decisive fashion. By the correlation it establishes, that schema had effectively cast the distinction between intelligible and sensible as a distinction between objects knowable by intellect and objects knowable through sensibility. The transition to the *Critique of Pure Reason* thus effectively abolishes one member of the distinction—or, more precisely, appropriates it to the other member. The purely intellectual is *absorbed* into sensible knowledge. Consequently, the distinction, *as* a distinction between two regions of knowable objects, is collapsed, *closed.*

The connections begin to take shape: In the transition from the *Dissertation* to the *Critique of Pure Reason* there takes place an *absorption* of the intelligible into the sensible and a consequent *closing* of the distinction itself. Scene 2 thus traces the contours of a Kantian occlusion of the distinction.

Scene 3 begins amid ruins. The metaphysical distinction and all that it supports, metaphysics itself, have collapsed. The ruined distinction remains only in the form of an empty limiting concept: From the thing as it appears to sensible experience, i.e., the phenomenon, is distinguished the thing in itself, the noumenon, which, utterly inaccessible to human knowing, is posited by the critique of pure reason in order to mark the limits of knowing. By rendering the limits legible, the concept of noumenon serves to enforce the assimilation of pure thought to sensible experience.

The retention of the traditional distinction, even though only as an empty, limiting concept, would already suffice to suggest that the Kantian occlusion is not total, that the obstruction piled up by the collapse is not totally impassable. But even if it could be total, there could be no question of merely granting utter occlusion—at least not as long as one remained unwilling to relinquish questioning as such once and for all. The aporia—as an aporia that attends the occlusion of metaphysics—is expressed by Kant at the very outset of the *Critique of Pure Reason*. The words with which he begins the Preface to the first edition are familiar: "Human reason has this peculiar fate that in one species of its knowledge it is burdened by questions which, as prescribed by the very nature of reason itself, it is not able to ignore, but which, as transcending all its powers, it is also not able to answer" (A viii). There is no choice but to reopen the metaphysical distinction on a new, more solid ground, to take up positively the question "How is metaphysics as science possible?" A new edifice must be constructed alongside the ruins. This work of construction constitutes the positive task of Kant's three critiques.

With due reservations, let me merely trace in three vignettes the contours of the edifice constructed through Kant's critical labors.

The *Critique of Pure Reason* establishes a new conception of the sensible—or, more precisely, it consolidates and extends that breach with the traditional conception of sensibility that was already marked in the *Dissertation*. Kant's celebrated comparison of the critical with the Copernican revolution is composed on this new conception and thus serves to announce it: One can henceforth suppose that, like the movement of a planet, objects must be regarded as resultants to be calculated by taking a subjective factor into account, one can henceforth suppose that objects must conform to our knowledge, precisely because they are invested with their form by the knowing subject. The breach is obtrusive: The form by which objects are informed is grounded, not in a pure intelligible beyond sensible experience, but rather in the subject of such experience. In the consolidation and extension of this breach, form no longer designates merely form of intuition but is extended to categorial form, the form grounded in pure understanding; as a result form takes on the sense of objectivity as such. Kant's "Copernican revolution" turns away from the intelligible ground, traditionally understood, to the subject as the ground of the objectivity of the object. In the new conception of the sensible, the constitutive opposition is not with the intelligible, traditionally understood, but rather with the grounding subject.

Nevertheless, this turning away from the traditional distinction between intelligible and sensible has the character of an *Aufhebung*, for the distinction is insuppressible, already reinvoked with the very speech that would banish it. It is a matter of reopening that distinction within the new conception of the sensible—or rather, a matter of establishing it, for in the assimilation of pure thought to sensible experience, the distinction has already been brought back into play within this new dimension. It is within this dimension that Kant finally situates that question which he silently passed over in the *Dissertation*: It is recast as the problem of the transcendental deduction of the categories, as the problem of vindicating the *a priori* applicability of pure concepts to objects of experience. The outline of the Kantian solution is well-known: Pure concepts can have objective validity precisely insofar as they belong to the conditions of the possibility of objects of experience; in order to show that and how such concepts function as such conditions, Kant focuses upon their character as concepts of synthetic unity and thus is able to show that they are connected, in a constitutive way, to intuition and thereby to objects as they appear in intuition. More specifically, the categories are vindicated by exhibiting their connection to a synthesis: They are concepts in which are thought those forms of unity that are instituted through synthesis in the manifold of intuition. Yet the synthesis itself is accomplished neither by thought nor by intuition. Kant is explicit: "Synthesis . . . is the mere result of the power of imagination" (A 78).

The first vignette is completed: in the *Critique of Pure Reason* a new conception of the sensible, its reference as object back to a grounding subject; within the sensible, thus conceived, the distinction between intelligible and sensible reopened and established. What holds open the distinction? What allows its terms to be distinct yet connected? What repairs, within the new dimension, the occluded distinction? Kant's answer: imagination.

The *Critique of Practical Reason* establishes a new conception of the intelligible. This conception surpasses the relative form that was established within sensibility; and, using precisely the schema provided by that vestigial form of the intelligible formulated in the concept of noumenon, the practical conception surpasses that form in such a way as to restore to it a content. The orientation to the new conception is already prefigured in the first Critique, namely, in that turning to the grounding subject which comes finally to focus on transcendental apperception, the empty positing of self as subject of all representations. The second Critique, in effect, completes the turn by presenting the subject as self-determining, as free, as intelligible. The course of this presentation is well-known: a fact of reason, a unique consciousness of the moral law, a pure feeling rigorously dismantled in Kant's analysis of respect—this fact presented as irrefutable testimony to practical reason, to reason's capacity to determine the will, to the subject's capacity for self-determination—that is, as testimony to freedom. Kant expresses with utter directness the new conception of the intelligible that is established through the primacy of practical reason: "If freedom is attributed to us, it transfers us into an intelligible order of things."[6]

So, the second vignette: in the *Critique of Practical Reason* a new conception of the intelligible as self-determining, primarily practical subject, as freedom.

The *Critique of Judgment* completes the critical edifice by establishing the connection between the new conception of the sensible (established by the first Critique) and the new conception of the intelligible (established by the second Critique). It is a matter of mediation between nature and freedom, a mediation possible only through the concept of purposiveness. In the "Critique of Aesthetic Judgment" in particular one may distinguish three principal stages in which this mediation unfolds, these stages corresponding to Kant's theories of the beautiful, of the sublime, and of beautiful art.

The beautiful, determined as formal purposiveness, corresponds to a certain harmony between imagination, in its apprehension of intuitive form, *and* understanding, by which such form could be brought under concepts. What kind of harmony? One that is not aimed at, that is unintentional—a free harmony. Such harmony between imagination and understanding should be contrasted with that connection which obtains at the level of theoretical knowledge: In aesthetic judgment the concepts of understanding do not function as rules governing imagination and rigorously determining the course of its synthesis; this is why one may, as does Kant, speak here of play. The stage of mediation corresponding to the beautiful thus takes place through a freeing of imagination, a releasing of it into its free play.

The second stage of the mediation between nature and freedom is broached by the violence done to imagination by the sublime in nature. Imagination is surpassed but precisely in such a way as to find itself directed beyond understanding and its realm, nature, to reason and its realm, freedom.

The unfolding of the mediation is completed in beautiful art, in the art of genius, in those productions of genius that Kant terms "aesthetic ideas." At this level there is no conformity whatsoever of imagination to understanding: Aesthetic ideas are representations of imagination which provoke thought but to which no concept of understanding is adequate. Now imagination is so freed from the rule of understanding that, conversely, it can govern understanding—though in its own playful way—by provoking thought.

The third vignette, bringing the entire Kantian play to conclusion, traces the freeing of imagination. Imagination is released to its free play, imagination becomes creative, at that moment when the mediation is genuinely accomplished. The keystone which crowns the arch binding into unity the critically reconstructed difference between intelligible and sensible is the *play of imagination*.

3. THE PLAY OF IMAGINATION

I want now to resume subversive interpretation at the more comprehensive level at which the play of critical metaphysics has moved, in order thus to install this play finally within the space of nihilism. Repeating the play within this space, I want especially to develop the outcome of the play, what becomes pre-eminently manifest in it, what in a sense the entire archaic reflection has served to make manifest: the play of imagination. This is the undeveloped possibility that I want to retrieve from the Kantian beginning and bring to bear upon the issue of utter occlusion, the crisis of metaphysics.

In order to transpose the Kantian play into the space of utter occlusion, let me outline a certain development pertaining to the relation between imagination and subjectivity as such. The development has as its point of departure a peculiar tension between these terms, a tension operative at several different levels within Kant's work. Most globally, it is the tension between that turning toward subjectivity which determines the entire critical system, in particular its reconstruction of the metaphysical distinction, *and* that ecstatic character by which imagination, though functioning as the keystone of the reconstruction, is, on the other hand, a turning of the subject away from itself, exposing it to captivation by the unruly play of images, threatening it with loss of self. One can trace the same tension at a simpler level and more explicitly in Fichte's reformulation. Within the section of his *Grundlage der gesammten Wissenschaftslehre* devoted to theoretical knowledge, Fichte takes up the Kantian problem of synthesis in a radical form which, though discernible in Kant's texts, is mostly suppressed within a more traditional framework. Fichte shows, more unequivocally even than Kant, that the fundamental synthesis is the work of imagination—that it is imagination that composes in their opposition those opposites whose synthesis is required: thought and intuition, phenomenon and noumenon, subject and object. What makes Fichte's formulation more radical, however, is that he foregoes simply installing imagination and its synthesis within an already constituted subject; on the contrary, the synthesis becomes the very condition of the possibility of finite subjectivity. On the other hand, returning to Kant's text, imagination is "one of the fundamental faculties of the human soul" (A 124). The tension is obtrusive: On the one hand, imagination is that by which subjectivity is first constituted as such; on the other hand, imagination continues to be reduced to a mere power possessed by the subject. Imagination is freed with one hand only to be suppressed, bound, with the other. But let me cut the knot! Let me free it once and for all!

By freeing imagination from subjectivity, by so radicalizing it that it ceases to be anything subjective at all, it is possible to transpose the issue of imagination into one of the primary dimensions opened up in that assault on the purely intelligible that has led to the utter occlusion of metaphysics. What dimension? That of the dissolution of the subject, the dismantling of subjectivity. This dimension must be distinguished from that in which Kant took up the antinomy of freedom and natural causality: It is not a matter of an alien causality that would invade an already constituted subject but rather of a force, a structure, an openness, that would constitute the subject "from within"—a "force" such as will to power, such structure as has been unearthed by structural anthropology, the openness of existent *Dasein*. However, the moment one takes up the dismantling of subjectivity, he thereby abandons the Kantian edifice and initiates its collapse by launching an assault against its conception of intelligibility as self-determining subject. One cannot transpose the issue of imagination into the new dimension without eventually undertaking a radical redetermination of imagination as such.

In order to prepare such a redetermination—and here it can be a matter only of preparation, with all the discontinuities and reservations thereby entailed—let me transpose the issue still more radically beyond subjectivity. Or rather, let me simply shift discontinuously from imagination to that play of images to which imagination, however it be determined, is always to some degree given over. Let me repeat the Kantian play within the space of nihilism by replacing Kant's turn toward subjectivity with a turn toward the play of images.

Yet, images in their play are also turned toward something which they image, and it would appear that in turning toward images one inevitably passes through them in such fashion as in the end to be turned away from them. The turn toward images would thus appear to revoke itself. But what is the character of that to which one would be turned by images? What is imaged in the play of images? Kant's answer is assured, at least at the level where imagination is genuinely freed to its play: In the play of images there is imaged the intelligible, i.e., practical freedom. This assurance is expressed in the title of the last major section of the "Critique of Aesthetic Judgment": "Of Beauty as Symbol of Morality." If, however, one lacks that assurance, that security, if one openly confronts the utter and recurrent occlusion of metaphysics, then there can be no question of simply establishing a new intelligible. On the other hand, an image is by definition attached to a dyadic structure—that is, it is an image *of* something, *even if* that of which it is an image cannot be declared an ultimate intelligible, an original beyond all imaging, a final security aloof from the play. It is not a matter of a domain of originals which, set apart from the play of images, would themselves be incapable of entering that play, of playing the role of image. Nothing escapes the play; one finds everywhere only the play of imaging, the play of indeterminate dyads. In turning toward images one is, in the end, turned to the play of imaging.

This turning, initiated by turning back into the metaphysical tradition, is not however a return to metaphysics, for it issues in no new determination of the intelligible. On the contrary, the metaphysical distinction between intelligible and sensible is radically displaced, decisively unsettled, by the turn to the play of imaging, for in that play there is incessant opening and closing of the distance between what the tradition, since its beginning in the Platonic dialogues, has thematized as intelligible and sensible. The play of imaging is nothing but the play of occlusion itself, of absolute occlusion.

A redetermination of imagination is now prepared: Imagination is original ecstasy; it is a standing out into the play of imaging, a being set out beyond oneself into that play, a being outside oneself in such radical fashion that the self is first constituted in a recoil from this ecstasy of imagination.

Let me recall a Platonic λόγος, one inscribed in the *Laws*, spoken there by the Athenian—recall it at least as a gesture: Man, at least his best part, is a plaything of the gods; and so we should live out our lives playing at the most beautiful play—sacrificing, singing, and dancing—so as to be able to win the favor of the gods and to repel our foes and vanquish them in battle.[7]

AFTERWORD TO THE SECOND EDITION: KANT AND THE GREEKS

The Gathering of Reason ventures a reinscription of Kant's thought that is oriented primarily to the Greeks. By translating reason back into λόγος while also reawakening the archaic sense of λέγειν and letting this sense resound in the Kantian critique of reason, this venture brings the entire critical project into communication with a decisive strain in Greek thought; indeed it puts this project in touch with an archaic dimension that begins to be closed off with—or, most certainly, immediately after—Plato and Aristotle. Both the gathering of reason in the broadest sense and the gathering of reason in the narrower sense treated in the Transcendental Dialectic are brought into a certain resonance with the recourse to λόγος that for the Platonic Socrates constitutes the beginning of philosophy, its assumption of its proper vocation. Beyond the formal logical apparatus and the extrapolations that are made to yield the table of categories and the forms of dialectical inference, beyond even the mechanism of synthesis and the orientation to the synthetic *a priori*, the operation of reason proves to be a gathering aimed at bringing into coherent presence. Once this connection is sounded, there are consequences throughout the critical project. Not the least of these is the possibility of reorienting the Kantian determination of imagination and of its constitutive operation to certain issues in Greek thought, including, most notably, those of φαντασία and εἰκασία, of what—by way of a very complicated itinerary—come to be called imagination.

Yet, in focusing on Kant and the Greeks, *The Gathering of Reason* only resumes—if differently—a preoccupation displayed by those of his younger contemporaries who were most profoundly touched by Kant's thought. Hölderlin is exemplary in this regard, for instance, in a letter to his brother-in-law written on Pfingston 1794. In the letter Hölderlin reports that his work has become "very concentrated"; it is known that at this time he was in fact working intensively on his epistolary novel *Hyperion*. Yet in the letter he continues by remarking that while indeed he occasionally tries to produce something original (referring presumably to his work on *Hyperion*), he otherwise divides his time between "the Kantian philosophy and the Greeks."[1] A few weeks later, in a letter to Hegel, he writes again of this preoccupation: "My work is now rather concentrated. Kant and the Greeks are almost my only reading."[2] What he writes two months later in a letter to Neuffer makes it clear that the preoccupation is not merely disjunctive. The letter concerns a possible contribution to a publication that has been planned. Hölderlin is careful to indicate, in advance, that there are several circumstances that might prevent him from sending a contribution (and presumably he did not in fact send one). But, with his reservations expressed, he then describes what he might contribute, describes it with a phrase that refers unmistakably to his preoccupation with Kant: "Perhaps I can send you an essay on *the aesthetic ideas*." Then, most remarkably, he adds that his essay "can count as a commentary on the 'Phaedrus' of Plato."[3]

Neuffer's later remark regarding Hölderlin's early poems confirms and further specifies Hölderlin's preoccupation. According to Neuffer, Hölderlin's hymns from the Tübingen period "were the result of years of striving to cloth in poetry certain abstract ideas, especially those of Plato and Kant."[4] Above all, Hölderlin sought to poetize the ideas of beauty and of love, as portrayed in the *Phaedrus* and the *Symposium*, together with the Kantian idea of freedom, all within the compass of the Kantian theory of ideas as elevating the human above the sensible world and the finite life sustained therein. Thus among Hölderlin's early poems there are hymns to love, to immortality, to freedom, and to beauty. Something of the attunement of his philosophical-poetic work during this time is expressed in these lines from *Hyperion*, which resonate with the famous lines from the Conclusion to the *Critique of Practical Reason*: "As Jupiter's eagle listens for the song of the Muses, so

I listen for the marvelous, unending euphony in me. . . . Full of divine youth, my whole being rejoices over itself, over all things. Like the starry sky, I am calm and moved."[5]

The same preoccupation is decisive for Schelling. In the same year (1794) in which Hölderlin's letters attested to his preoccupation with Kant and the Greeks, Schelling composed a commentary on Plato's *Timaeus*. This *Timaeus*-essay, only recently published, is an extended, coherent, self-contained text. The first of its two parts is devoted to an interpretation of the first of Timaeus' three discourses (27c–47c); the second part is addressed to the initial portion of Timaeus' second discourse (47c–53c), including the discourse on the χώρα. One remarkable feature of this text is the absence of the Fichtean terminology that figures so prominently in Schelling's very first publications, which are almost contemporaneous with the *Timaeus*-essay. It seems that at the time of this essay Schelling had not yet begun to appropriate the *Wissenschaftslehre* but rather, as with Hölderlin at the same time, was oriented to Kant and the Greeks, specifically to Kant and Plato.

This orientation is unmistakably displayed by the interpretations that Schelling offers, especially by his way of construing the initial passages of Timaeus' first discourse. For instance, Schelling cites the passage in which Timaeus distinguishes between *being* (τὸ ὄν), which is ungenerated and is apprehended by νόησις with λόγος, and *becoming* (τὸ γιγνόμενον), which is generated, which never is, and which is apprehended by δόξα with αἴσθησις. Schelling then proposes his interpretation. He writes: "Thus here Plato himself explains ὄν as something that is the object of pure understanding [*das Gegenstand des reinen Verstandes*]." Noting that it is purely and fully knowable and not merely the object of an uncertain and incomplete opinion, Schelling then remarks that "all these are characteristics that are suited to the ideas of *pure* understanding and of *pure* reason." On the other hand, Schelling interprets becoming as "the empirical, that which has arisen through experience."[6] Thus Schelling's interpretation fuses the Platonic-Timaean distinction between being and becoming with the Kantian distinction between the two stems of human knowledge, the rational and the empirical. At the same time, this interpretation reduces, even effaces, the difference between ideas in the Platonic sense (abstracting here from all that is problematic in determining such sense) and ideas in the Kantian sense. His interpretation virtually identifies Platonic ideas as correlates of pure understanding or of pure reason.[7] The Timaean story of the making of the cosmos in the image of the ideal paradigm becomes, with Schelling, a drama of pure reason, demonstrating that nature is not merely a product of empirical receptivity but rather is properly fashioned by our power of representation (*Vorstellungsvermögen*), by pure reason in the broadest sense.

One could hear an echo of this fusion of Kant and the Timaean Plato–and indeed a certain development of it—in a passage in Hegel's *Faith and Knowledge*, written in 1802 for the *Critical Journal of Philosophy*, coedited by Hegel and Schelling. The passage occurs in the context of Hegel's critical discussion of Jacobi, specifically of Jacobi's conception of knowledge as analysis, as a process of positing an analytic unity over against the manifold of experience. In opposition to this conception, Hegel insists that the transcendental imagination, in which knowing is centered, constructs an "absolute and original identity of universal and particular," that is, of unity and manifold. Hegel's explanation, cast as an explanation of Kant, leads him to refer back to Plato's *Timaeus*: "this is the identity that Kant calls synthetic, not as if a manifold lay before it, but because it is in itself differentiated, bi-polar so that unity and manifold do not supervene each to the other in it; rather they detach themselves from one another within it and are held together forcefully, as Plato says, by the middle."[8] Plato—or, more precisely, Timaeus—says this—almost—in the course of describing how the god formed the soul of the cosmos. What is said is that he blended it in the middle (ἐν μέσῳ [35a]) between indivisible, ever selfsame being and divisible, generated being.[9] Thus blended in the middle, this third thing, the soul, would therefore hold together the extremes, so that one might say—as Hegel declares Plato to say—that they are held together "by the middle [*von der Mitte*]." The pertinence of the reference is especially enhanced if, with Schelling, the Platonic distinction between these extremes is allowed to fuse with the Kantian distinction between the rational and the empirical. The third, the middle, the soul of the cosmos, becomes the transcendental imagination as the originary formation of synthetic identity.

And yet, what of Kant himself and the Greeks? How does Kant himself understand the connection of the critical project to Greek thought and, in particular, to Plato? In what ways does he regard critique as resuming Platonic thought? At what points does he insist on differentiation?

To be sure, Kant does not simply reduce Greek thought to Platonic philosophy. This is evident in the final chapter of the *Critique of Pure Reason* entitled "The History of Pure Reason," though Kant is careful to observe that with this title he is merely indicating a remaining segment of the system that must be actually filled out in the future. In this chapter Kant turns to Greek thought and draws a contrast with respect to the object of knowledge. On the one side are the intellectualists, represented in antiquity by Plato. They declare that "in the senses there is nothing but illusion, that only the understanding knows the true." On the other side are the sensualists, represented in antiquity by Epicurus. These declare that "reality is to be found solely in the objects of the senses, that all else is imaginary" (A853–54/B881–82). Kant leaves the contrast merely as a contrast without the slightest indication that one term of the contrast, that represented by Plato, might need to be regarded as governing—and indeed as having first made possible—the contrast as such.

In this same chapter Kant draws another contrast that he takes to be exemplified in Greek thought, a contrast with respect to the origin of knowledge. On the one side are the noologists, represented in antiquity by Plato. These take knowledge to have its origin in reason independently of experience. On the other side are the empiricists, represented in antiquity by Aristotle. These declare experience to be the origin of all knowledge. Again, Kant leaves the contrast simply as such, moving on to modern times, pairing Locke with Aristotle and Leibniz with Plato. There is not the slightest indication that one might need to recognize that the differentiation between Aristotle and Plato presupposes the utmost solidarity between their thinking, that one might need to consider the extent to which, whatever the difference, Aristotle remained within the compass of Plato's thought. Thus, while indeed it extends the domain of Greek thought beyond Plato, Kant's admittedly sketchy account of the history of pure reason does not offer much insight into the connection between the critical project and Greek thought.

It is quite otherwise with the account that Kant offers near the beginning of the Transcendental Dialectic. This account occurs in the first section of the First Book of the Dialectic, in the section entitled "On the Ideas in General." Though the account is limited almost entirely to Plato, the subtlety of the discourse and the insight it offers into the connection with Greek thought make it incomparably superior.

What prompts Kant to turn to Plato is his decision to adopt the word *idea* for critical purposes and his insistence therefore on establishing and consistently maintaining the precise sense of the word. What is remarkable is the extent to which this sense turns out to coincide with the Platonic sense of the word.

Kant begins by observing that Plato used the word *idea* to mean "something that not only can never be borrowed from the senses but that far surpasses even the concepts of understanding" (A313/B370). Kant declares, almost as an aside, that the concepts of understanding were the concern of Aristotle. But, he observes, for Plato ideas do not merely make experience possible but are rather the archetypes of things themselves (*Urbilder der Dinge selbst*). Kant takes Plato to have regarded ideas as issuing "from the highest reason [*aus der höchsten Vernunft*]" and as coming to be shared in by human reason only from that source; he takes Plato also to have held that since human reason is no longer in its original state, since the ideas are now much obscured, human reason must recall the ideas through the effort of remembrance, which is called philosophy. At this point at least, Kant lets the phrase "highest reason," designating what Plato took to be the source of ideas, remain indeterminate; he does not identify this source, in its Platonic guise, with divine reason but leaves open the possibility of taking it to be, even for Plato, simply reason as such, reason as it comes to be enacted by subjects who also are submitted to the other stem of human knowledge. Kant's strategy in this regard is no doubt linked to the remarkable hermeneutical principle that he proceeds to enunciate: that it will often happen that we understand an author "better than he has understood himself." Kant explains why this is so: "As he has not sufficiently determined his concept, he has sometimes spoken, or even thought, in opposition to his own intention" (A314/B370). Clearly Kant's goal in the present account is to understand Plato better than he has understood himself, at least as regards the appropriate sense of ideas. What this would require is setting aside whatever Plato said or thought that was in opposition to his own intention. This requires, in turn, that Plato's intention be identified.

According to Kant, Plato's intention was to be attentive to a certain transcendence. This transcendence is such that our power of knowledge surpasses the mere language of experience: "Plato very well realized that our power of knowledge [*Erkenntniskraft*] feels a much higher need than merely to spell out appearances according to a synthetic unity, in order to be able to read them as experience; he realized also that our reason naturally soars upward [*sich aufschwingen*] to modes of knowledge that go so much further that no object given in experience can ever coincide with them" (A314/B370–71). Kant attests, moreover, to Plato's recognition that such knowledge has its reality (*Realität*), that it is not mere fiction.

What are these modes of knowledge that Plato is taken to have recognized, these modes of knowledge toward which our reason naturally (*natürlicherweise*) soars upward, thus by nature surpassing nature? Kant identifies two fields in which Plato recognized such modes of knowledge as are linked to ideas. The primary field is, says Kant, that of the practical. Kant immediately launches into a discussion of freedom and of the idea of virtue, indicating thus, in terms very much his own and quite remote from Plato, the reality of practical ideas. Yet even before launching this discussion, Kant adds a note in which, following his hermeneutical principle, he sets aside certain things that Plato allegedly said or thought in opposition to the proper intention that Kant has now identified. Kant declares that he cannot follow Plato in certain extensions beyond the practical, namely, to pure speculative knowledge and to mathematics. Neither, says Kant, can he follow Plato "in his mystical deduction of these ideas or in the extravagances whereby he, as it were, hypostatized them." Kant gives not the slightest hint as to which discourse in which dialogue he is referring to, nor even as to whether he has in mind some particular Platonic discourse, as opposed to secondary accounts such as that given by Brucker (mentioned later in this passage). What is most significant in this connection is the way in which Kant goes on to open the possibility of an interpretation that would bring the otherwise questionable discourses into accord with Plato's proper intention. The note concludes therefore by pointing to its own self-retraction: "although the exalted language that he employs in this field is quite capable of a milder interpretation that accords with the nature of things."

In defense of Plato's recognition of ideas in the field of the practical, Kant turns to criticism of Brucker, who in his writings on the history of philosophy had ridiculed Plato for certain assertions put forth in the *Republic*. This is Kant's only mention of a particular Platonic text. And rather than refuting Brucker by explication of this text, Kant simply declares a certain hermeneutical openness to it: we should follow up the thought expressed in the text (Kant mentions the thought that a prince can rule well only insofar as he participates in the ideas), and, where the great philosopher leaves us without further resources, we should undertake fresh efforts and place the thought in a proper light rather than dismissing it as impractical. Again, Kant launches into a discourse cast very much in his own terms and quite alien to that of Plato's *Republic*, a discourse on the idea of a constitution as allowing the greatest possible human freedom.

Kant identifies a second field in which Plato "rightly discerns clear proofs of an origin from ideas," namely, nature. Kant mentions plants, animals, and the orderly arrangement of the cosmos, which, he says, "clearly show that they are possible only according to ideas" (A317–18/B374). Thus, in his reference back to Plato, Kant anticipates the appropriation of teleology to the critical project as this will be carried out in the *Critique of Judgment*.

Kant concludes his discussion of Plato's thought by expressing virtually unlimited respect and solidarity with it, stipulating only the condition that one must "set aside the exaggerations in the expression." Otherwise the ordering according to ends is "an enterprise that reserves respect and imitation." Such is the case even more with the practical: "It is, however, in regard to that which concerns the principles of morality, legislation, and religion, where the ideas first make possible the experience itself (of the good)—though they can never be fully expressed therein—that Plato's enterprise exhibits a quite characteristic merit" (A318/B375).

In the end, one cannot but wonder about the difference. One cannot but wonder where exactly the difference is to be marked between Kant's own thought and that of Plato as Kant interprets him. Assuming that it is Plato's thought that determines the very parameters of Greek philosophy as Kant understands it, what, in the end, is the fundamental difference between Kant and the Greeks?

Certainly there is no fundamental difference in the field of the practical, even though in any particular regard Plato may have gone only so far, so that a fresh effort, indeed an elaboration in quite different terms, would become necessary. Neither is there a fundamental difference in the field of nature, that is, as regards the pertinence of ideas to the teleology displayed in nature. The difference between Kant and Plato (as Kant interprets him) would seem, then, to lie solely in the expression, in the exaggerated expression, the exalted language, of which Plato avails himself. This would seem to be the only difference, granted that Plato's thought and language have been submitted to that "milder interpretation" that Kant holds open, that "milder interpretation that accords with the nature of things."

And yet, how thoroughly is this difference sustained? How rigorously does Kant secure his expression against the workings of metaphors that would set it soaring? After all, even in his discussion of Plato, just as he is about to add the note referring to Plato's exalted language (*hohe Sprache*), Kant describes reason as by nature soaring up to the ideas. It is almost as if the passage merely reinscribes the metaphorics of the famous passage in the Introduction in which, referring to Plato, Kant describes reason as a light dove cleaving the air in its free flight, feeling the resistance, and imagining that its flight would be still easier in empty space. Is the discourse on the upward flight of reason any more secure from the drift of metaphor than the discourse in which, immediately following his discussion of Plato, Kant describes the critical project itself as a matter of leveling the ground, of preparing it so that it might support the majestic moral edifices that philosophy in its proper dignity would then erect? Such groundwork is necessary—says Kant, as his language drifts into a still more fanciful metaphorics—because "in this ground are to be found all kinds of mole-tunnels [*allerei Maulwurfsgänge*] that reason has dug in its futile but confident search for treasures" (A319/B375–76).

NOTES

INTRODUCTION

1. 95 e–99 e.

2. In many of Nietzsche's texts a reversal of the traditional recourse to reason (a reversal of "Platonism") is directly announced, that very directness generating an internal contradiction (usually unexpressed) in which the self-referential turning of the crisis of reason is enacted. An example from that section of *The Twilight of the Idols* entitled "'Reason' in Philosophy":

> —Finally, let us contrast the very different manner in which *we* conceive [*in's Auge fassen*] the problem of error and appearance (—I say "we" for politeness' sake . . .). Formerly, alteration, change, any becoming at all, were taken as proof of mere appearance, as an indication that there must be something there which led us astray. Today, conversely, precisely insofar as the prejudice of reason [*das Vernunft-Vorurteil*] forces us to posit unity, identity, permanence, substance, cause, thinghood, being, we see ourselves somehow caught in error, *compelled* into error. So certain are we, on the basis of rigorous examination, that this is where the error lies (*Werke: Kritische Gesamtausgabe*, ed. Giorgio Colli & Mazzino Montinari [Berlin: Walter de Gruyter & Co., 1969], VI 3, p. 71).

3. Immanuel Kant, *Kritik der reinen Vernunft*, A xii. Reference to this work (KrV) will be given according to the pagination of the first (A) and second (B) editions, as presented in the edition by Raymund Schmidt (Hamburg: Felix Meiner Verlag, 1956). Reference to Kant's

other writings is by volume and page number of *Kants Gesammelte Schriften*, edited by the Preussische Akademie der Wissenschaft (Berlin: 1902 ff.).

4. Cf. Brief 112: An Marcus Herz. 24. Nov. 1776. X, 199.

5. Nietzsche, *Werke*, VIII 1: *Nachgelassene Fragmente, Herbst 1885–Herbst 1887*, p. 123.

6. In addition to the numerous statements to this effect in the main critical texts (e.g. KrV, B xix–xxi, B xxxvi, B 22 f.), there is Kant's direct statement in an early letter to Lambert: "Before true wisdom [*Weltweisheit*] can come to life, the old one must destroy itself" (*Brief* 34: An Johann Heinrich Lambert. 31. Dec. 1765. X, 57).

7. Cf. *Brief* 112: An Marcus Herz. 24. Nov. 1776. X, 199: "It must be possible to survey the field of pure reason, that is, of judgments that are independent of all empirical principles, since this lies a *priori* in ourselves and need not await any exposure from our experience." Cf. also KrV, B 23.

8. "*Idee zu einer allgemeinen Geschichte in weltbürgerlicher Absicht*," VIII, 19.

9. "*Beantwortung der Frage: Was ist Aufklärung?*" VIII, 35 f.

10. One should in this regard attend closely to the gesture with which Kant concludes the *Critique of Pure Reason*—or rather, the gesture, the "cursory glance" (A 852/ B 880) which he substitutes for the concluding division of the system, the division that would deal with "The History of Pure Reason." The glance back at the "infancy of philosophy" (*Kindesalter der Philosophie:* A 852/B 880) provides the most favorable possible context for Kant's final appeal to the judgment of his reader as regards the prospect of achieving *security* for human reason: "If the reader has had the courtesy and patience to accompany me along this path, he may now judge for himself whether, if he cares to lend his aid in making this path into a high-road, it may not be possible to achieve before the end of the present century what many centuries have not been able to accomplish; namely, to secure for human reason complete satisfaction in regard to that with which it has all along so eagerly occupied itself, though hitherto in vain" (A 856/ B 884).

11. *Brief* 166: An Marcus Herz. *Nach* d. 11. Mai 1781. X, 269.

12. *Brief* 205: An Christian Garve. 7. Aug. 1783. X, 339.

13. It is quite significant that here Kant explicitly correlates the concept of whole in that material determination appropriate to critique

with the unity of reason. One would need eventually to thematize the deforming of the hermeneutical principle that could be borne by this correlation: Should the unity of reason be undermined, should reason prove not to be one with itself, should it prove to be separated from itself (perhaps by intrinsic self-concealment), the relevant whole would be deformed, as would the hermeneutical principle defined in terms of that whole.

14. It was initiated by Heidegger in *Sein und Zeit* (Tübingen: Max Niemeyer, 1960⁹), § 7B, 34; and rigorously executed in reference to the Heraclitus fragments in Heidegger's text "Logos (Heraklit, Fragment 50)" (*Vorträge und Aufsätze* [Pfullingen: Gunther Neske, 1954²]); various elaborations are given in the text of a seminar on Heraclitus given in 1966–67 by Heidegger and Fink: *Heraklit* (Frankfurt a.M.: Vittorio Klostermann, 1970). I have undertaken an analogous recovery of λόγος in the Platonic dialogues: *Being and Logos: Reading the Platonic Dialogues*. Third Edition (Bloomington: Indiana University Press, 1996), esp. pp. 7 f., 149 ff., 524–31.

CHAPTER I

1. The distinction goes back to that section of the *Phaedo* to which reference was made above (95 e–99 e): Socrates contrasts that "second sailing in search of causes" which he undertook eventually by having recourse to λόγοι *with* his earlier involvement in περὶ φύσεως ἱστορία.

2. *Kritik der Urteilskraft*, V, 168.

3. Perhaps the most succinct formulation of this distinction is that given in the Preface to the Second Edition: "To *know* an object I must be able to prove its possibility, either from its actuality as attested by experience, or *a priori* by means of reason. But I can *think* whatever I please, provided only that I do not contradict myself, that is, provided my concept is a possible thought" (B xxvi).

There are several passages in which Kant addresses himself directly to the issue of such unlimited knowing as something to be *thought* at the outset of critique, as determinative of its opening:

(1) Near the end of the Transcendental Analytic (A 256/B 311): "For we cannot in the least represent to ourselves the possibility of an understanding which would know its object, not discursively through categories, but intuitively

in a non-sensible intuition." The concept of such an understanding will prove to be a specification of the concept of divine or unlimited knowing. Kant is insisting that such knowing can be neither represented as actual (i.e., known) nor even represented as possible in that sense of possibility determined in the postulates of empirical thought, i.e., real or objective possibility in contrast to mere logical possibility (noncontradiction) (cf. A 218/B 266–A 224/B 272; A 596/B 624 n.). Such knowing can merely be thought.

(2) *Critique of Judgment*, § 77: "We can, however, *think* an understanding which being, not like ours, discursive, but intuitive . . ." (V, 407—Italics added).

(3) Again: "It is here not at all necessary to prove that such an *intellectus archetypus* is possible, but only that we are led to the idea of it—which too contains no contradiction—in contrast to our discursive understanding, which has need of images (*intellectus ectypus*) and to the contingency of its constitution" (V, 408).

4. This role of the distinction is most directly expressed—parenthetically—in the *Critique of Judgment:* "But if this be so, the idea of a possible understanding different from the human must be fundamental here (just as in the *Critique of Pure Reason* we must have in our thoughts [*in Gedanken haben*] another possible [kind of] intuition if ours is to be regarded as a particular kind, namely, that for which objects are valid only as appearances) . . . (V, 405).

Among the commentators who have called attention to the role of this distinction, the following should especially be mentioned: Heinz Heimsoeth, *Studien zur Philosophie Immanuel Kants* (Köln: Kölner Universitäts-Verlag, 1956), p. 192 f.; Martin Heidegger, *Kant und das Problem der Metaphysik* (Frankfurt a.M.: Vittorio Klostermann, 1973[4]), pp. 23 f.; Ingeborg Heidemann, *Spontaneität und Zeitlichkeit: Ein Problem der Kritik der reinen Vernunft* (Köln: Kölner Universitäts-Verlag, 1958), p. 81. Gottfried Martin discusses the issue in terms of analogy, citing a *Reflection* in which Kant speaks of using "the concept of our understanding elevated to completeness to represent to ourselves the divine understanding" (*Kant's Metaphysics and Theory of Science*, tr. P. G. Lucas [Manchester University Press, 1955], p. 164).

5. *De mundi sensibilis atque intelligibilis forma et principiis*, II, 397 (§ 10).

6. *Ibid.*, 392 f. (§ 4).

7. See Kant's development of the distinction between the real use and the logical use of the intellect. *Ibid.*, 393 f. (§ 5).

8. In a letter written to Schultz in 1788 Kant expresses his concern that hostile critics might seize upon this apparent contradiction: "On this occasion I take the liberty of remarking that, since the enemies of critique [*die Antikritiker*] gnaw at every expression, it would be advisable to make a little change in the passage on page 27, lines 4, 5, 6 [Kant is referring to the first edition of the *Critique of Pure Reason*], where a *sensible* understanding is mentioned and the divine understanding appears to have a *thinking* ascribed to it" (*Brief* 340: *An* Johann Schultz. 25. Nov. 1788. X, 557).

9. Cf. A 249 where Kant identifies nonsensible intuition with understanding.

10. Cf. A 50/B 74–5; A 68/B 93; Heidemann, *Spontaneität und Zeitkichkeit*, pp. 187 f., 191.

11. The character of such thought is perhaps most rigorously elaborated in that series of determinations given in § 77 of the *Critique of Judgment* (V, 405–410):

(1) Human understanding is determined as discursive: "Our understanding is a faculty of concepts, i.e., a discursive understanding, for which it must indeed be contingent of what kind and how very different the particulars may be that can be given to it in nature and brought under its concepts."

(2) From this determination is distinguished a more general sense of understanding, a sense which could still be applied to divine knowing even though the latter is not discursive: "But still, to knowledge also belongs intuition, and a faculty of a *complete spontaneity of intuition* would be a faculty of knowledge distinct from sensibility and quite independent of it, in other words, an understanding in the most general sense; thus one can also think an *intuitive* understanding (negatively, merely as not discursive), which does not proceed from the universal to the particular and so to the individual (through concepts) . . ."

(3) Such intuitive understanding proceeds "from whole to the parts"—"in contrast to our discursive understanding which has need of images . . . and to the contingency of its constitution."

12. Thus Kant sometimes uses the expression "original apperception" (A 111; B 132).

13. It is also anterior to the division between possibility and actuality. It "would have none but actual objects" (*Kritik der Urteilskraft*, § 76. V, 401–404).

14. The phrase "to man at least" was added in the second edition, in which generally the role of the distinction between human knowing and divine knowing is more explicit.

15. Cf. A 277/B 333; B 67; and especially Kant's letter to Reinhold of May 12, 1789, in which he writes: "Of no object whatsoever can man know the real essence (the nature), that is, the primary *inner* ground of all that necessarily belongs to a given thing" (*Brief* 359: *An* Carl Leonhard Reinhold. 12. Mai 1789. XI, 36). Also Heimsoeth, *Studien*, 75 f., 194 f.

16. In a letter to Herz, Kant broaches this distinction in relation, specifically, to the antinomies: "The antinomies of pure reason could provide a good test stone for that, which might convince him [Maimon] that one cannot assume human reason to be of one kind with the divine reason, distinct from it only by limitation, that is, in degree—that human reason, unlike the divine reason, must be regarded as a faculty only of *thinking*, not of intuiting; that it is thoroughly dependent on an entirely different faculty (or receptivity) for its intuitions, or better, for the material out of which it brings forth knowledge . . ." (*Brief* 362: *An* Marcus Herz. 26. Mai 1789. XI, 54). The point of the connection with the antinomies is that divine thought, since it is not essentially removed from its content, cannot fall into conflict with itself (antinomies) regarding its content.

17. "Now the understanding in us men is not itself a faculty of intuitions, and cannot, even if intuitions be given in sensibility, take them up *into itself* in such manner as to combine them as the manifold of its *own* intuition" (B 153). The words italicized by Kant serve to outline the disunity of thought: Its content must come from elsewhere, and, even if it takes that content up into itself, the content remains one brought "from elsewhere," not its own.

18. The specific way in which thought is related to this level depends on the character of the thought, on whether it takes the form of understanding, judgment, or reason and on whether it is pure or empirical. In every case the relation involves peculiar complexities,

and those relevant to the present interpretation will be taken up in due course. Nevertheless, despite the complexity and the modalization of the relation and the qualifications thus required, there remain several decisive senses in which thought unconditionally requires a "matter" that must be provided by intuition.

19. This peculiar character of pure intuition not only grounds the possibility of mathematics but also serves to give mathematical thought its distinctive *creativity*. In fact, it is in Kant's considerations of mathematics that this character of pure intuition becomes most evident. Thus, in the course of considering geometry he says that "objects, so far as their form is concerned, are given through the very knowledge of them, *a priori* in intuition" (A 87/B 120–21). In a more extended consideration of mathematical construction he writes: "As regards the formal element, we can determine our concepts in *a priori* intuition, inasmuch as we create for ourselves, in space and time, through a homogeneous synthesis, the objects themselves—these objects being viewed simply as *quanta* (A 723/B 751). In *Über eine Entdeckung* (1790) Kant clarifies further what such construction involves and relates it explicitly to imagination (VIII, 191–2 n.).

20. *Logik*, IX, 91.

21. *Ibid.*, 94 f.

22. In this connection Kant writes in the *Prolegomena*: "For the specific nature of our understanding consists in thinking everything discursively, that is, by concepts, and so by mere predicates, to which, therefore, the absolute subject must always be lacking. Hence all the real properties by which we know bodies are mere accidents . . ." (IV, 333).

23. In this regard especially it should be observed that many of the formulations at the level of the Transcendental Deduction prove inadequate, i.e., in need of qualification, elaboration, deepening, at the subsequent levels. Thus in Kant's consideration of the principles, especially of the anticipations of perception and the analogies of experience, this specific formulation gets carried over into a more adequate and complex account of the issue. Such procedure is typical of Kant, that of beginning with relatively simple (but ultimately inadequate) formulations and then deepening and transforming them as the inquiry proceeds. If the resultant stratification that informs his texts is not observed, incoherence in interpretation is inevitable.

24. This identification, unqualified within the context of the Transcendental Deduction, proves at a deeper level to have been provisional. In the last chapter of the Transcendental Analytic ("The Ground of the Distinction of all Objects in general into Phenomena and Noumena") the problem of the transcendental object gets reopened in relation to the problem of the noumenon.

CHAPTER II

1. Cf. B 69–71 where Kant expresses this distinction between appearance and illusion from the perspective of the problem of appearance rather than that of illusion.

2. Cf. *Anthropologie in pragmatischer Hinsicht*, VII, 146 (§ 11), together with XV (I), 92.

3. The concept of such an encroachment of sensibility upon thought occupies a prominent place in the *Inaugural Dissertation*. Kant writes: "Every method of metaphysics concerning sensible things and intellectual things comes back to this precept above all: Great care must be taken *lest the domestic principles* of sensible knowledge transgress their boundaries and affect intellectual things" (II, 411, § 24). In the context of the *Dissertation* such encroachment has of course a fundamentally different significance from that which it assumes in Kant's critical works, since in the former thought, in the sense of the "real use" of the intellect, is taken to have access to the intelligible rather than being placed in service to intuition.

In the *Prolegomena* Kant stresses that the mixing of objective with subjective constitutes illusion: ". . . all illusion consists in holding the subjective ground of our judgments to be objective" (IV, 328). Although this confounding of subjective with objective is repeatedly exhibited in the course of the Transcendental Dialectic, Kant does not develop the thesis that sensibility plays a role in provoking it, that there is an "unobserved influence of sensibility on the understanding." I shall return to this issue in Chapter VI.

4. In the *Anthropologie* (§ 40) Kant explicitly assigns to "understanding" a twofold sense structurally identical with the ambiguity that "reason" has in the *Critique of Pure Reason* (VII, 196 f.).

5. Cf. Heinz Heimsoeth, *Transzendentale Dialektik: Ein Kommentar zu Kants Kritik der reinen Vernunft* (Berlin: Walter de Gruyter & Co., 1966–1971), Vol. I, p. 15.

6. Cf. *Logik*, IX, 114 ff.

7. Here Kant touches upon that function of inference to which I referred in delineating the modes of gathering (Ch. I, 3).

Heimsoeth suggests that Kant's view of logical procedure was heavily influenced by the example of classical modern physics in which there was progress toward ever more universal laws, as in the working out of the laws of motion from Galileo and Kepler to Newton (*Transzendentale Dialektik*, I, 21).

8. Cf. *Logik, IX, 94*; also above, Ch. I, 3.

9. Kant explains in a letter to Schultz: "In a syllogism a general rule is stated by the major premise, whereas the minor premise ascends from the particular to the general condition of the rule; the conclusion descends from the general to the particular, that is, it says that what was asserted to stand under a general condition in the major premise is also to be asserted of that which stands under the same condition in the minor premise" (*Brief* 221: *An* Johann Schultz. 17. Febr. 1784. X, 367). Because this conception is not, however, applicable to the disjunctive and especially the hypothetical syllogism except with rather severe qualifications, Kant does not in his *Logik* define the syllogism in terms of movement toward greater universality but rather in terms of subsumption under rules: "The general principle on which rests the validity of all conclusions through reason may be expressed in the following formula: What stands under the condition of a rule stands also under the rule itself" (IX, 120).

10. Cf. *Logik*, IX, 134.

CHAPTER III

1. *Logik*, IX, 134 f.

2. Leibniz first used the word "apperception" in the relevant connection in the *Nouveaux Essais*, where it denotes consciousness in distinction from perception, which does not necessarily involve consciousness (*Die philosophischen Schriften* ed. Gerhardt [Hildesheim: George Olms, 1965], Vol. V, p. 148). Later he came to use it as the specific designation for self-consciousness or reflective knowledge of the inner state (cf. "*Principes de la Nature et de la Grace, fondés en raison,*" *ibid.*, Vol. VI, p. 600).

3. Thus Kant says regarding the representation "I": "Whether this representation is clear (empirical consciousness) or obscure, or even whether it ever actually occurs, does not here concern us" (A 117 n.). In this regard Fichte's interpretation is most incisive (cf. *Zweite*

Einleitung in die Wissenschftslehre, *in Werke*, ed. I. H. Fichte [Berlin: Walter de Gruyter & Co., 1971], Vol. I, p. 459).

4. This dependence is most explicitly, but not exclusively (cf. A 108), expressed in the second edition. Cf. H. J. Paton, *Kant's Metaphysic of Experience* (London: George Allen & Unwin Ltd., 1936), Vol. I, pp. 512–515.

5. Kant accounts for the different order followed here (in contrast to that in the table of categories) by adding: ". . . with this difference only, that since our starting-point is a given thing, 'I' as thinking being [rather than the informed manifold of intuition], we begin with the category of substance, whereby a thing in itself is represented, and so proceed backwards through the series, without, however, otherwise changing the order adopted in the table of the categories."

6. *Prolegomena*, IV, 334.

7. See Descartes' Second Meditation (*Oevres*, ed. Adam & Tannery [Paris, 1904], Vol. VII, esp. p. 28).

8. Cf. *Logik*, IX, 135.

9. Cf. Heimsoeth, *Transzendentale Dialektik*, I, 105. At the end of the chapter Kant remarks that he is not yet in a position to explain how the simple corresponds to the category of reality (A 405).

10. See Descartes' Sixth Meditation, where the difference between mind and body is specifically expressed as a difference between something entirely indivisible and something by nature divisible (*Oevres*, VII, 85 f.); and especially Leibniz's statement in the "Monadology" that "there is no conceivable way in which a simple substance can perish naturally" (*Die philosophischen Schriften*, VI, 607).

11. At the beginning of the *Anthropologie* Kant presents this transcendental concept of personality from a positive perspective: "That man can have the representation I, elevates him infinitely above all the other beings living on earth. By this he is a *person*; and by virtue of his unity of consciousness throughout all the changes he may undergo, he is one and the same person, i.e., a being altogether different in rank and dignity from *things* . . ." (VII, 127).

CHAPTER IV

1. Herman-J. de Vleeschauwer, *The Development of Kantian Thought*, tr. A.R.C. Duncan (London: Thomas Nelson, 1962), 49 f., 82 f.

2. "It was not from the investigation of the existence of God, of immortality, and so on, that I started but from the antinomy of pure reason. . . . These were what first awoke me from the dogmatic slumbers and drove me to the critique of reason itself in order to end the scandal of reason's ostensible contradictions with itself" (*Brief* 820: *An* Christian Garve. 21. Sept. 1798. XII, 257 f.). A similar testimony, stripped of the autobiographical element, is given in the *Prolegomena:* "It serves as a very powerful agent to rouse philosophy from its dogmatic slumber and to stimulate it to the arduous task of undertaking a critical examination of reason itself" (IV, 338).

3. On the historical background of the various positions and arguments in the antinomies, see especially, Martin, *Kant's Metaphysics and Theory of Science*, Ch. II. For a detailed presentation of the proofs of the individual theses and antitheses, see Heimsoeth, *Transzendentale Dialektik*, II, 215–259.

4. See the Leibniz-Clarke Correspondence, *Die philosophischen Schriften*, VII, 364.

5. See *ibid.*, 377 f.

6. Cf. Martin, *Kant's Metaphysics and Theory of Science*, 46 f.

CHAPTER V

1. Kant's usage here corresponds to that of Baumgarten and Wolff: *realitas* pertains to what a *res* is, not whether it is; and so *realitas* is synonomous with *quidditas*. See A. G. Baumgarten, *Metaphysica* (Hildesheim: George Olms, 1963), pp. 11 f. (§ 36); and Christian Wolff, *Gesammelte Werke*, ed. Ecole & Arndt, II. *Abteilung. Lateinische Schriften*. Band 3, p. 196 (§ 243).

2. Kant observes that the positing of this totality is global in character: This idea, "insofar as it serves as the condition of the complete determination of each and every thing, is itself undetermined in respect of the predicates which may constitute it and is thought by us as being nothing more than the sum-total of all possible predicates . . ." (A 573/B 601).

3. Descartes and Leibniz may in general be regarded as having simply revived the versions of the proof put forth in the Middle Ages by Anselm and Duns Scotus respectively. Cf. Efrem Bettoni, *Duns Scotus: The Basic Principles of His Philosophy*, tr. Bernardine Bonansea (Washington, D.C.: Catholic University of America Press, 1961), pp. 133 ff.

4. *Oevres*, VII, 65–67.

5. In his "Meditationes de Cognitione, Veritate et Ideis" Leibniz writes: "I was once instigated to make a more exact investigation of this question by the famous scholastic argument for the existence of God, which Descartes recently revived. Whatever follows from the idea or the definition of a thing—so the argument runs—is predicable of the thing itself. Now existence follows from the idea of God as the most perfect or greatest possible being. For the most perfect being includes all perfections within himself, and existence is one of them. Therefore, we can predicate existence of God. In truth, however, this argument permits us only to conclude that God's existence follows if his possibility is already proven. For we cannot use a definition in an argument without first making sure that it is a *real* definition, or that it contains no contradiction. From concepts which contain a contradiction, we can draw conclusions contrary to one another, which is absurd" (*Die philosophischen Schriften*, IV, 424).

6. *Oevres*, VII, 66.

7. V, 161.

8. Here, as throughout the consideration of the ideal, the issue is thought in general, thought of already constituted things. By contrast, at the level of *a priori* thought (pure understanding) this second moment of dependence does not hold.

CHAPTER VI

1. Especially from this point on, constructions involving forms of "to be" will often need to be understood horizonally, i.e., as including a tacit reference to a certain interpretive horizon. Thus, in the present case, "is" would expand into: "within the horizon constituted by the issue of gathering, is manifest as . . . ."

2. VII, 153 f.

3. "*Die Sinnlichkeit im Erkenntnisvermögen (das Vermögen der Vorstellungen in der Anschauung) enthält zwei Stücke: den Sinn und die Einbildungskraft*" (*Ibid.*).

4. VII, 167 ff.

5. In § 31 (VII, 174–77), entitled "On the Sensible Inventive-Faculty" (*Von dem Sinnlichen Dichtungsvermögen)*, Kant identifies and discusses three ways in which this giving of form can take place: (1) by

the sensible inventive-faculty of constructing spatially, (2) by the power of association, and (3) by the power of connecting on the basis of affinity.

6. This role of imagination in the moment of actual gathering, apparently limited to the cosmological phase, is identified in the *Critique of Judgment* (§ 57), where it serves as the basis for an explicitly formulated inversion: "As in a rational idea the *imagination* with its intuitions does not attain to the given concept, so in an aesthetical idea the *understanding* by its concepts never attains completely to that internal intuition which the imagination binds up with a given representation" (V, 343).

7. IV, 257 f.

8. VII, 178.

9. A related passage from the Preface to the second edition connects this invasion of reason by sensibility-imagination with the danger of a correlative disruption of reason in its practical employment: ". . . the principles with which speculative reason ventures out beyond its limits do not in fact *extend* the employment of reason, but, as we find on closer scrutiny, inevitably *narrow* it; for these principles actually threaten to extend over everything the bounds of sensibility, to which they properly belong, and so to supplant reason in its pure (practical) employment" (B xxiv f.).

10. VII, 212–220.

CHAPTER VII

1. In a letter written in 1791, J. S. Beck brought up this issue in one of its most direct forms: "The *Critique* calls 'intuition' a representation that relates immediately to an object. But in fact, a representation does not become objective until it is subsumed under the categories. Since intuition similarly acquires its objective character only by means of the application of categories to it, I am in favor of leaving out that definition of 'intuition' that refers to it as a representation relating to objects" (*Brief* 499: *Von* Jacob Sigismund Beck. 11. Nov. 1791. XI, 311). Kant's answer, in part: "Perhaps right at the outset you can avoid defining 'sensibility' in terms of 'receptivity,' that is, the kind of representations in the subject insofar as he is affected by objects, and locate it in that which, in knowledge, constitutes merely the relation of the representations to the

subject, so that the form of sensibility, in this relation to the object of intuition, makes knowable no more than the appearance of this object" (*Brief* 500: *An* Jacob Sigismund Beck. 20. Jan. 1792. XI, 315).

2. Cf. F. H. Jacobi, *Werke* (Leipzig, 1812–1825), II, 304.

3. Cf. Fichte, *Zweite Einleitung in die Wissenschaftslehre*, *Werke*, ed I. H. Fichte (Berlin: Walter de Gruyter, 1971), I, p. 487 ff.; also *Grundlage der gesammten Wissenschaftslehre*, *Werke*, I, 215, 280 f.; also my discussion in *Spacings—of Reason and Imagination. In Texts of Kant, Fichte, Hegel* (Chicago: University of Chicago Press, 1987), chap. 2.

4. *De mundi sensibilis atque intelligibilis forma et principiis*, II, esp. § 3–6, 10, 12–15 (pp. 392–406).

5. *Brief* 70: *An* Marcus Herz. 21. Febr. 1772. X, 129–135.

6. V, 42.

7. 803 c–e.

AFTERWORD TO THE SECOND EDITION

1. Friedrich Hölderlin, *Sämtliche Werke und Briefe* (Munich: Carl Hanser Verlag, 1970), 2:602.

2. Ibid, 610.

3. Ibid, 620.

4. Cited in Dieter Henrich, *Der Grund im Bewusstsein: Untersuchungen zu Hölderlins Denken (1794–1795)* (Stuttgart: Klett-Cotta, 1992), 153.

5. Hölderlin, *Sämtliche Werke*, 1:624.

6. F. W. J. Schelling, *"Timaeus." (1794)*, ed. Hartmut Buchner (Stuttgart-Bad Cannstatt: Frommann-Holzboog, 1994), 23.

7. As the interpretation proceeds, Schelling specifies that ideas are, first of all, concepts in the *divine* understanding, which would become possible in human understanding only through intellectual communion of man with the divine origin. See my discussion in *Chorology: On Beginning in Plato's "Timaeus"* (Bloomington: Indiana University Press, 1999), 154–67.

8. G. W. F. Hegel, *Jenaer Kritische Schriften*, vol. 4 of *Gesammelte Werke*, ed. Hartmut Buchner and Otto Pöggeler (Hamburg: Felix Meiner, 1968), 372.

9. This passage is one of the most difficult and disputed in the entire dialogue. Its precise sense has been the subject of dispute from the time of the early Academy. See *Chorology*, 65–70.

INDEX